The American Recorder Society and Me... *a memoir*

by Martha Bixler

The American Recorder *Society and Me . . . a Memoir*

Copyright © 2014 Martha Bixler

All rights reserved. Except for the use in any review, the reproduction or utilization of this work in whole or in part in any form by any electronic, mechanical or other means is forbidden without the express permission of the author.

ISBN 978-1-908904-93-5

Published by Peacock Press
Scout Bottom Farm
Mytholmroyd
Hebden Bridge HX7 5JS (UK)
Tel: 01422 882751
Fax: 01422 886157
www.northernbeebooks.co.uk

Design and artwork, D&P Design and Print

Contents

FOREWORD		iv
CHAPTER ONE	Beginnings	1
CHAPTER TWO	Faltering Forties	6
CHAPTER THREE	Flourishing '50s	14
CHAPTER FOUR	Soaring '60s	35
CHAPTER FIVE	Some Slippage and Some Saviors in the '70s	64
CHAPTER SIX	Expansion in the '80s	95
CHAPTER SEVEN	Afterword: the '90s and Beyond. More changes, and politics galore	196
CHAPTER EIGHT	The Millennium—a very brief look.	226
APPENDIX I	History of the American Recorder Society Chapters	232
APPENDIX II	ARS Chapters (1939–1995)	235

Foreword

The following memoir originated as a gleam in the eye of the American Recorder Society (ARS) Board of Directors at the Fall 1988 meeting. Its planned appearance as a "History of the American Recorder Society" in 1989 was to be a feature of ARS 50, a year-long celebration of the founding of the Society designed to publicize the ARS and recruit new members. The Board designated me to be in charge of this history.

I accepted this assignment with some misgivings, as I knew there would be a lot of work involved, but I was given two helpers: Ken Wollitz, an ex-President of the ARS, a good writer, and one who had had a lot of experience with the inner workings of the ARS, and Marcia Blue, an enthusiastic member of the Society, who was willing to put in (as it turned out) thousands of hours of work on the project.

According to the original plan Ken Wollitz was to contribute a chapter on the ARS workshops and Marcia Blue would write another on the history of the ARS chapters. Ken soon found that his task required more time than he could devote to it, so he eventually dropped out of the endeavor. Marcia devoted many years to the Sisyphean labor of gathering data on the 90-plus chapters—much of the material that she assembled is available to the public at the Recorder Music Center at Regis University in Denver—but she found that this mass of information did not lend itself to organization in the form of a chapter. Her summary of this work is included here in two appendices. Other assistance came from Judith Wink and a former student of mine, Giocille Terenzio, but the responsibility for what is written here is mainly mine.

As part of the research for this document, Ken Wollitz, Marcia Blue, Sigrid Nagle, and I conducted a number of interviews with people who had been involved with the ARS in the '60s, '70s, and '80s. We even interviewed the founder of the ARS, Suzanne Bloch, twice, since the tape of the first interview turned out to be untranscribable. (The second was also almost impossible to transcribe—Suzanne spoke softly, with great rapidity, and with a particularly heavy German accent.) Peter Seibert interviewed Winifred Jaeger, in Seattle. These interviews, which were all taped and then carefully transcribed, have been a very valuable source—an "oral history" of the ARS. The transcriptions and tapes are now also at the Recorder Music Center.

Around 1990 I was lucky enough to visit the Erich Katz Archives, which were then at the University of Colorado, Boulder. These archives, generously donated to the American Music Research Center at CU by Winifred Jaeger, Erich Katz's companion, are a treasure-trove of information concerning The American Recorder Society in the '40s and '50s. The entire collection has since been relocated to the Recorder Music Center at Regis University.

There were, of course, many other textual sources. I have minutes of meetings that took place as far back as the '40s, and other documents from the '40s and '50s. I had access to office records going back to the time of our secretary Clara Whittaker, in the '60s, through the tenures of Bill Leatham, Andrew Acs, and Mary Ann Fleming, our administrative directors in the '70s, and Waddy Thompson, our executive director in the '80s. I have my own voluminous correspondence, dating back to the very early '60s, when I was editor of The American Recorder, and then in my two presidencies of the ARS in the '70s and '80s. I have used the minutes of meetings of the Board of Directors from 1960 until 1990 as well as 15 "Letters to the Board," written during my presidencies. These "letters" were written to Board members in an attempt to keep them apprised of what was happening in the ARS, which in those days mostly meant what was happening in New York. In addition there are the earliest editions of the ARS Newsletter, from 1950–1960; all issues of The American Recorder from 1960 to the present, later (after a 20-year hiatus) editions of the *Newsletter*, from 1980 to the present; and other publications, such as the British *Recorder News*, later re-named the Recorder Magazine.

As time passed it became apparent that writing a history of the ARS was a much bigger project than any of us had thought, and it would take much longer than anyone had anticipated. Moreover, there was no way I could write a "history of the ARS" without its turning into a personal memoir. I am the one who has been there longer than anyone else, and I was so heavily involved with so much that happened that it was impossible for me to write about some issues without introducing my own personal slant. So this document is not a "history"; it is a memoir. I have tried to avoid misstatements of fact, and to be fair, even when writing about situations where I had strong opinions. This is not a scholarly paper, and I have no footnotes or references to sources for some of my assertions of fact, but I have done my best to see that I've said nothing that is untrue. In some cases I have had to rely on my own memory or that of others. There will be errors—this is inevitable—but they will be corrected.

A few matters of style: I have struggled with such issues as, for instance, whether I should say "chairman," "chairwoman," or the modern "chair" when writing about the head of a committee (I never did make a decision about this); I use whatever word seems appropriate in each situation. Should I capitalize "Board of Directors," "President," "Executive Director"? Should I write "70s and 80s" or "'70s and '80s"? How often should I put the name of a committee of the Board in bold letters? I finally decided to follow what appear to be the most generally accepted rules whenever I could, but above all to aim for consistency.

In closing, I must acknowledge those who have been "cheerleaders" in this endeavor—Valerie Horst, Gene Murrow, Connie Primus, and others—and those long-suffering witnesses to many of the events herein recorded who have been good enough to read the manuscript, or parts of it—John Nelson, Scott Paterson, Judy Whaley, Gail Nickless, Connie Primus, John Nelson, Winifred Jaeger, and, especially for his helpful editing, Mark Davenport.

Finally I wish to dedicate this memoir to the memory of my husband, Richard Sacksteder, who died before it could be published but without whose editing, proofreading, technical help, and never-failing aid and encouragement, I would never have been able to complete it.

MARTHA BIXLER

Suzanne Bloch, 1955.

CHAPTER ONE
Beginnings

A letter addressed to Erich Katz and signed by Douglas Perrin, which is preserved in the Erich Katz Archives at the Recorder Music Center at Regis University in Denver, Colorado, makes the following assertion: in 1939 J. Homer Wakefield, who was teaching at Brigham Young University in Utah, gave a series of concerts with some friends. They called themselves "The American Recorder Society." This group of players, for the most part anonymous, has vanished without a trace, and the tale may be apocryphal, for, as anyone over a certain age knows, for a long time every piece of stationery, every brochure, every important document connected with the American Recorder Society bore the legend at its head: "Founded in 1939 by Suzanne Bloch." To the end of her life, Suzanne herself was firm in her recollection that she was the founder of The American Recorder Society, now a 75-year-old organization of recorder players not only from the U.S. but from all over the world: young, old, from every walk of life, including professional musicians and amateurs, those who are "serious" about the instrument and those who use it only as a source of recreation and social intercourse.

In a letter addressed "to whom it may concern," dated March 30, 1939, and signed by Suzanne Bloch, a lutenist, devotee of early music, and daughter of composer Ernest Bloch, the birth of the American Recorder Society was announced to the world. In this document Suzanne Bloch tells of the founding of the ARS "in answer to the growing need for a center of information regarding the instrument, its players and its literature."

The aims of the fledgling society were rather grandiose considering its small size—perhaps a dozen amateur players who gathered in a

NewYork City schoolroom once a month to entertain themselves with music-making. "Members will be entitled to a monthly bulletin answering questions pertaining to the recorder received by the American Recorder Society, and the use of a lending library of recorder music. The encouragement of ensemble playing will be stressed; members will be asked to form groups wherever they are. . . . More recorder music for school, home and concert use will be the Society's greatest aim. . . . Contemporary composers will be urged to write for the recorder." And, most important, "Dues for members will be $2.00 yearly, payable every sixth month on April first and October first." For the magnificent sum of $1.00 every six months the recorder players of America could belong to a society of their very own. A copy of the above-mentioned document was received at the national headquarters of The American Recorder Society at the end of October, 1987. It had been forwarded by a member of the Chicago chapter of the ARS, Ruth Feucht, who had been given it by an older member, Jane Cooke. Jane had told Ruth that the document was "from the first organization of The American Recorder Society." Although Suzanne Bloch had no memory of the document or its contents, it appears to have been signed by her, and was presumably sent to recorder players she knew around the country as an invitation to join. Suzanne herself thought it might have been sent to colleges as well. In any event, in view of the date on the letter, April 1st, 1939 seems a convenient date to set for the founding of The American Recorder Society. In the summer of 1935 Suzanne Bloch went to Haslemere, in Surrey, England, to study the lute (then an almost-obsolete instrument, like the recorder) with the celebrated antiquarian, musical instrument maker, and lutenist Arnold Dolmetsch. Dolmetsch's son Carl, then 25 years old, was already coming into his own as a recorder player, and he persuaded Suzanne that she should learn to play. After a half-hour lesson with Carl, Suzanne became, in her own wry words, an "instant professional," although, to give her credit, she was always modest about her recorder skills.

Carl Dolmetsch came to New York City on tour in the winter of 1936 or 1937 and performed with Suzanne. Carl played the recorder and Suzanne played recorder, lute and virginals. One of the places they visited was the City and Country School, an independent school in Manhattan. One of their listeners was a young music teacher, Margaret Bradford. So enraptured was she that she, too, went off to Haslemere to study recorder with the Dolmetsches. She, too, became an instant professional, not performing but teaching recorder to adults at New York University, and children at the City and Country School. G. Schirmer published *How Two Play the Recorder* by Margaret Bradford and Elizabeth Parker in 1938/39. Suzanne Bloch in the meantime had started importing Dolmetsch recorders to sell in the United States, mainly as a favor to the Dolmetsch family, and publicizing the recorder in concerts along with her lute. There is no doubt that Suzanne played a large part in getting the recorder movement started in this country. Her contributions, she believed, were three: 1) bringing recorders to the U.S., 2) popularizing them by playing them in concerts, and 3) founding The American Recorder Society.

Suzanne's aim, stated in an interview many years after the founding of the Society, was to get people to play better. Even in those very early days it became obvious that the recorder was an easy instrument to learn to play badly, and for true musicians it was often a trial to listen to the squawks of beginners. "We've got to start a Society where people can meet," said Suzanne. "I want to have them learn to hear each other."

Suzanne Bloch and Margaret Bradford had a recorder-playing friend, Irmgard Lehrer, whom they considered a true professional; they asked her to be the first president of The American Recorder Society. Conflicts arose almost immediately—between those who wanted to use the Society for the benefit of the amateur members (Suzanne and Margaret) and those who were mainly interested in furthering their own careers (according to Suzanne, Irmgard Lehrer, who "was using it [the ARS] for herself," as in printing ARS stationery with her name on it, for instance). Others involved with the Society in its infancy, who were undoubtedly motivated by a combination of both altruism and self-interest, were: Alfred Mann, musicologist, conductor, college professor and recorder-player; Theodore Mix, founder of Magnamusic, first a retail storekeeper, then a distributor, then a publisher of recorder music and importer of recorders and harpsichords; Carleton Sprague Smith, chief of the music division of the New York Public Library, and Harold Newman, an accountant called in to help with practical matters who later became a distributor, arranger, and publisher of recorder music as well.

Perhaps a word or two concerning the use of the words "amateur" and "professional" in this memoir are due here. The American Recorder Society was founded by Suzanne Bloch, a brilliant professional musician, teacher, and performer on the lute, devoted to early music. In her day there were no professional recorder players; the Society was founded for the amateurs—those who professed, as the name implies, a love for the instrument. As the 20th century progressed so did knowledge of early music history, notation, performance practice, and the playing of early instruments other than the recorder, to say nothing of the art and science of making copies of early instruments. A true professional class began to emerge in the latter part of the century—those who made their living or part of it playing and teaching early instruments, including the recorder. In the early days of The American Recorder Society musicians like Suzanne Bloch and Erich Katz did not consider themselves professional recorder players. But from the very beginning there was a strange schism between those who considered themselves amateurs in recorder playing (if they thought about it at all), and those who wanted to be considered professional, like Irmgard Lehrer. This schism has been the cause of some deep distress among the members and the administration of the ARS, as will be seen later.

Irmgard Lehrer was persuaded to resign as president of the ARS about a year after she took office, and Harold Newman became the second president. Newman was not a professional, according to Suzanne, but was "the one man who can handle things. He knows about business, things we don't know. And he also is not in the profession. He's not trying to make a living from the recorder, so he's ideally suited."

CHAPTER TWO
Faltering Forties

Meetings of The American Recorder Society were held fairly regularly in the early '40s in schools, apartments, and, occasionally, Steinway Hall, in New York City. Sometime in 1943 it was decided to suspend operations until after the end of the distractions of the Second World War. Recorder playing in the United States, however, did not cease. Two interesting documents from that time are two issues of The American Recorder *Review*, "a quarterly devoted to the Revival of the Recorder" dated "Summer, 1942," and "Winter, 1943–44." They turned up in the archive of the late Dr. Emmanuel Winternitz, a former curator of musical instruments at the Metropolitan Museum of Art in New York, and have found their way to me. In the first issue its editor, Dr. William Charles Carle, wrote: "This is the first issue of a magazine devoted entirely to a single musical instrument: the recorder or block flute. The American Recorder *Review* will try to become an information center, a clearing house for different opinions and an encouraging guide in future developments."

The first issue of *A.R.R* contains contributions by Irmgard Lehrer and Carleton Sprague Smith ("Standards [should be] maintained at a high level. . . . The recorder is not as easy to play well as many people think."); an article on the "renaissance of the recorder" in the United States; a "survey [of the movement] from coast to coast," including discussions of possible uses for the recorder as a therapeutic instrument for soldiers at war and handicapped children at home. There were also advertisements for recorder courses at Smith College and the Juilliard School (both taught by Irmgard Lehrer); advertisements for American-made instruments by William Koch, David Dushkin, and Irmgard Lehrer; notices of recorder performances (Irmgard Lehrer in

Elizabethan costume); and reports of recorder activities in Washington, D.C.; Pittsburgh; Chicago; Portland, Oregon; San Francisco; and, of course, New York City. The ubiquitous Irmgard Lehrer was at the forefront of recorder activities in New York; she also had advertisements in the *A.R.R.* for recorder classes and music published by her "Center for Recorder Music" on West 119th Street. There is even a musical supplement to The American Recorder *Review*, ostensibly the beginning of a supply of "more recorder music for school, home and concert use" that was one of the original aims of The American Recorder Society.

The second issue of *A.R.R.*, the "Winter 1943–44" edition, describes more of the activities of Irmgard Lehrer. A short article about the Trapp family's use of the recorder is included. Curiously, there is no mention of The American Recorder Society in either of the two issues of *A.R.R* that have been preserved. (And yet there may have been a connection: In its first issue of a *Newsletter* in 1947 the ARS announced plans to "reissue the ARS Review.")

In 1947 Harold Newman was the "Director" of The American Recorder Society, and Carleton Sprague Smith its Honorary President. Meetings were a combination of concerts and "supervised playing time for members." Membership dues were $3.00 per year or 50 cents a meeting. One could become a Friend of the Society for $5.00. To save money, meetings were moved from Steinway Hall to branches of the New York Public Library, starting with the Nathan Straus branch on East 32nd Street.

Two issues of an American Recorder Society *Newsletter* published in 1947 (since aborted; *ARS News Letter* [sic] No. 1 reappeared in 1950) give programs of mini-concert performances, under the aegis of the ARS, of both early and new music for the recorder. Erich Katz's many arrangements and original music make frequent appearances on the concert programs including "Old Christmas Carols and Songs" for three recorders, his "Sonatina" for two altos, and his "Trio" for alto recorder, flute, and viola. There are reports of the New York appearances of Suzanne Bloch, Alfred Mann, and Erich Katz, of recordings of recorder music (on "unbreakable material,") and of the new Dolmetsch plastic recorder. Some rather grandiose plans are presented to the ARS membership. The October 1947 *Newsletter* announces a re-issue of the ARS Review and more ARS *Newsletter*s to come. "Outstanding American Composers will be encouraged to write for the recorder, and if funds are available, some commissions will be offered for compositions." As far as I can tell, none of these plans was carried out, at least not immediately.

We owe some of the earliest chronicles of The American Recorder Society to Lois M. Hutchings, who as a graduate student in biology at Cornell University in the winter of 1939–40 read an ad in the New York Times that changed her life. Margaret Bradford was teaching a course in recorder playing at New York University. Lois joined the course in the fall of 1940, and was soon invited to attend meetings of The American Recorder Society. Like many a new convert, then as now, Lois quickly found herself involved in the administration of the ARS. Lois Hutchings was probably the very first secretary of The American Recorder Society.

"An incident of the early days," she writes, "does the Society [little] credit. In 1941 we were assembled on the stage of the Metropolitan Museum of Art to perform a concert. Three times the conductor tried to get us started and failed. So, Alfred Mann and his talented, professional mother, harpsichordist Edith Weiss-Mann, took over and presented the concert." Saved by the professionals! Then, as now, the yen to perform sometimes took over from the common-sense recognition that one might not be ready. From the minutes of The American Recorder Society, October 27, 1942:

> During the business meeting, which was called to order by the President, Mr. Harold Newman, . . . many different members of the society voiced opinions and offered suggestions. . . . Several people

expressed the opinion that the original purpose motivating the formation of the Recorder Society was to bring together proficient players, and, also . . . that each one might receive stimulation. . . . We are an association of amateurs and professional standards are not applicable. . . . Regarding the last spring concert (May, 1942, at the Metropolitan Museum of Art), the general consensus of opinion was that there was a lack of careful planning. For instance, most of the players did not even know the order of the program. . . . It was recognized that the most successful numbers were those in which the participants had rehearsed together several times.

From a later memo:

World War Two took more and more of the men so in 1943 it was decided to suspend meetings until more normal times came back. An interesting incident occurred in 1943 while we were still holding meetings. To one of our meetings someone brought a distinguished recorder conductor who had recently come to the United States from Germany. We found him unnecessarily precise according to our lax standards. I'm not certain, but it may have been Erich Katz [it was].

Erich Katz, early 1940s.
(Photo courtesy of The Erich Katz Papers, Recorder Music Center, Archives and Special Collections, Regis University, Denver, CO)

If Suzanne Bloch was the mother of the American Recorder Society, Erich Katz was its father. A distinguished German-Jewish musicologist, with a doctorate from the University of Freiburg, Erich Katz had escaped to England in 1939 from Nazi Germany, and from there to the United States. Like many of his compatriots, he had endured the horrors of concentration

Erich Katz leads a playing session in the late 1940s, probably in an adult education class given by City College of New York at a high school.

(Photo courtesy of The Erich Katz Papers, Recorder Music Center, Archives and Special Collections, Regis University, Denver, CO)

camp, life in a foreign country (England, where he taught music at a girls' boarding school from 1941–1943), and a harrowingly dangerous trip across the Atlantic in a small passenger ship escorted by a U.S. military convoy. With his second wife, Hannah Labus Katz, Erich Katz journeyed by train from Halifax to New York, where the couple's first residence was a tenement Hannah derisively called "Buckingham Palace." Although trained as a physician, Hannah could only find work as a nurse. Erich started copying music at 45 cents a page.

The children of Columbia professors Paul Tillich and Reinhold Niebuhr were among his first students at Riverside Church. Later Erich secured teaching positions at the City College of New York, the New School and, most fortunately for the ARS, the New York College of Music in 1944. The College of Music later came to be, for many people, the headquarters of the American Recorder Society.

Erich Katz was not accepted by the ARS with open arms at first. A postcard dated December 2, 1943 from then-President Harold Newman, preserved in the Erich Katz Archives, invites Erich to attend and perform at the Christmas meeting of the ARS at Steinway Hall in New York. Whether he performed or not, the distinguished musicologist did not make a terrific impression upon the members. Suzanne Bloch, who was by then beginning to lose interest in the Society, concluded that Erich Katz "was a very dull man." (But then she also held that Edith Weiss-Mann was "a sour-faced woman who played as though she were doing the family wash.")

Erich Katz was, however, an extraordinary man, a musician who was also a magnetic and inventive educator. He was also a composer, conductor, musicologist as stated, and a completely free spirit.

Program from a March 13, 1944 concert of early music including ARS members Suzanne Bloch and Erich Katz.

Determined not to be fettered by convention, he dressed casually, living close to squalor in a cramped New York City apartment, and yet he loved the out-of-doors with something close to passion. He was passionately devoted to music, too, though he often wrote and spoke of the joys of silence. Another of his passions was The American Recorder Society. Probably the greatest service to the ARS ever performed by Harold Newman was his introduction of Erich Katz to the Society.

In a February, 1961 letter to then-vice president A.C. Glassgold Erich Katz mentions that when he got seriously involved with the ARS it had 18 members. This confirms his letter of March 12, 1961 to Rhoda Weber, stating that when he "took over" in 1947 or '48 he "started to reorganize with the 17 remaining members." The first postwar meeting of the ARS was held on October 29, 1947 at the New York College of Music, 114 East 85th Street. Erich had started teaching there, and the ARS was fortunate to be able to use its auditorium as a convenient venue for meetings for many years.

In 1949 LaNoue Davenport joined The American Recorder Society. A jazz trumpet player of extraordinary musical gifts, he had come to New York to study music and, especially, composition with Erich Katz at the New York College of Music. Of that period Davenport recalls:

> Of course if you studied with Erich you were drawn into all of his activities, so I began to sing with a group he directed called the Musicians' Workshop. At some point around 1948 or 1949 Erich arranged to do a concert of early music over WNYC. We needed someone to play a recorder, which I'd never heard or had in my hands. The concert was about a month away.... So a month later I made my debut on alto recorder.... I think [the music] was an arrangement of a DuFay piece. After that I was hooked. I became a disciple and began to do a lot of things with Erich, one of which was The American Recorder Society—which he resuscitated about that time. [Interview 6/8/88]

In the 25th-anniversary issue of The American Recorder (November 1964) LaNoue writes: "In 1949 [the ARS had] . . . several visions of projects which would further the interests of the recorder in particular, and early music in general."

1. The establishment of ARS chapters [these were begun in 1955]
2. A teachers' certification program [started in 1961]
3. Publication of a national magazine of high quality [begun in 1960]
4. Summer schools for recorder players [the first "American Recorder Society Seminar" was held at the National Music Camp in Interlochen, Michigan in August of 1961]

CHAPTER THREE

Flourishing '50s

In 1950 membership in The American Recorder Society was still very small (20–25, according to LaNoue Davenport [interview, 6/8/88]), and still confined to New York City, but this tiny flower was about to burst into bloom. The influence of Erich Katz on the Society was making itself felt. He often performed at or conducted meetings of the Society, using his own arrangements of early music and his own original music for recorders, which was being published by Harold Newman's newly organized Hargail Music Press. Erich was also "spreading the news" about the recorder by teaching adult classes through the City College Extension Division and giving a series of lessons on the radio entitled "You Can Play the Recorder!" In 1950 the first meetings of the Society were held in summer months.

An important event for the development of the ARS was the arrival of Winifred (Wini) Jaeger upon the scene. Wini was an accomplished musician herself who became a student of Erich Katz at the New York College of Music. In the beginning she helped out with managing the American Recorder Society, and then became more and more involved. In the end she was Erich's colleague and collaborator, a performer, arranger, and teacher, as well as an indispensable member of the administration of the ARS. Wini's kitchen table and Erich's studio apartment on East 85th Street alternated as the ARS "office." Erich and Wini, in a "complete reorganization," set out to make the American Recorder Society a viable organization for recorder players.

Erich Katz was appointed "Musical Director" of the ARS in 1950. His assistant musical directors were Betty Krohn, Eleanore Scovill, LaNoue

Musicians' Workshop, New York College of Music, mid 1950s. Erich Katz is directing. Winifred Jaeger is in the front row, third woman from the right.
(Photo courtesy of The Erich Katz Papers. Recorder Music Center, Archives and Special Collections, Regis University, Denver, CO)

Davenport, and Bernard Krainis. It should be stated here that LaNoue Davenport and Bernard Krainis were the "young Turks" of the '50s. They were possibly the first two bona fide professional recorder players in the United States. Each was, as a young man, strongly influenced by Erich Katz, but each was self-taught on the recorder. Each discovered, on his own, how to create a truly beautiful sound and to make music on the recorder in a way that had surely not been heard in professional music circles for some 200 years.

Bernie Krainis, like LaNoue Davenport, came to the ARS via Erich

Katz. Bernie had played the trombone, but his introduction to the recorder came in the form of a 21st-birthday present of a Dushkin alto recorder from his father on December 28, 1945. Krainis recounts:

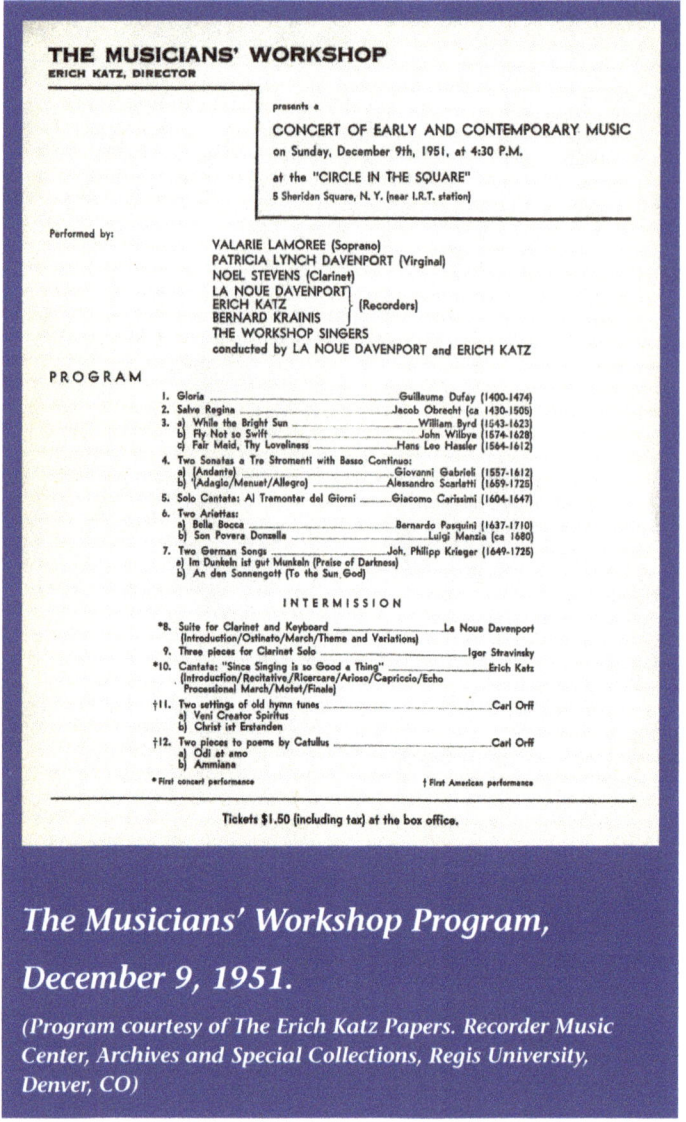

The Musicians' Workshop Program, December 9, 1951.

(Program courtesy of The Erich Katz Papers. Recorder Music Center, Archives and Special Collections, Regis University, Denver, CO)

> Until that moment, until I had the thing in my hands, not only had I never seen or heard the instrument, but I had never even heard of it. It was the absolute first. I stayed up all night and figured out the notes, and since no one told me that it was supposed to be an easy instrument, I started to practice. I've kept practicing ever since.

In 1949 I tuned into station WNYC and heard, all by accident, a program by the Musicians' Workshop. It was maybe a half hour of unusual madrigals and two- and three-part recorder things. I was very excited. It was the first time I had ever heard anybody else play the recorder with any degree of fluency. The group was directed by Erich Katz. . . . I got in touch with him. I expressed interest in playing with the Musicians' Workshop. He suggested I come to an ARS meeting and asked if I was a member of the Recorder Society.

I said no. I had heard of the ARS, but it's such an imposing name that I thought it consisted of seasoned professional players, that I couldn't really keep up. . . . I walked in and there were . . . eight or ten people sitting around very casually and unprepossessingly. One of the great culture shocks of my life was hearing them play for the first time.

It quickly became clear to me that this would be a quid pro quo, that in order for me to gain entree into the Musicians' Workshop, I was expected to put in my time with the ARS. That first year or two I believe I conducted every ARS meeting [that I was asked to conduct] with absolutely no experience in conducting. [Interview 9/12/88]

By 1951 Harold Newman had, according to an interview in AR in February of 1972, "turned over" the ARS to Erich Katz. As Newman became more involved in the mercantile area of the recorder world—selling recorders and publishing and selling recorder music, the ARS became Erich Katz's domain. Erich's administrative help came from devoted amateurs—Druscilla Evans, Isabel Benedict and Lucinda Ballard—who, according to Bernard Krainis, "held things together in the early '50s." With the musical director and his "assistants" (soon two prominent teachers—Gertrud Bamberger and Johanna Kulbach—were added to their number) the group formed a loosely organized "administrative council." Bernard Krainis edited the *Newsletter* from 1950 until June of 1953 and LaNoue Davenport edited it until the summer of 1959. Winifred Jaeger was Treasurer and served as Secretary for some time. This unincorporated "Board of Directors" continued to function in much the same way until 1959, when Erich retired to California. In 1950 the first "membership committee" of the ARS was formed, to actively recruit and maintain membership.

The ARS *Newsletter* was reborn January 20, 1950 with Bernard Krainis as its first editor.

With this first issue of its News Letter, The American Recorder Society inaugurates a policy, long awaited and hopefully discussed, of presenting a fairly regular periodical devoted exclusively to the interests of the growing number of recorder players throughout the United States.

Krainis went on to say that "the recorder movement is at the present time mainly concentrated in the New York City area," but he felt, evidently, that what interested New Yorkers would interest the nation. The first *Newsletter* reported on classes in recorder given by Gertrud Bamberger at the YMHA, Reba Mirsky at the New School for Social Research, and Erich Katz at the City College of New York.

Newsletter 2, April 1, 1950, tells of a Honolulu Recorder Society started by Dr. and Mrs. Leonard J. Goldwater during the war when Dr. Goldwater was stationed at Pearl Harbor.

> It is believed that this group has introduced some new combinations into ensemble playing, particularly through developing ukulele accompaniments for the recorder. Our informant states that he does not believe that this combination is one which will find widespread adoption outside of the Hawaiian Islands.

Newsletter 2 tells of meetings, concerts, and live radio broadcasts of recorder playing, of newly released recorder publications and recordings, and complains of the difficulty of finding places to buy recorder music (then lists some). It also lists places to study the recorder and gives news of the activities of the British Society of Recorder Players.

The ARS *Newsletter* was published fairly continuously until 1960. For a decade it was a valuable source for its readers, not only of news of the recorder world and the activities of the Recorder Society, but of places to find instruments, music, and instruction on the recorder—three basic needs of recorder players. And it was the first source, for players, of educational and scholarly articles in the emerging field of early music performance practice.

An announcement was made in *Newsletter* 4, November 1, 1950, of an exciting new project, the "ARS Editions," a music series for recorder ensemble to be published by Clarke & Way. These modest editions were priced at 60 cents a copy—40 cents for members. AMP (Associated Music Publisher) became the publisher and distributor with No. 13 in April, 1954. Erich Katz was editor-in-chief in every sense of the word. One of Katz's most important contributions to The American Recorder Society was getting members of the ARS interested in early music, both to listen to and to play. Like a number of musicologists and composers of the '50s, Erich was deeply interested in early music. He had founded the Musicians' Workshop, a group devoted to the performance of both early and new music, that attracted students at the New York College of Music soon after he started teaching there in 1947. He started publishing music for recorders, both arrangements and original works, with Hargail Music in the 1940s. As editor-in-chief of the new ARS Editions, Erich made quantities of early and new music accessible to recorder players at ARS meetings. Some examples of the early editions are: Salamone Rossi, *Five Sinfonie a Tre Voce* (SAT) arranged by Erich Katz; Melchior Franck, *Four Dances* (SSAAT) arranged by Erich Katz; and Girolamo Frescobaldi, *Canzona* (SSAT) arranged by Bernard Krainis.

Early ARS editions ran heavily toward Renaissance and early Baroque music— though there are some original compositions, such as Henry Cowell's *Three Pieces for Three Recorders*, one of which, "Pelog," is based on an Indonesian five-tone scale. Bass recorders were rare in the '50s, and the ARS editions did not make much use of them, trying to make do with very low tenor parts. "The publications are not presented with any musicological pretensions," Erich wrote in ARS *Newsletter* 9 (3/3/52):

> Our intention is to add valuable material to the existing literature for group playing, serving mainly those many people who are amateurs in the true sense of the word: music lovers for whom recorder playing is a means—sometimes the only one—to active

participation in music. The joy of music making—not just listening—for which there is no substitute, is the main reason for the growing popularity of recorder playing. There is always a need for more literature to satisfy the yearning for good music in this field.

The early ARS editions were, in short, designed to make early music accessible to recorder players. The recorder-playing community of the '50s did not, on the whole, worry much about authenticity. There were, however, even from the beginning, a few voices of concern. A letter to Erich from David Way (one of the publishers of the early ARS Editions) of March 19, 1952 said in essence that he (Way) thinks some authenticity is important, at least insofar as stating original instrumentation and scoring (transposition, etc.) are concerned.

> The person with real knowledge of this field will, of course, recognize our additions [sic] for what they are. It is the half-learned that we must beware of and it seems to me that we should make some effort to persuade him that we know what we are talking about.

In those years Erich's views prevailed. Indeed, many of Erich Katz's publications for recorder, including his superb method, *Recorder Playing*, are famous for the amount of pure Katz that is interpolated into folk songs, Christmas carols, and arrangements of early music. Erich's purposes were pedagogical and pragmatic; he wanted to provide material for the growing ranks of recorder players, and this he did, indefatigably and successfully.

The year 1950 brought the first of the two Newman brothers, who are not related to Harold Newman, into the web of the American Recorder Society. Joel Newman, a Columbia graduate student later to become a distinguished musicologist, met the talented and charismatic Bernard Krainis, started studying with him, and was soon involved in a "mini-performance" at a meeting of the ARS that Bernie was conducting. Like many other practicing musicians before and after him, Joel was taken aback at the sound of a roomful of 40 or 50 people playing the recorder simultaneously, but he was intrigued nevertheless. Joel moved rather quickly into the top echelons of the American Recorder Society, as a performer, musical director, education director, and later as editor of the ARS Editions. With LaNoue Davenport and Bernard Krainis, Joel Newman brought the aura of the professional musician to this society of amateurs. This aura was in many ways beneficial, as it helped to bring about standards in recorder playing that the amateurs—often derisively called "tootlers" in the early days—could never have attained by themselves, but it also brought the beginnings of conflict between the views of those who thought the recorder should be a purely recreational instrument and those who thought it should be an instrument for professionals only.

This conflict, as stated in Chapter One, has been the source of one of the primary problems faced by the various administrations of the ARS during its first 60 years, beginning with the goals of the "professional" Irmgard Lehrer vs. those of the "amateur" Suzanne Bloch and lasting until sometime in the '90s. There have been strong partisan feelings on both sides of the question. On March 15, 1967, Erich Katz, then living in Santa Barbara, wrote to Joel Newman:

> The real problem, and I think you will agree with me, is not East-West, but 'professionals' against 'amateurs.' The ARS, for better or worse, is an organization of amateurs and can't be compared with . . . an organization of professionals like the AMS [American Musicological Society].

Now that the lines between amateur and professional players have been clearly drawn, with professionals of astounding virtuosity the world over playing on instruments of a much higher caliber than those of the 1950s and '60s, the recorder is fully recognized as a musical instrument, not merely a toy for children or a stepping-stone to a "real" instrument like a clarinet. Due in part to the consciousness-raising done in this country by the ARS and by similar organizations in other countries, notably the Society of Recorder Players in England, the argument seems to be settled: the recorder is many things to many people. It is a true instrument, heard in concerts not only of early music, but with "mainstream" classical groups as well, in jazz performances, in television commercials, movie scores, pop recordings, classical CD's, and wherever music is played, in many different venues. The recorder is also a source of cultural enrichment, musical fulfillment, and enormous pleasure to amateur players. Both pursuits of the recorder have their legitimate place, and both are supported by the ARS.

Plans were made, and announced in *Newsletter* 1, January 20, 1950, for an annual concert of the ARS to be presented at Carl Fischer Hall in New York City. The ARS concert presented at the New York College of Music on May 23, 1950 was free to members and $1.00 for others. Recorder-playing performers were Erich Katz, LaNoue Davenport, and Bernard Krainis. A problem of the time, duly noted in the *Newsletter*, was balancing the recorder in concert with the modern violin, cello, and piano. ARS concerts were not, of course, the only early music concerts in the New York of the '50s. There were other performers on the recorder; Suzanne Bloch gave concerts at Town Hall with her mathematician-cum-recorder player husband Paul Smith; "The Weavers" used recorders; and Pete Seeger was a proficient player. Bach's Brandenburg Concerto No. 4 was a favorite, as people discovered it had been composed for recorders, not flutes. Safford Cape's Pro Musica Antiqua, a Belgian group, was giving U.S. tours. Again Bernard Krainis in the *Newsletter*: "We can only wistfully regret that there is not yet such an organization in the United States."

Concerts under the aegis of the ARS (really the New York group) continued through the 1950s, adding performers like LaNoue's wife Patsy Lynch Davenport, Herbert Kellman, Alfred Mann, Lois Wann, Johanna Kulbach, Tui St. George Tucker, Robert Dorough, Martha Bixler, Joel and Morris Newman, and many others. An ARS concert

A concert at the New York College of Music in the early 1950s. Left to right (seated on stage) Carl Cowl (ARS Secretary in the 1950s) and Rod Evans; (playing) LaNoue Davenport, Winifred Jaeger, Herbert Kellman.
(Photo courtesy of The Erich Katz Papers; Recorder Music Center, Archives and Special Collections, Regis University, Denver, CO)

at the Circle in the Square Theatre was given a favorable review in the New York *Herald Tribune* on May 6, 1952. Reviewer Jay Harrison's concept of the recorder is, however, in some ways curious. Although he states flatteringly that "the participants [in the concert] were of a technique equal to the demands of the music and of a sensitivity commensurate with its content," he goes on to say that "the personality of the recorder is a strange one, being based not upon the skill with which it is played but upon the inherent delicacy of its timbre." And then, appallingly, after stating that the pieces included in the performance "are compositions of elegance and power, spilling over with life, and everywhere neatly made," he continues, even using the "t-word," with: "As *tooted* [italics mine] across the centuries by the members of the American Recorder Society they told a tale as vibrant and contemporary as though they had been put to paper not 24 hours before their performance."

The debut performance of the New York Pro Musica Antiqua, the pioneering group of the early music movement in the United States, took place at the New School for Social Research in Manhattan on April 26, 1953. The recorder soloists were Bernard Krainis and LaNoue Davenport. This was a significant event for many reasons. The New York Pro Musica was not only a pioneering group but also the leading American professional group devoted to the performance of early music for 20 years or more. Bernard Krainis and LaNoue Davenport, already engaged in a rivalry that stimulated the development of recorder playing in this country, were at different times regular members of this influential group—Krainis until 1959 and Davenport from 1960 to 1970. Both Bernie and LaNoue were extremely influential in the recorder movement in this country, for several important reasons: their travels with the New York Pro Musica, their numerous recordings, the large number of people they taught, and because of the involvement of both in the administration of the ARS. Each was president for a time, LaNoue twice, from 1959–1962 and again briefly in 1966, and Bernard from 1962–1964.

A cultural milestone of the '50s was the beginning of commercial recordings featuring the recorder and/or early music. These were not promoted by The American Recorder Society financially, but they were made possible partly by the atmosphere created by the existence of the ARS. In 1953 Esoteric put out a recording of the "Primavera Singers" (an antecedent of the New York Pro Musica Antiqua) under the direction of Noah Greenberg. Classic Editions issued Recorder Music of Six Centuries performed by the "Recorder Consort of the Musicians' Workshop" (LaNoue Davenport, Bob Dorough, Erich Katz, Bernard Krainis, and Herbert Kellman). Both recordings were reviewed in the New York *Times* on August 12, 1953.

An awakening interest in professionalism among recorder players can be noted in an editorial by LaNoue Davenport in *Newsletter* 14, October, 1953. He emphasized the role of the ARS in encouraging performance of Baroque music on Baroque instruments, i.e., recorders.

"While the main endeavor [of The American Recorder Society] will continue to be towards informal music-making, the *professional* [italics mine] aspect of the recorder also has a definite place in a recorder society, particularly in concerts."

Another "first" for the '50s: *Newsletter* 6, April 20, 1951 mentions contact with a summer resort, South Wind, near Woodburn, NY, for use for a week or weekend organized by The American Recorder Society for its members. Quoted rates by the resort for one room, double occupancy, were $42 a week through July and August and $14 for a weekend. Nothing came of this first attempt, but the groundwork was laid for what eventually became an important and influential part of the infrastructure of the ARS: the summer and weekend workshops held in increasing numbers in the 1960s, '70s and '80s. Along the way, David Dushkin started a series of summer recorder weeks at a camp in Kinhaven, Vermont, beginning in the summer of 1954.

The ARS's interest in and involvement with the education of recorder players began in the 1950s and has never ceased. Erich Katz's previously mentioned *Recorder Playing*, a method based on his amazing "massed recorder" classes at City College teaching soprano and alto players simultaneously, was published by Clarke and Way in 1951. A list of 20 members who taught the recorder was published by the ARS in 1953. (Here again it must be stated that The American Recorder Society at the time was an almost completely provincial organization based in New York City. There must certainly have been teachers of recorder in other parts of the United States, but we didn't know about them!) Lists of teachers and places for instruction continued to be published through the '50s, but it was not until 1960 that a scheme for testing teachers was worked out, and the ARS got into the business of deciding who should be doing the teaching, that is, endorsing teachers, schools, and workshops on the recorder. This was opening Pandora's Box, as will be seen later.

On February 1st, 1954 The American Recorder Society boasted of having 220 members, of whom only 73 lived outside the New York metropolitan area and 24 away from the East Coast. The ARS clearly had a long way to go before it would live up to its name: American Recorder Society. In July of that year annual dues were raised to $4.00 for members living in the New York metropolitan area and $2.50 for "those outside." This small group, the non-natives, however, was getting restless. For their modest dues they were getting *Newsletters*, of course, and news of all the exciting doings in New York, and indeed constant news of the rapid expansion of the world of the recorder and early music in other countries (recorder playing in Quebec, the founding of the Society of Recorder Players in New Zealand in 1953, and the astonishing claim in *Recorder News*, the magazine of the British Society of Recorder Players, that there were over 8000 recorder players in New South Wales), but they wanted more. They wanted organized playing in their own areas. There were groups outside New York: the San Francisco and Seattle Recorder Guilds are mentioned early in the '50s. An article published in House Beautiful, June, 1954, and reprinted in *Newsletter* 17, reported on the formation of the Southern California Recorder Association; a Chicago Recorder Society was germinating. *Newsletter* 18, October 1954, told us that "several inquiries have been received about establishing chapters of the ARS . . . and perhaps this year will see the first ARS organizations outside of New York."

At a meeting of the officers of the ARS on July 1, 1954 "the American Recorder Society decided, in response to numerous inquiries, to establish chapters outside of New York City." Six or more members of the ARS could constitute a chapter, and the chairmen of the various chapters would be members of an advisory committee to the Board of Officers of the ARS. On April 2, 1955, 16 years after the founding of the American Recorder Society, the Boston chapter of the ARS was unanimously and officially welcomed by the officers of the national organization. Chapter membership dues were to be $3.50 annually, with $2.50 going to the ARS. A condition of chapter membership was individual membership in the national organization, but this first chapter and future chapters were to have "considerable freedom of method, organization and objective."

The Philadelphia chapter of the ARS followed close behind Boston, becoming official in July of the same year. In 1956 the Memphis chapter came into being; in 1958 Chattanooga, Washington (D.C.) and Chicago (over 80 members and four musical directors by June, 1959— their first chapter concert was on May 15, 1959). In 1959 Austin, Milwaukee, and Buffalo formed their own chapters. The ARS *Newsletter* started carrying chapter news in its pages in recognition of the needs of its members in the "'hinterlands."

Other developments of the mid- to late-'50s: Meetings of the American Recorder Society were held regularly at the New York College of Music. At a typical meeting the "assistant musical director" would conduct 30–50 recorder players in arrangements for recorders published by Schott or Bärenreiter, or one of the new ARS Editions, and, with a few friends, give a short performance.

The ARS continued to publish lists of teachers of the recorder for its members (in 1955 there were 22 names on the list; in 1956, 29). In April, 1957 the ARS *Newsletter* began publishing a series of 10 articles on recorder technique by the English pedagogue Anthony Rowland-Jones. LaNoue Davenport taught at a Labor Day weekend in 1954 at the Indian Hill Music Workshop in Stockbridge, Massachusetts. David Dushkin continued to run summer music and recorder camps in Vermont. The National Federation of Music Clubs included recorder for the first time in its 1954 Festival. Patty Grossman taught at a recorder workshop at the Idyllwild (California) Arts Foundation, and Eric Leber began teaching recorder at Folk Music Week at Pinewoods Camp (Massachusetts).

A recorder seminar under the direction of LaNoue Davenport was held in two weekend installments at a hotel in Lakeville, Connecticut, September 20–21 and 27–28, 1958. Days were spent with small ensemble classes in the hotel rooms. In the evenings the faculty (LaNoue Davenport, Martha Bixler, Shelley Gruskin) performed. We were paid $25 for each weekend. I thought it a fortune at the time. The two weekends were "produced" by Ted and Alice Mix of Magnamusic Distributors, Inc., in Sharon, Connecticut. The Mixes were much involved in the founding of the ARS, and were always strong supporters; their firm remains a business member of the ARS to this day. This event was not an ARS event per se, but it was probably the model for the very first week-long recorder summer seminar under the auspices of the ARS in 1962.

The noted English recorder maker and player Carl Dolmetsch and his accompanist, harpsichordist Joseph Saxby, came to New York at the beginning of an American tour (the last had been 20 years earlier, in 1937) and were presented in a concert on October 6, 1957 by the American Recorder Society. Dolmetsch conducted a meeting of the Society at the New York College of Music on October 7.

The ARS's own concerts and those of its individual members continued at an increasing rate. The "assistant musical directors" performed as well as taught at members' meetings. Suzanne Bloch organized a series of solo concerts for children at the New York College of Music, playing lute, virginals, and recorders. In a New York Philharmonic Young People's concert 60 children played transcriptions of music by Mozart, Handel, and Beethoven. The grandly-named New York Recorder Ensemble and Telemann Society (I hasten to say neither had any connection with the ARS) gave astonishingly amateurish performances in that innocent age, at places like New York's Town Hall, Carnegie Recital Hall, and the Museum of the City of New York. Erich Katz was still Musical Director of the ARS and nominally in charge of the ARS concert presented at P.S. 6 on May 22, 1955, but it was LaNoue and Bernie who, each directing his own consort, brought the first hints of professionalism to an ARS performance. (ARS members were still admitted free, with non-members paying $1.50 a

Musicians' Workshop, New York College of Music, mid 1950s. Left to right: Martha Bixler, Robert Dorough, Winifred Jaeger.
(Photo courtesy of The Erich Katz Papers. Recorder Music Center, Archives and Special Collections, Regis University, Denver, CO)

ticket.) In July, 1957 a review in the *Musical Courier* of the annual ARS concert at Carl Fischer Hall states that "though many of its members are amateurs, it [the Society] demonstrated the power to present concerts of genuine musical excellence." On January 9, 1956, recorders were played in Carnegie Hall for the first time.

My own involvement with The American Recorder Society, which has continued until the present day, began in 1955. As a conservatory graduate deeply attracted to early music, I was easily drawn into the ARS orbit. I started singing with the Musicians' Workshop, then directed by Davenport, heard him play, and decided I must study the recorder with him. When LaNoue "turned pro," that is, began to play for money, I turned right along with him. We played in concerts, (including those for school children funded by the New York State Council for the Arts), made radio broadcasts and recordings, and taught at early music workshops. Later we entered the lucrative world of television commercials. I owe my entire career in early music to

Manhattan Consort rehearsing at the headquarters of the New York Pro Musica, c. 1960. Left to right: Sheila Schonbrun, Donald Plesnicar, Judith Davidoff, Martha Bixler, Shelley Gruskin, LaNoue Davenport.

LaNoue and to the ARS. But I certainly paid my dues. I played in my first ARS concert in May of 1955 as part of LaNoue's consort, the Manhattan Recorder Consort. I became one of Erich Katz's assistant musical directors, and began conducting meetings of the Society. Later I was a member of the ARS Board of Directors, still later president, twice. In October of 1958 I became associate editor of the ARS *Newsletter*, then editor in 1959. In 1960 I found myself the first editor of the new quarterly, The American Recorder. Later I went back to editing the *Newsletter*. All of these jobs were unremunerated at the time that I held them. And I have been, over the years, on the education, workshop, office, nominating (sometimes chair), Katz competition, executive, publications, music, scholarship, and various search committees. As the afore-mentioned editing positions began to be compensated, I would find myself in a new job I could do gratis, like that of editing the Members' Library Editions.

Morris Newman, a brilliantly talented bassoon player, became involved in the ARS as a teacher, performer, and administrator, through his brother Joel and Bernard Krainis, circa 1957. The American Recorder Society and Morris Newman had a big influence on each other; the ARS got Morris interested in early music, and Morris brought a militant spirit of professionalism to the Society. There were two aspects to this professionalism: the first, and most obvious, was the "pay me for whatever I do" attitude; the second, perhaps more important, was an increasing demand that the Society's exponents, or those with some pretensions toward professionalism at least, actually practice and play like professionals on other instruments. This was an idea that was still fairly new at that time. Although this "professional" attitude had its destructive aspects, it was on the whole a shot in the arm for the ARS, at least at the administrative level, and the beginning of the end of the ambience of mediocrity and amateurism in the worst sense that had clung to it from the beginning.

On September 28, 1957, a momentous event took place: the Board of Officers of the ARS met and agreed to approve a newly drafted constitution and bylaws for the ARS. Erich Katz was beginning to think about moving to his beloved Santa Barbara, California, where he and Wini had been building a cottage for themselves for years, stick by stick, during her two-week summer vacations. After a decade of running the ARS with an iron hand, Erich wanted, in his careful way, to make sure that his (also beloved) Society would be well organized and off-and-running when he left it on its own.

The American Recorder Society was legally incorporated on July 18, 1958. At the first annual business meeting of the Society (of course only New York metropolitan area members were physically able to attend) on May 16, 1959, the new bylaws were presented to the membership and a Board of Directors for the newly-incorporated Society was elected by secret ballot among the members present. Board members elected were, for two years: Martha Bixler, LaNoue

Davenport, Shelley Gruskin, Bernard Krainis, and Joel Newman; for one year: A. C. (Cook) Glassgold, Albert Hess, Johanna Kulbach, Marvin Rosenberg, and Elizabeth Watson. LaNoue Davenport, chosen in a unanimous vote of the Board of Directors on May 28, 1959, was the first constitutional president of the ARS; Cook Glassgold was chosen vice president. We thus had one professional and one amateur player in the two key administrative posts, and the seeds of later dissent between the two groups were immediately sown.

Other new appointments were Donna Hill, a writer, artist, and amateur recorder player, as secretary, and Yrsa Damman Geist, a student of Erich's and a colleague at the New York College of Music, as assistant secretary. Donna was a real find: she had discovered the ARS *Newsletter* in the New York Public Library and offered to make an index of it. She soon discovered, however, that she was needed badly as a secretary of the organization, and she took over from Winifred Jaeger the members' lists, mailings, and minute-taking at Board meetings. Marvin Rosenberg became treasurer (replaced a year later by Rhoda Weber, who became at the same time, informally, an assistant secretary), and Ralph Taylor, co-owner and CEO of Caswell-Massey, a company manufacturing men's cologne, also an amateur recorder player, was made assistant treasurer. Thus it took six people to take over the work of two.

The newly appointed officers, all very hard-working volunteers, plus a representative from each chapter of the ARS, were to comprise the Executive Board of The American Recorder Society. At this meeting also Joel Newman was appointed general editor of the ARS Editions and educational director of the Society, and I was appointed editor of the ARS *Newsletter*. We were the obvious candidates for these positions; Joel was already making his name as a musicologist, and had the sources, the knowledge and the musical intelligence to make him a competent editor of musical editions. I had been for some time helping the newly-appointed president with the *Newsletter*, so it was natural for me to take it over, thus putting my head firmly into that particular yoke.

LaNoue had a wonderful time as president, presiding over the beginning of this halcyon period. He was extremely good at getting others (as I remember it, mainly me) to do whatever legwork was required for any particular project. I remember a reception given by the ARS after a concert presented by Carl Dolmetsch and Joseph Saxby in Town Hall. LaNoue directed me to ask a student of mine if she would let us have her beautiful town house for the reception. That was all well and good; the student was delighted. However, a couple of days before the concert, I realized that my student and I were responsible for the whole thing. I still remember her startled words: "Then I guess we're doing it, you and I!" As we made drinks, peeled and cut vegetables and fruits and made dainty sandwiches for the visiting bigwigs and local ARS brass, I understood once again the role of a volunteer in a not for-profit Society: be there for whatever is needed!

Erich Katz resigned as Musical Director of the ARS in July, 1959 after he suffered his first stroke, and at the May meeting he was named "Honorary President" by the members of the ARS. (Erich suffered a second stroke in 1972 and died July 30, 1973.) Winifred Jaeger was named "Honorary Vice President." At the end of 1959, with 10 chapters, two publication series—the *Newsletter* and 40 ARS editions of music—600 members in the United States and foreign countries including Norway, Turkey, Vietnam, England, Canada and Australia, and a yearly budget of $1,150, the ARS embarked upon its third decade full of hope for becoming at last a truly national organization worthy of the name.

Erich Katz at the toy piano in his Santa Barbara home, March 13, 1972.

CHAPTER FOUR

Soaring '60s

"I feel lost," said I to LaNoue at the first meeting of the Board of Directors of The American Recorder Society, after Erich Katz deserted us for sunny California. "I feel found," was LaNoue's rejoinder, and in that brief exchange lay the essence of what was happening in the ARS and the difference between our two personalities. We were both "lost" and "found." Erich Katz, the musicologist, teacher, and father figure who had ruled the ARS for so long, had left us, his spiritual children, to take care of the ARS by ourselves. He had left us with a new organization, new bylaws, and a new freedom that LaNoue found exhilarating and I found scary.

My fears were, at first, unfounded. There was astonishing growth for The American Recorder Society in the '60s. Elections were held every year, with Board members holding staggered two-year terms. Board meetings were held monthly or bi-monthly in New York. Bernard Krainis was elected second president of the ARS in 1961. The number of members increased from 600 in July of 1959 to 2,700 in 1970. Some membership figures presented by the Treasurer at Board meetings follow (they fluctuated wildly according to the season): 858 in 1961; 1,485 as of 4/15/63; 1,645 on 6/1/63; 1,843 on 9/25/64; 1,726 on

LaNoue Davenport, 1962.

1/15/65; 1,923 on 9/21/65; 2,026 on 11/27/66; 2,205 in January 1967; 2,384 at the end of 1968.)

The number of chapters increased during the decade from 10 to 62. The New York chapter, Recorder Guild (now New York Recorder Guild), was formed—after a tremendous hue and cry from a committee of New York recorder players for a chapter of their own and many noisy meetings—on October 16th, 1960—with Bernard Krainis as president and Martha Bixler as vice-president. (I was musical director by 1961.) Besides responding to the needs of New York members of the ARS, who felt they were being ignored by the ARS leadership, Recorder Guild was formed, according to a letter from Cook Glassgold to Erich Katz dated 12/12/60, partly to allay fears of other chapters that "New York is running the whole show." From the beginning there was this paradox of discontent: too much/too little is going on in New York!

From the beginning also, the chapters of the Society have been, like children, a mixed blessing. All chapters were founded with the idea that they would be real chapters of The American Recorder Society, with all their members being by definition members of the national organization. Within a short time, however, the Board of Directors began to discover that this was often not the case. Vice President Glassgold wrote to a chapter leader, Frank Plachte in Los Angeles, on April 7, 1961, reminding him that all members of the Southern California chapter must be members of the ARS. Bernard Krainis arranged a meeting with officers of the Boston chapter on October 10, 1961 to discuss this question. In the minutes of the Executive Board meeting of September 11, 1961, it is noted that Diana Blair had designed a charter to be sent to all chapters, on the reverse side of which would be printed the articles of incorporation of the ARS under the laws of the state of New York. Since, the Board agreed:

> The charter will specifically bind chapters to abide by the By-Laws and Articles of Incorporation of the ARS, and since, by extension,

> any act of a chapter not in accord with either might jeopardize the Society's corporate status and tax-exempt privilege, it became evident that any decision made by a chapter in which non-ARS members are permitted to vote would be null and void. . . . The Board made its position perfectly clear; there can be no deviation from its principles which will apply without exception to all chapters, requiring mandatory membership in ARS of all voting chapter members.

But it wasn't until the mid-'80s that the "national ARS" took serious steps to make sure all chapters were "obeying the law," with disastrous consequences (see Chapter Six).

The ARS continued to re-invent itself during the '60s. Life membership was established at $100 in 1961. In 1961 also, legal counsel Ben Arnest worked on a revised charter for the ARS, establishing it as a non-profit and a nationwide organization, not just a New York State one. The bylaws were revised in 1961 and again in 1962, 1964, and 1969, reflecting the growth in size and activity of the organization. Annual dues for individuals were raised from $2.50 to $3.50 per year effective September 1, 1962. By the end of 1965 dues had risen to $5.00 a year.

Workshops

The first-ever ARS Workshop, called an ARS "seminar" (this somewhat pretentious name was used in the early years) for adults, took place at the end of the National Music Camp season in Interlochen, Michigan in August, 1961. LaNoue Davenport was the director. Bernard Krainis initially agreed to be on the faculty but chose instead to start his own school, the Berkshire Recorder School, at his summer home in Great Barrington, Massachusetts, thus continuing the rivalry with LaNoue that had begun in the early '50s when both were disciples of Erich

Katz. Bernie held his session earlier in the summer than the Interlochen workshop, thus enabling him in years afterward to justifiably claim the "first" recorder summer school as his own, beating out the ARS. From all reports, Bernie's school was every bit as good as LaNoue's, so this healthy competition harmed nobody.

At an informal meeting of some ARS Executive Board members held at the Krainis School, the idea was presented for the ARS to sponsor traveling workshops (The Viola da Gamba Society of America now does this!) given by professional teachers visiting chapters. Nothing ever came of this idea, but it was an interesting one, reflecting Bernie's ever-present hope that the ARS would support professional musicians and at the same time improve the level of playing of American amateurs. Funding was always a problem! As early as the spring of 1960 the ARS had started making approaches to foundations for grants to support teaching workshops around the country, especially in places where there were no chapters that might be able to help with funding,

Leo Christiansen playing with LaNoue Davenport at the harpsichord. Interlochen, MI, August, 1962.

Interlochen, MI, August, 1962. Left to right: Judith Davidoff, Donna Hill, LaNoue Davenport, Martha Bixler.

Faculty members at Interlochen, MI, August, 1962. Left to right: Friedrich von Huene, LaNoue Davenport, Judith Davidoff, Martha Bixler.

Picnic returning from Interlochen, MI, August, 1962. Left to right: Martha Bixler, Judith Davidoff, Friedrich von Huene.

but it soon became clear that the money would have to come from the members themselves, and they were unwilling to pay so much for recorder instruction. This was the beginning of Bernie's long dissatisfaction with the ARS for "fostering mediocrity," as he often liked to say.

With the presentation of its first early music workshop in August of 1961 the ARS did get seriously, if modestly, into the business of the education of its members. Besides appointing itself the judge of who should be teaching the recorder and other early instruments (study of the viol was an early addition to the curriculum) to vacationing amateur players, and where, The American Recorder Society made itself the keeper of the imprimatur, or "teacher's certificate," which was to be a license to teach the recorder to anyone anywhere. A teacher-training program was part of the curriculum at Interlochen and examinations were given. Teachers' certificates were presented at the seminar to those who had completed the program and passed the exam. In the fall of 1961 the Board voted to give honorary certificates to past and future faculty members of the ARS seminar at Interlochen (that's the way I got mine the next summer).

We talked grandly about an expanded program of summer seminars, regional committees, and exams by tape, but what mostly came from that discussion was the formation of an education committee consisting of the usual suspects—LaNoue Davenport, Bernard Krainis, Joel Newman and Martha Bixler—to study the problems of teacher accreditation. This committee was probably the first of a string of special "committees of the Board" that by the '80s were functioning as independent study and research groups. Some have not lasted, but the education committee has remained an important subcommittee of the ARS Board until the present day.

Faculty For Recorder Seminar

FRIEDRICH VON HUENE

FRIEDRICH VON HUENE is a music graduate of Bowdoin College. He served as flutist in the Air Force Band, and is currently no the faculty of the Longy School of Music in Cambridge and Brandies University. He is a recognized authority in recorder building, having spent four years in the flute workshop of Verne Powell.

•

KATHERINE BOWERS of Chicago, a respected and successful teacher in the 1961 Seminar will also be on the 1962 faculty.

MARTHA BIXLER

MARTHA BIXLER is Musical Director of Recorder Guild, Metropolitan New York Chapter of the American Recorder Society; a member of the Board of Directors of ARS; and a former editor of its quarterly publication, *The American Recorder*. She is a graduate of Smith College and the Yale University School of Music. A member of the Manhattan Consort and the Canticum Musicum, she is a performer on both the harpsichord and the recorder. Teaching appointments include the New York College of Music and the Dalton School.

JUDITH DAVIDOFF

JUDITH DAVIDOFF is a native of Boston, and a graduate of Radcliffe College and the Longy School of Music. She has made extensive concert and television appearances on the East Coast, in Europe, and the Middle East. She was a guest artist in the festival "Music at Compostela" at Santiago, Spain, in the summer of 1960.

She is a member of the Camerata of the Boston Museum of Fine Arts, The Manhattan Consort, and is the director of classes in viola da gamba and consort playing at the Boston Museum of Fine Arts.

SHELLEY GRUSKIN

SHELLEY GRUSKIN, a native New Yorker, is a graduate of the Eastman School of Music. He has played with the Rochester Philharmonic and the N.B.C. Opera Co., and has taught at the Dalton School and the N.Y. College of Music. Presently, he is a memebr of The Manhattan Consort and the New York Pro Musica.

ARS Recorder Seminar faculty, Interlochen, MI, 1963. Left to right: Friedrich von Huene, Martha Bixler, Judith Davidoff, Shelley Gruskin.

Its primary function in the '60s was the writing and re-writing of the teachers' exams and the appointment of ARS "examiners" who were licensed to give the exam. 17 "examiners" were appointed.

ARS summer schools proliferated. In the summer of 1962 the second ARS "seminar" was held at Interlochen. The faculty consisted of LaNoue Davenport, director, Martha Bixler (my first ARS summer workshop), Kay Bowers, Judith Davidoff (viol), Shelley Gruskin, and Friedrich von Huene, a young German-American player and teacher becoming known as a maker of fine recorders. The curriculum included recorder, baroque flute, viola da gamba classes, and recorder pedagogy. In 1963 Interlochen was host to an ARS workshop again, and the first two-week ARS summer workshop was held at Goddard College in Plainfield, Vermont. Faculty members, most of whom had been at either the Interlochen seminar or at the Berkshire Recorder School, or both, were the best-known American instructor-performers of the day.

In 1964 LaNoue Davenport directed the first West Coast ARS workshop at the Mendocino Arts Center in Mendocino, California. Ken Wollitz and Peter Ballinger directed the Mendocino Workshop in the summer of 1966. And in that year the ARS sponsored its fourth annual Recorder Festival at Hartt College in Hartford, Connecticut, which included a recorder seminar. In 1964 also the ARS started putting big "ads" into The American Recorder for its summer workshops. In that year the directors of the workshops received $300 each. Members of the faculty were paid $200 weekly plus three cents a mile for travel. The surplus for Goddard was divided among the faculty. In August of 1965 a "Meadowbrook Festival" was held at Oakland University in Rochester, Michigan under the directorship of Shelley Gruskin. In December of 1967 the directors of the ARS summer workshops were announced: LaNoue Davenport for Interlochen, Martha Bixler for Goddard, and Ken Wollitz for Idyllwild—all members of our still very ingrown community. In 1967 also an ARS summer school was begun at the University of Notre Dame in South Bend, Indiana. In 1968 another

California workshop was started at the Idyllwild School of Music and the Arts. Mexico City was the exotic location for additional ARS summer workshops in 1966, 1967, and 1968. The ARS continued to support summer workshops at Interlochen off and on through the summer of 1970. (Gloria Ramsey, the Director in 1968, invited me to teach that year, but I couldn't afford to go! Transportation was not paid in those days.) ARS workshops continued at Goddard through 1971.

The formula for instruction at all of these ARS workshops was essentially the same: the schools, held for one or two weeks during the summer, were for adults past the beginner stage; recorder technique and repertoire classes were held for small groups divided, as well as could be determined, into levels of proficiency. Often there was singing and some massed playing; instruction and coaching in "related instruments" like baroque flute, krummhorn, and other double reeds were added, while viol playing had been taught from the beginning. Faculty and student concerts were always a part of the schedule. For exercise, volley-ball was popular, particularly at Goddard, for both faculty and students, who were all roughly the same age; later, because so many of the faculty members (and later of course the students)

ARS faculty at Goddard College, 1963. Left to right: Gian Lyman, Morris Newman, Miriam Samuelson, Alex Silbiger, Arnold Grayson, Barbara Mueser, Friedrich von Huene, Martha Bixler, Bernard Krainis.

Faculty performance at Goddard College, July, 1966. Left to right: Barbara Mueser, Alex Silbiger, Eric Leber, Martha Bixler, Morris Newman.

Faculty performance at Goddard College, July, 1966. Left to right: Jean Hakes, Martha Bixler, Barbara Mueser.

enjoyed it, Renaissance and English country dancing were made a part of the regular schedule; theory and musicianship classes were also popular at many of the workshops. At the end of the week, after the faculty concert and a night of revelry, an exhausted faculty gave a few brave and bleary-eyed students the exam for the ARS teacher's certificate; gradually the number of certified teachers on the ARS membership list grew.

One of the grandest of the summer schools presented under ARS sponsorship was the "International Recorder School" directed by Bernard Krainis and held at Skidmore College in Saratoga Springs, New York, in the summers of 1965 and 1966. Here for the first time some of the "stars" of the recorder world from outside the U.S. were lured to this country for two weeks each summer. We Americans hoped to show them how advanced we were in all aspects of recorder playing. Bernard Krainis was the master of this ambitious endeavor.

In this milieu the sheep began to be separated from the goats. The

European "stars"—Frans Brüggen from Holland, Han-Martin Linde from Switzerland, and Hans Ulrich Staeps from Austria—joined Bernie as the super-faculty at the Skidmore workshop, along with Barbara Mueser, an American viola da gambist, and Eric Leber, harpsichordist. Bernie also invited a host of Americans as "junior faculty" who would teach the consort classes and act as foils to the stars. Classes were held in Baroque and contemporary solo literature, consort playing, and pedagogy. Lectures were presented by Joel Newman (by then a professor at Columbia University) and recorder-maker Friedrich von Huene, Linde, and Brüggen. The junior recorder faculty consisted of 17 recorder player-teachers from points scattered around the U.S., with the notable exceptions of Morris Newman (it didn't pay enough) and LaNoue Davenport.

Bernie had expected to dazzle us all, including the Europeans, with his superior playing (he was acclaimed as "the greatest recorder player in the world," at least on his record jackets), but it soon became clear that Europe was "ahead of" America in every aspect of recorder playing—performance, scholarship, and pedagogy. Our eyes and ears were opened by the scholarly lectures and sizzling playing of the Europeans, and with some humility we began to realize that we Americans had a lot to learn from them, particularly in the just-beginning field of historical performance practice, something most of us had not given much thought to heretofore. It was a sad experience for Bernie, and I don't think he ever recovered from it. He and LaNoue were the virtuosos of The American Recorder world, but they had much to learn from some of their European counterparts, especially the emerging Dutch players.

Through the '60s and '70s, and well into the '80s, the workshops were "ARS workshops," with locale, director, a good part of the program and, above all, the financial arrangements tightly managed by The American Recorder Society. All were given free publicity in The American Recorder. Until the mid-'70s all were advertised in one brochure mailed from the national office to all members of the ARS. Fees for students were low (around $100 including tuition and room and board); the director of a workshop earned $425 per week by the end of the decade—the faculty $275 each.

Other educational ventures

In March of 1962 Eric Leber (then Education Director of the ARS), Bernard Krainis, and I were sent by the ARS to the annual Music Educators National Conference at the Conrad Hilton Hotel in Chicago to blow the horn of the American Recorder Society. We demonstrated our instruments, discussed the use of the recorder in schools, gave a sample lesson to local children, gave away literature, and discussed music for recorder—both for teaching and for adult playing. We also gave a half-hour performance. This was the first of many visits by the ARS to national and regional meetings of MENC and, later, Orff conferences, in an effort to make our presence known to music educators around the country.

Publications

American Recorder Society Editions boomed in the '60s, with a new editor, Joel Newman, and a new publisher, Galaxy Music Corporation, who was able to make the editions longer and more complete and gave them a classier look. In the three-year agreement negotiated with the new publisher one of the six publications per year was to be a free members' edition. The price per edition was higher: ARS Edition No. 41, published January 13, 1962, cost $1.00. By the end of 1969 the price had doubled to $2.00. 40 ARS Editions had been published by 1960; by 1970 the number had increased to 73. The ARS Editions were published by Galaxy until 1985 with Joel Newman as General Editor. The free members' editions were tolerated by Galaxy until 1969, when the publishers decided that the ARS had become too large, and they could no longer afford to give away free copies of one of the editions annually to all the members.

With Joel Newman the ARS Editions began to reflect the musicological consciousness-raising of the early music community in general, and of recorder players in particular, during this decade. The very beginnings of "musicological" (not merely musical) editing began with a few explanations (and sources) of articulation marks. Howard Mayer Brown's arrangements of Chansons for Recorders, ARS Edition No. 52, published in 1964, was the first ARS Edition in which a printed preface gave the buyer some information concerning the source (Attaingnant), and the editing interpolated by the arranger.

ARS Edition No. 60, a transcription by I.H. Paul of a Bach flute sonata (more currently thought to be by C.P.E. Bach), represents an early brave attempt, in an ARS publication, to contribute to the literature of the recorder while at the same time presenting some musicological authenticity. Alterations from the Urtext edition (a copy by C.P.E.) are freely acknowledged in both the recorder (originally flute) and obbligato keyboard parts. The original source is given, and, most important, the editor states that the "phrasing and articulation indications in this version are the editor's, and they are meant to serve merely as suggestions." Better versions of this sonata have been published since 1968, the date of I. H. Paul's, and nobody would even think of using this edition now. Not only are the marks of articulation changed from the original (and made exceedingly fussy) but ornaments are re-interpreted, not necessarily correctly. Particularly old-fashioned, in editing for recorder, are the ubiquitous breath marks, many of which are placed, in my opinion, in completely unmusical places. Still, this edition, like others of the '60s, was perhaps "halfway there," in terms of authenticity, and it certainly was enjoyed by ARS members at the time.

More successful was ARS Edition No. 66, a delightful sonata for transverse flute and continuo by John Reid, an 18th-century Scottish general who was also a composer of some repute. It was arranged and edited for recorder and keyboard by Alexander Silbiger. Articulation marks are sparingly applied, and suited to both the recorder and 18th-century performance practice, and the continuo part is beautifully realized.

Joel Newman not only discovered the musical treasures that appeared in the ARS Editions published by Galaxy but he also edited many of them himself. Additionally, he introduced quite a few modern works into the canon during this decade, some by contemporary composers of note, like Katz, Linde, Staeps, Bartók (arranged by David Goldstein), and the American composers Jack Beeson, Seymour Barab, and Alvin Etler. When added to the original pieces for recorders published by Erich Katz, including LaNoue Davenport's *A Day in the Park*, the Henry Cowell pieces noted above, and Erich's own *Santa Barbara Suite*, those early ARS Editions played an important role in introducing original contemporary recorder music to the repertoire.

The American Recorder

I had been editing the ARS quarterly *Newsletter* for a couple of years; during that time we always had barely enough money to cover the costs of printing and mailing to our members. But I will never forget the meeting of the Executive Board in the fall of 1959 when I was told that there was no more money at all. We could not afford to put out the January, 1960, issue of the ARS *Newsletter*. What in the world to do? In an almost quixotic sort of decision (I don't really remember being consulted—only informed), the Board decided to put out a magazine instead. The name of the new magazine would be *The American Recorder*.

The original name we picked was *The Recorder*, but that was being used by the Boston chapter for their *Newsletter*. To my naïve surprise the Boston chapter was not the slightest bit interested in relinquishing this title to us! (The name of the magazine was changed to *American Recorder* in 1990 by its editor of the period, Ben Dunham. I refer to the magazine in this history sometimes as The American Recorder, sometimes as *American Recorder*, sometimes as AR, and sometimes simply as "the magazine.")

I would be the editor. Since I was already the *Newsletter* editor that would be a given—I had no choice and Cook Glassgold, who had had previous experience as a publisher of "little" magazines, agreed to be my managing editor. He would deal with layout, paste-ups, and the mechanical aspects of putting out a magazine, about which I knew absolutely nothing. There were assistant editors, too. Bernard Krainis was named publications editor, and Joel Newman and LaNoue Davenport were welcome early reviewers of both concerts and music. Marvin Rosenberg agreed to be the editor of record reviews. In the second issue of the magazine Joel Newman started his thinly disguised and delightful column called "Flauto Piccolo's Corner," in which he aired "his lively preferences and animadversions on a variety of musical subjects." Joel Newman was a very valuable contributor to the magazine throughout the '60s, writing scholarly articles and also a column he called "Roses and Brickbats," which was a compilation of what reviewers were saying about the ARS Editions.

The task of being editor-in-chief of the magazine seemed to me so monumental at the time that I hardly noticed the way in which the biggest problem—money—was solved. It wasn't until I interviewed Ralph Taylor for this history years later, in the spring of 1992, that I found out that both Ralph and Cook had hit up friends, relatives, business acquaintances, and customers for loans and financial help with the first magazine. Probably the biggest hero in that endeavor was Ralph Taylor, as he evidently really twisted some arms. The funny thing was that, because he had made such a large contribution (he was well-to-do, and undoubtedly contributed some of his own money as well), Ralph began to think of himself as entirely responsible for that first issue of the magazine. In later years he referred to himself—in print—as the first editor of the AR. This was the source of some chagrin to me! But by the time I interviewed him, elderly and ailing, in 1992, there didn't seem to be much point in arguing. It gave him great pleasure to give himself that distinction.

Volume I, No.1 of *The American Recorder*, a quarterly publication of the American Recorder Society, was issued in the winter of 1960. It had a newly-designed three-color cover, with calligraphic-type lettering for the name of the magazine and a handsome "ARS" logo, and it was printed on rag paper. The price was 50 cents, but not many people paid this price; it was sent gratis to members of the ARS, and, in a frank attempt to advertise the Society and woo new members, extra copies were sent to chapter representatives and prominent recorder players around the country, in hopes that they would generate interest in and bring new members to the ARS, thus paying for the cost of printing the new publication. President and editor joined in extolling the brave new world of the recorder player, and all were hopeful that we would draw thousands of new members into the Society in that decade.

I actually enjoyed editing the first three issues of *The American Recorder*. They were handsome (though not very fat) issues, reflecting Cook's artistic eye. After the first issue Susan Brailove, a music editor at Oxford University Press, was hired, at $100 an issue, to be managing editor of the magazine. I very much enjoyed working with her. We were both vastly overworked, but exhilarated by our involvement in the new venture. Finally, after three issues, I felt I could not manage the editing any more so I handed it to Ralph Taylor, who was willing and eager to take over.

Right away there were problems; the fun of editing went directly to Ralph's head, and he began to do things with the magazine that others found offensive. In April of 1961 Susan reported to the ARS Board that the editor-in-chief was neither bothering to edit before sending material to her nor proofreading afterward. Ralph had an unfortunate predilection for limericks, which he used as space-fillers in the magazine. But the "professionals" (I put this word in quotes because professionalism was still a new distinction among recorder players) really became irritated when Ralph began putting musical opinions into his editorials. They didn't think he had the right or the musical savvy to do it, and of course this attitude offended him. In the same 1992 interview Ralph complained bitterly to me about the "censorship" he felt he was getting from both LaNoue and Bernie. It was the beginning of Ralph's increasing resentment (after early hero worship) of LaNoue. After a committee on educational policy reported to the October 10, 1961 Board meeting that "AR editorials should not contain personal opinions of the editor on topics requiring musical judgement," Ralph Taylor, much insulted, resigned.

Donna Hill was appointed editor of *AR* in October of 1961. The magazine was a classy one under her aegis, full of interesting material and carefully edited. She relinquished this post because of illness in the fall of 1963. Elloyd Hanson, appointed editor-in-chief in November 1963, was the first paid editor; he received $250 an issue.

The American Recorder has been a show publication of the Society since its inception, something we have been able to point to with pride in all the decades since. The ARS has published, through its magazine, articles on technique, ornamentation, literature, and the history of the recorder. There have been translations of important treatises, such as that of Étienne Loulié's "Method for Learning How to Play the Recorder." There have been articles about recorder makers, performing groups, and, of course, pedagogy. There are profiles of celebrities in the recorder world. There have been bibliographies of method books. There are minutes of Board meetings, chapter news, and cheerleading columns from the president of the ARS. In every issue there are reviews of music, books and recordings of music of interest to recorder players (a regular column on recordings was begun in the December,

1990 issue of AR). There is news of important recorder happenings—performances, conferences, and contests. The American Recorder advertises early music workshops, those brought into the world by the ARS and others as well. From time to time there has been free music published in the magazine, both original (some avant-garde) and arrangements for recorder. Styles in both appearance and content have changed over time with the various editors of the magazine, but its essential mission has remained the same: as the primary organ of communication it keeps the members of The American Recorder Society abreast of the events of the recorder world, it educates and entertains them, and it attracts new members into the Society. Since its inception the magazine has been a quarterly; in 1994 the editor, Benjamin S. Dunham, began putting it out five times a year. The editor since 2002 has been Gail Nickless.

Administration

Letters written to Erich Katz in Santa Barbara (now in the Erich Katz Archives at the Recorder Music Center at Regis University in Denver, Colorado) in the years following his move to California are a rich source of information about the ARS in the '60s. Erich was an energetic letter-writer and very demanding of replies. Few of his letters to us, his ex-disciples, are preserved, but ours to him are safe and sound. Most of our letters begin with a pitiful apology for being so late in answering his, and a plea for forgiveness. Our early messages were enthusiastic: Rhoda Weber wrote to Erich on March 1, 1961: "We now have close to 1000 members—double the amount we had last year at this time." Vice President Glassgold notes:

> . . . a remarkable improvement in the level of amateur playing in New York. Where formerly it was like descending into Dante's Inferno to attend an ARS meeting with a hundred eager beavers blowing in a dozen sundry keys, now it's generally endurable and

at times even pleasant to hear [12/19/61].

The letters reflect, also, some of our problems without our mentor. Interestingly our problems, like those of a small "developing" country ruled first by a strong dictatorship and then with power distributed among tribal chiefs, were mainly political. Martha to Erich (6/10/61): "The problems seem to multiply instead of resolving themselves. Marvin Rosenberg did such a miserable job as Treasurer he was replaced by Rhoda Weber." And again on 9/12/61: "The national Exec Board has actually little to do now except fight, and we've had some lulus." LaNoue to Erich (9/13/61): "I had a terrific, name-calling fight with Ralph Taylor at last Exec. Bd. meeting over the editing of the *AR*."

In the '60s the administrative apparatus of the American Recorder Society was called the Executive Board. This consisted of the ARS officers, the Board of Directors, and chapter representatives, many of whom lived near New York and could get to the bi-monthly Board meetings. One of the ARS heroes of the early '60s was A. C. (Cook) Glassgold, a labor organizer with strong artistic interests, an editor of art publications married to a dancer, and a devoted amateur recorder player. He was one of the founders and producers of the new *American Recorder*, as noted above. In 1961 he was appointed vice president (Bernard Krainis was president); although modestly reluctant to take this high office, Cook was president from 1963 to 1965.

Cook's labors for the ARS were incessant. From me to Erich in Santa Barbara (2/14/60): "The people who run ARS now are Cook and Rhoda. Another Erich and Wini." Joel Newman to Erich (1/23/60): "Cook Glassgold has been a marvel." The Board meeting minutes for September 11, 1961 show that Cook tried for grants from four foundations: the Arthur Jordan Foundation, the Martha Baird Rockefeller Foundation, the Mary Louise Curtis Bok Foundation, and the Fairfield Foundation. He never gave up trying for grant money during his tenures as vice president and president of the ARS, but he never succeeded in raising any. In 1962 Cook set up an orderly procedure for elections to the Board of Directors of the ARS, arranging for ballots to be sent first class to all the members. About 300 members voted in the 1962 election.

However, as the first "non-professional" president of the ARS, Cook bore the brunt of the growing antagonism of the so-called "professionals" toward amateur recorder players. This was unfortunate, because not only was Cook a much better administrator than those who came before him, but he was conscientious in trying to save money for the forever struggling organization. Those ARS members who gave of their professional musical services, particularly at workshops, caused him many difficulties. In January of 1964 the regular teachers at the Goddard summer workshop, myself included, signed an "ultimatum" stating that they (we) wouldn't teach there or anywhere the following summer for less than $350 a week, and the director must receive $580. But there was no way the ARS could afford what were, in those days, seemingly astronomical fees.

We were clearly at an impasse, and an emergency meeting was held at Cook's apartment on January 17, one of the stormiest of the stormy meetings we used to have. Glassgold offered the ARS share of a possible surplus under the existing set-up at Goddard, which was supposed to have been shared equally between Goddard College and the ARS, to the teachers alone. It was not enough. LaNoue, then "Director of Summer Seminars," would have none of the "professionals'" ultimatum. (LaNoue always had a quite different attitude: in the fall of 1964 he returned to the ARS the remuneration for one-half his travel costs to the Mendocino seminar because, as he wrote, his "income from the seminar covered this amount. I see no reason why the ARS should spend this money.") Bernard Krainis refused to direct the Interlochen seminar for the pittance offered.

I immediately regretted my own part in the "ultimatum." I was easily swayed! I was at first on the side of the members of the ARS administration who were trying to save money and protect the Society from the grasp of the "professionals." Then I was sympathetic to the economic needs of my colleagues, both imagined and real. Then I was influenced once more by the opinions of those, like LaNoue Davenport, who thought the professionals were simply too greedy. Indeed, my own relationship with LaNoue was seriously jeopardized at that meeting, and I was nearly dropped, in retribution, from the New York Pro Musica Renaissance Band, of which he was the director. What a mess! Two days after the January Board meeting Cook wrote a rather despairing letter to Erich Katz (1/19/64): "The lid is just ready to blow off the Society, or perhaps it already has."

   We eventually solved the financial problem (and I wasn't fired from the Pro Musica!). Shelley Gruskin (he was another "non-greedy one" or "cheapskate," depending upon how you looked at it) accepted the job of directing Interlochen for $300. New arrangements were finally made in March for Goddard that summer: the college was no longer to be involved in any financial arrangement except for being paid a $50 fee per student—and presumably per faculty member—for room and board. The ARS would receive $50 for tuition per student per week. All other income would go to the director ($410 guaranteed plus room and board plus travel) and faculty ($260 each plus room and board and travel). This was quite a change from the early Interlochen days, not so long before. I remember earning $75 for that week, and being paid nothing for travel, which meant driving to Michigan in a borrowed car! So Goddard went on as usual in 1964, but there were more snafus concerning re-imbursement of the ARS for expenditures made by the faculty. Probably Cook's worst moment came when he received a letter from one of the "'professionals" accusing him of conducting ARS's affairs "like a pushcart peddler" [9/14/64]. This to a man who had been donating his own professional skills to the administration of the ARS for years! I don't think Cook ever quite recovered from this terrible letter.

In the mid-'60s Cook was getting flak from other quarters as well. Rhoda Weber quit her monumental efforts as membership chair and treasurer of the ARS in the summer of 1964 because she was paid too little ($250 annually) for her work. She thought Cook was unresponsive to her needs, and quite possibly he was. In a letter to Erich Katz on 8/1/64 Weber writes:

> I suppose you have heard by now that I have quit my job with the ARS. It was a sad moment, but I had really reached the end of the rope with Cook. We had worked together peacefully for three years, but the moment he became president he was a different man—increasingly difficult to get along with and driving a wedge between the Executive Board and the musicians.

(In her interview with Ken and me much later Rhoda stated that her problem with Cook was that she wanted a raise, now that the ARS had 11 chapters and 600-odd members, and Cook had said, "Don't be greedy." A remark like this would be very much out of character for him.)

Saviors appear when they are most needed. In September 1964 Clara Whittaker, a retired secretary with impeccable writing, accounting, and organizing skills, who had been doing clerical work since 1961 (for a pittance) as secretary of the ARS, was named secretary-treasurer and membership secretary of the organization. She was working part-time (and presumably avoiding any danger to her social security income) and her salary, in combining these jobs, must have been around $750 annually. Elloyd Hanson, editor of The American Recorder, was being paid $250 per quarterly issue. The managing editor, Susan Brailove, made $100 per issue. In 1965 Clara's friend Bob Rhodes, a printer and an amateur recorder player, took over the job of membership secretary of the ARS. Bob also gave the ARS office space in his print shop, the American Name Printing Company, for $25 a month. Clara and Bob did all the administrative work of the Society until September 1971. They were the administrative glue that held the ARS together in the '60s.

On July 1, 1965, Cook Glassgold wearily gave up the reins of the ARS as President. In a letter to Erich Katz (6/15/65) Glassgold writes:

> In a week I hand over all official documents, signs, seals and perquisites to the new administration and may I add, with a heavy heart for I fear for ARS's future. Thanks to the hostility created by some of our supercilious Easterners and to the childish regional chauvinism of some of our insecure Westerners the ARS is now about to reap a bitter harvest.

What Cook is referring to here is not the continuing battle between "amateurs" and "professionals" but the burgeoning battle between East and West. From the moment that the first chapter of the American Recorder Society was chartered, members from the hinterland have complained of feeling shut out of the organization and that the national headquarters was not doing enough for them. (Chapters continued to spring into being, however, and there were 48 by the end of 1965.)

Cook Glassgold retired, thoroughly embittered, from the presidency and from active participation in ARS affairs. He died in February of 1985, and his New York Times obituary makes no mention of his work with the ARS in its account of the life of this distinguished man, a member of the art faculty of the City College of New York in the 1920s, a museum curator, a government housing official, a director of international refugee and relief operations, and a trade union administrator. Although he died feeling little love for us, I was thankful that we had finally pulled ourselves together to present him with a life membership in the ARS a few years before his death.

After Cook, the ARS took its first step in "nationalizing" its administration. The Board of Directors selected the busy musicologist Howard Mayer Brown, a professor at the University of Chicago, as president in the summer of 1965. Cook had been certain this would never work out and he was absolutely right.

Howard Brown tried to keep the wheels rolling in an orderly fashion. One of his first presidential acts was to write to the members of the administrative board, all of whom lived in the New York area (although Vice President Colin Sterne lived in Pittsburgh and other members of the Board of Directors were scattered around the country), asking them to keep in touch (by mail!) with him and with the other members of the Board of Directors. He planned for five meetings of the combined boards, which comprised the Executive Board, in fiscal year 1965–1966, in New York, Chicago, and San Francisco. Meetings were indeed held in Chicago (2/20—with very few attending) and in the San Bernardino Mountain area in California (6/19 at a conference at Lake Arrowhead, where ballots were counted and three new members of the Board elected. Of course only western Board members—Californians Shirley Marcus and Leo Christiansen—could attend). He also proposed, and got the Board to agree to, a raise in national dues to $5.00. This raise did not take effect until 1969 however.

A large issue faced by Howard Mayer Brown was Bernard Krainis's "Proposal for the Reorganization of the American Recorder Society," which was discussed seriously by the education committee of the ARS, approved (by a small margin) by the executive committee, then sent to the entire membership as a proposal to be approved or disapproved. In essence, what Bernie Krainis wanted was for the ARS to appoint a program director (himself) for a "first term" of a minimum of five years, who would

> . . . plan and administer a stepped-up instructional program, a secretary to deal with membership and administrative details, and a regular part-time treasurer or controller, to manage its finances. . . . The program director would be responsible for planning and organizing all ARS activities except the ARS Editions and the magazine. He would, however, work closely with the editor of ARS Editions . . . and with the editor of The American Recorder.

Bernie's proposal goes on to suggest annual workshops for chapters, taped lessons, recordings, a teacher's manual, and other goodies for the members. The salaries of the program director ($5,000), secretary ($1,200), controller ($1,000), AR editor and managing editor ($1,400) and expenses of the traveling workshops and taped lessons would be paid for by increasing the annual dues of the 2,000 members of the ARS to $10.00.

From this distance this seems a modest proposal indeed, and President Howard Brown, in his letter to the membership describing it, did his best to present it fairly, but the membership was up in arms. Their ire was compounded by the fact that a third-class mailing and the Christmas rush delayed some ballots containing the proposal, which was to be voted on yea or nay before December 1. Many members, particularly those on the West Coast, received their ballots after the deadline had passed. In a fit of paranoia, the members "were convinced," as Brown wrote in a letter to the ARS Executive Board, that

> . . . ballots had been sent them purposely late so that their vote could not be counted. Indeed, the vicious personal tone of many of the ballots has distressed me a good deal, for it shows that there has been a serious lack of communication between the national organization and the membership.

In spite of the fact that the ballots were late in some areas, or perhaps because of it, the membership of the ARS would have none of Bernie Krainis's proposal. The possibility of a raise in dues to $10.00 was unthinkable, although some members thought much of the proposal was commendable. But ARS members were not ready to pay for, nor did they want, so much instruction, and they did not want to put so much power into the hands of one individual.

Despite its political troubles, The ARS was in pretty good shape in the fall of 1966. We had nearly 3,000 members and 53 chapters. In July of 1966 *Time* Magazine had printed a two-column article—"Pipe with a Pedigree"—on recorders and recorder playing in the U.S. The writer claimed the existence of some 750,000 players in the United States and gave some free publicity to the ARS. Back issues of the AR were now being sent to University Microfilms in Ann Arbor so they could be put on microfilm and preserved for eternity. There were 86 "starred" names in the ARS Directory, meaning that the members listed had either passed the ARS Teachers Exam or been approved as a teacher by *fiat*. 18 of these were examiners as well. The examiners had all been approved by *fiat*, except for Daniel Waitzman, who paid $25 to apply for and pass the "examiners' exam." Bernie Krainis, who never approved of the appointments by *fiat*, had applied to take the exam as well, but the Board refused to take him seriously, leaving him willy-nilly with his position as an honorary examiner.

There were some difficulties at The American Recorder. Questions arose as to how scholarly a magazine it should be. Erich Katz, always a maverick when it came to scholarship, started complaining in letters to Joel Newman about the abundance of footnotes in the magazine. Worse, there were problems with production. Minutes of the California Board meeting show members worrying over the fact that the ad for a recorder weekend at the UCLA conference center did not appear in the AR until after the weekend. Complaints began appearing from the general membership about the lateness of AR, particularly for Westerners, the tardiness of the editor in answering letters, and articles that were either too scholarly or not scholarly enough. Correspondence between Erich Katz and Joel Newman in 1967 reflects Erich's dissatisfactions with the magazine and Joel's dissatisfactions with the various presidents: Cook Glassgold (non-musician), LaNoue Davenport (didn't work hard enough), and Howard Mayer Brown (a non-member until he was elected).

The problems of Howard Brown, the first "out-of-town" president, and of Elloyd Hanson, the first "out-of-town" editor of AR, were similar in that each was trying to serve a national constituency, in the days before faxes and e-mail, on a budget that was not of national proportions. Now, in the year 2000+, the ARS, with no more members on its rolls but quadruple the dues of 20 years ago, is able to float a truly national Board and paid administrative staff. Electronic mail brings any one member in touch with any other at negligible cost; our president in Madison, Wisconsin, our administrative director in St. Louis, Missouri, our magazine editor in Denver, Colorado, and our scattered Board members are in constant communication often without the cost of airfares. But the rapid expansion of the '60s really gave us growing pains.

By the summer of 1966 Howard Brown had decided, wisely, that he no longer had the time or inclination to be president of the American Recorder Society. LaNoue Davenport was made president pro tem in the fall. In the spring of 1967 Peter Ballinger, a Californian and a new member of the ARS Board, was elected president of the ARS by the Board of Directors and, like Howard Mayer Brown, he tried to do the right things. In a letter of August 17 to the new Board he admits that "quite frankly, I am very much in the dark as far as running the organisation [sic] is concerned, at least by mail, and I rely on your help and advice to a large extent." Poor Peter was immediately accused by a member of the East Coast hierarchy of appointing Gloria Ramsey, from Los Angeles, as education director only to spite the East Coast (!), which must surely have been disheartening, but the real problem, as always, was communication between him and the chief administrator, Clara Whittaker. In our interview of July 27, 1988, Clara stated, gently, her complaints about both the "out-of-town" presidents of 1967:

> That's when it [running the ARS] started slipping away. Howard Brown didn't help a lot. I never understood why. They were both
>
> quite capable. . . . He was always somewhere else. . . . I could never pin him down. . . . I know that it got away. You see, everything was so convenient, with Cook being across the street, and with Bob

> having the shop on Twentieth Street. It was so handy and we had everything just at our fingertips. Then when there was a new president [Ballinger], he had a new wife and a baby and he was on the West Coast; you couldn't function.

This was really the crux of the problem. There was always a lot of pressure from members of the Society not in New York City to have Board members and officers from "out-of-town," but the Society was just too small to function properly over long distances.

Peter Ballinger resigned on April 29, 1968, without appointing a nominating committee (which should have been hard at work since March) for the Board elections that were still being held annually by the ARS. Vice President Gerhart Niemeyer, the acting president, made me chair of the nominating committee (by telephone!—it was an emergency). I was on the ballot; it's amazing how frequently—in the old days—we made this illegal mistake! We hastily put together a slate of seven candidates for the ARS Board. We managed to get the ballots out to the membership by third-class mail (at $4.00 national dues we decided that we couldn't afford first class) on May 25, with a deadline date for return of June 22. Most of the membership had time to vote, but the ballots didn't arrive on the West Coast until June 25!

Rage and consternation! It seems that in those days nobody ever gave anyone else the benefit of any doubt. The worst possible motives were immediately suspected. Erich Katz in Santa Barbara was irate. In a letter of 25 June to "the election committee" (me—his old friend) he wrote:

> I don't know who is responsible for the stupid mishandling of this matter. . . . It should be obvious to anybody that such important mail must be sent first class. . . . A large section of ARS members has been disenfranchised, which should make this election automatically invalid.

A letter from Frank Plachte, a West Coast pediatrician who soon became known as a persistent gadfly tormenting the administration of

the ARS, to Clara Whittaker, the long-suffering secretary, rants of "preposterous managerial incompetency," and "grotesque lack of communication between the Administrative Board and Board of Directors and the membership at large, the ruling clique."
Even the members of the "ruling clique" itself were disgusted, blaming each other for the disaster. LaNoue to Erich on June 17:

> We are having a meeting of the ARS ex. bd. here this evening to try and pick up some of the shambles left by our ill-fated attempt to have presidents outside New York. Things are in a mess at the moment, and I can't say as I can get very excited about it. Clara Whittaker is a notoriously difficult person. . . .

The Administrative Board rushed around to make amends. The terms of the existing Board of Directors were extended to September 3, 1968. Elections were held all over again and a new Board was elected, properly, by secret ballot, and the Board gratefully selected Ken Wollitz, a talented performer, teacher, and transplanted Californian now firmly ensconced in New York, as president, and a new, more efficient era seemed to have dawned.

Ken assumed the ARS presidency on September 3, 1968. One of his early tasks was to find a new editor for AR. There had been trouble brewing for some time. In the spring of 1966 the UCLA conference center placed an ad for a recorder weekend in AR but AR did not come out until after the weekend was over. Letter from Erich Katz to Joel Newman in 1967: "I know that scholars love footnotes, but everybody, absolutely everybody else hates them, and I must say that of late we have had too many . . . in the magazine." A July 10, 1967, letter from Joel Newman to Erich Katz: "The pending issue of A.R. [sic] is going to be scandalously late. . . ." Elloyd Hanson resigned as editor just before the embarrassing appearance, on the front cover of the Summer '68 issue of the magazine, of the table of contents from the Spring '68 issue as well as the wrong volume number. Although these were printer's errors, they reflected some other inefficiencies and deficiencies we were suffering from in the publication of this increasingly important symbol of the usefulness of the ARS. In the same issue of AR, in a gracefully written editorial on the first page, Ken announced the appointment of John Koch, son of the recorder maker William Koch, as the new editor.

1969 was a good year for the ARS. I was on the Board again and I made sure, by means of a Postcard campaign to other members of the Board, that Ken was re-elected president for a full term of two years. In May of that year new bylaws were sent to and voted on by the members. They included a change to four-year terms for the members of the Board of Directors with elections held, after the first two years, every four years. This excellent measure saved a great deal of time and money for the administration of the ARS. The new bylaws provided that all ballots were to be sent to the members of the Society by first-class mail. At the same time, national dues were raised to $5.00.

A letter from me to Erich on September 11, 1969 is joyous: "Ken is doing a very good job with the ARS." But membership was beginning to drop. There were 572 lapsed memberships in fiscal year 1967/68, but we still had 2,384. By December 1969 we were down to 2,270. Still, new chapters and new workshops (one-day, weekend and week-long) continued to form and flourish. The administration was on an even keel again, and the ARS Editions were going well. Galaxy Music, the publisher, announced that, because of the increasing size of the membership, no more free members' issues would be distributed after 1969, but bigger discounts (up to 25%) would be given to ARS members who purchased them in the future. The future of the ARS did indeed look bright.

CHAPTER FIVE

Some Slippage and Some Saviors in the '70s

I am sometimes tempted to compare the political fortunes of the ARS to those of the United States of America. For a time ARS national elections and changes in administration came every four years, as they do to the nation, and they seemed to happen at times of crisis. The correspondence is particularly striking in the '70s when the ARS was like a miniature parallel universe reflecting in a minor way the major national events: disaster in Vietnam, Watergate and the loss of confidence in government, the Saturday night massacre, the resignation of a president, economic hardship, and general malaise. The '70s were a time of continuous crisis for both the nation and our organization, and it seemed at times as though the ARS, at least, might disappear altogether.

At the beginning of the decade all was well with the ARS. The prevailing optimistic view is reflected in the following statement issued in 1970 by Donna Hill, a former editor of The American Recorder, then archivist of the American Recorder Society. It reads in part:

> The purpose of The American Recorder Society is to stimulate appreciation of the musical arts, particularly the art, history and literature of the recorder and related instruments. The Society aims to take an active part in the revival of early music, to inspire musical scholarship and to advance professional playing as well as to encourage the practice of music by amateurs everywhere.

The Society had its beginning in 1939, when twelve people interested in early music and the instruments on which it was played met periodically and performed under the direction of Suzanne Bloch, daughter of the composer Ernest Bloch. Dr. Erich Katz joined after World War II, and the group began to grow and to take on a more formal aspect. . . . In 1950, the Society began publishing a small quarterly, the *Newsletter*, and the ARS Editions for recorder consort, which Dr. Katz edited for the first forty numbers. In 1955, chapters were organized in Boston and Philadelphia. By the time of his retirement in 1959, when he was elected honorary President, Dr. Katz had seen the Society grow to a national organization of ten chapters and six hundred members, with business conducted by a board of ten elected officers and additional appointed officers, and an advisory committee of chapter representatives.

Among the Society's national activities are summer workshops and a teaching certification program, and its publications which include a Membership Directory, the ARS Editions, and the quarterly magazine, The American Recorder.

The Society's Membership Directory is a list of members, officers, chapters, teachers and examiners, published annually to aid in the formation of chapters and playing groups. The ARS Editions are published in response to the need for serious music in inexpensive format for recorder groups of moderate to advanced skill. . . . Seventy-two editions have so far been issued, the first forty by Associated Music Publishers, New York, and the new series by Galaxy Music Corporation, New York.

The American Recorder, which succeeded the old *Newsletter* in 1960, offers articles by distinguished scholars and musicians, reviews of books, music, phonograph records, and concerts, and accounts of national and local activities of the Society.

Local activities of the ARS depend on the energy and initiative of chapters, and are usually vigorous. Many local groups, such as that of the Metropolitan New York area, known as Recorder Guild, publish chapter *Newsletter*s in which they offer short articles and announcements of meetings, concerts, and other activities. The Recorder Guild holds regular meetings conducted by professionals, sponsors week-end workshops and has a consort coordinator who keeps lists of players to help in the formation of playing groups. Chapters in Boston, Chicago and Los Angeles have similar programs.

Highlights of the year 1970: Membership in January stood at 2,408. Always in flux, the number grew to 2474 in February, to 2,532 in May, and to 2,553 in June, but was back down to 2,391 in December. Clara Whittaker was hired as a full-time executive secretary-treasurer, at a salary of $140 a month, commencing July 1, 1970. Most of the Board members still lived in New York City, and meetings were held once a month. Advertisements for the ARS summer workshops were taken in the *Saturday Review*, the *New York Review of Books*, and the *Village Voice*. The entire budget of the ARS in 1970 was, astonishingly, under $2,000. Visions of a Junior Recorder Society danced in Board members' heads and were written about by the president of the ARS in the Spring 1970 edition of AR. This vision of the future was not to be fulfilled until some 25 years later. Likewise the idea of informational pamphlets for the benefit of chapters—these began appearing in the productive 1980s.

President Ken Wollitz approached the New York City Board of Education with the idea of starting pilot programs in teaching public school music teachers how to teach the recorder, with ARS members serving as faculty. The Board of Education was all in favor of starting a program of this sort, but had no money to pay our teachers, so the project was reluctantly abandoned. In November the Board of Directors dissolved the old education committee and appointed a new one, with Ken Wollitz as its chair. Martha Bixler was made the Director of Adult Amateur Education (that meant I was to keep rewriting the Teachers'

Exam and keep track of the Education Program), Gerald Burakoff was made Director of Public School Education (that meant he represented the ARS at MENC meetings), and Howard Mayer Brown was made Director of Musicology (goodness knows what that was supposed to mean).

Donald Waxman, editor-in-chief of Galaxy Music, proposed a recorder composition contest sponsored jointly by the ARS and Galaxy, with the winner to be given a prize of $500 and publication in the ARS Editions. The judges for this contest were Ken Wollitz, Martha Bixler, Donald Waxman and Joel Newman, ARS editor of the series. This plan came to splendid fruition with the publication in 1975 of *Spectra*, a fine quartet for recorders by the Brazilian composer Eduardo Alemann, the first piece in the ARS Editions with even a faint tinge of avant-gardism.

Although we did not know it at the time, the ARS Executive Board meeting held on December 6, 1970 was the last ever for Clara Whittaker, secretary-treasurer of the ARS, and Robert Rhodes, membership secretary, who were the administrative mainstays of the ARS. Clara's desk and typewriter were in the office of Bob's company, the American Name Printing Company at 141 West 20th Street in Manhattan. Bob had an addressograph and did all the mailings, notices, and dues statements; he even mailed the magazine. The two went on an extended vacation to Mexico in the winter of 1970–1971, which made things a bit difficult, but we fully expected them to come back and put everything clerical to rights. The bombshell came in the form of a letter to President Ken Wollitz from Clara in March announcing her resignation as executive secretary of the ARS. This terrible news was broken at the March, 1971 meeting of the Executive Board attended at my apartment by three people: Ken, Daniel Waitzman, and myself. The February meeting had been canceled (for no apparent reason), and it is evident from this and from the report of the pathetic number of Executive Board members at the March meeting that things were really beginning to go awry. I was never quite sure, until I quizzed Clara at the interview I conducted with her in 1988, about what her motivation was, but I suspected that it was pure pique, and I turned out to be right. Clara had simply "had it." She was disgusted, probably with some justification, with the vilification she had received over the years from the "recorder professionals" on our Board, and with the lack of cooperation and communication from the "nonprofessionals," mostly Board members, who seldom responded to her requests with the alacrity she would have liked. It was a great pity, because the people she punished, including herself, were not those with whom she was so angry. Clara was sharp, but she was a very good, careful administrator, willing to work for peanuts. She not only kept the list of our peripatetic members up to date; she paid the bills, kept the books and took care of all correspondence. From the interview: "One of the time-consuming jobs Bob and I had was to attend to changes of address—about 20% of the membership changed addresses every year." Clara made sure the ARS brochure for summer schools got printed (this involved a great deal of nagging of the personnel involved) and that the expenses and profits from those workshops were paid and distributed. As a good secretary does, she reminded Board members and the president of the things they should be doing. And as a good amateur recorder player, she was devoted to the ARS. She left us very much in the soup.

Letter from me to Erich dated March 22, 1971:

> Things are bad at ARS. Clara has quit and everything is sliding backwards. . . . Goodness knows when if ever there will be a Goddard brochure, or there will be any elections, or when a new teachers' exam will be written, or when, if ever, Wini [Erich's companion, honorary vice president of the ARS] will get her teachers' certificate [I had proposed this at the February Board meeting, but there was now no one, of course, to implement the suggestion]. But when I get most

irritated with Ken I stop to think that at least he is willing to be Pres. of the Society, when there is just nobody, I mean nobody else. My worst nightmare is that it might some day devolve upon me.

Needless to say, there was a backup of clerical work in the ARS office of horrendous proportions. Rhoda Weber had a friend, a young single woman with two small children who needed money very badly and wanted to work at home, who volunteered for the job of secretary. All of the ARS files were consequently moved into her apartment with high hopes and many promises for a quick cleanup. Unfortunately, the young woman, who had been formally appointed secretary-treasurer of the ARS, took one look at the material, shuddered, stuffed it all into a closet, closed the door and never opened it again, except to stuff more mail—bills, checks, and angry letters—inside. Minutes of the April, 1971 Board meeting tell of a "discussion of ways the increasing chorus of complaints [my words as secretary pro tem] from chapters and individual members can be answered." The June Board meeting minutes introduce one of our saviors, Arthur Nitka, the proprietor of Terminal Music in New York. Arty had long been a friend to all the recorder players in New York and many around the country. At first a clerk, then the owner of Terminal Music, he had built up an "early music" department, both retail and mail order, upon which many of the members of the ARS depended. A recorder player himself, he found and sold music, instruments, and recorder supplies. He was friendly and knowledgeable; he would let you try out his recorders (stuffy classical music stores in the city, worried about germs, did not) and was free with his advice. And he gave everyone a 20% discount.

Although members of the ARS were slightly fearful of the possible conflict of interest involved, they elected Arty to the ARS Board in 1969. He repaid their confidence and trust. From the minutes of the Board meeting in June of 1971:

The major portion of the meeting was given over to a report by Arthur Nitka on projects he has undertaken at the request of the Board, soliciting material for pamphlets and articles, writing letters to chapters, ARS teachers, publishers and individuals with various specialties.

Mr. Nitka presented a comprehensive plan for the solicitation of many kinds of material for the magazine. This plan includes articles from teachers, performers, educators, etc., on a variety of topics including music lists, choosing recorders, and various technical problems.

Mr. Nitka was appointed Executive Assistant to the Board of Directors to facilitate his activities and in order to pursue these projects. The Board expressed a vote of thanks to Arthur Nitka for his extraordinary efforts.

Arty also promised to act as Ken's secretary; he took on this task with enthusiasm: "I'll be Ken's 'rememberer.'" In other words, he was offering to run the ARS. Although Arty was one of the "professionals," he did not balk at doing some of the nitty-gritty needed to keep the ARS going.

Of course, even with all of his good intentions, Arty Nitka, a busy professional person, could not keep the ARS afloat single-handed. Board elections were not held in the spring of 1971—a bad move. Trouble was brewing again at the magazine—lateness, delays, and problems with the printers all being cited as excuses for irregularity in its issue. An overdue Board election was put off until February, then March, 1972. Louise Austin, Marilyn Carlson, Colin Sterne, Daniel Waitzman,

Kenneth Wollitz at Amherst in 1989.

and Ken Wollitz were elected to the Board and took office June 30, 1972. Continuing members of the Board were Arnold Grayson, Gerhart Niemeyer, Arthur Nitka, Alexander Silbiger, and Rhoda Weber. I was given a four-year reprieve. Only four members of the Board lived in New York City and could attend Board meetings. Ken was re-elected president (by means of phone calls to the Board) in April, and Rhoda Weber became vice president. This was the last election held until the fall of 1976, which was well after the expiration dates of the terms of half of the Board members.

As always, the problems of the ARS in the early '70s can be at least partly explained as monetary—that is, things were not being done or not being done well because we could not pay for them. Ken Wollitz stated the situation well in his "Message from the President" in the February, 1972 issue of the magazine:

> This 'increasing chorus of complaints' is a sincere response to a very real problem in the administrating of the society's affairs. The basis of this problem is economic, a vital fact of which our critics, vocal or silent, are probably not aware. Presently our society is in the uncomfortable position of being too large (approximately 2,500 members) to be run by a volunteer, unpaid administration, and yet is too small to be able to afford the full-time direction that an efficient and expanding operation requires. . . . I will present a few rough figures to explain the society's financial situation. Income for the fiscal year of September 1, 1970—August 31, 1971, totaled a bit over $17,000 (membership dues—$11,000, A.R. ads and subscriptions—$4,000, profit from summer workshops— $1,500, and misc.) Expenses totaled somewhat less than $17,000. Almost half of this sum was for printing. Postage, mailing, office supplies, rent etc. consumed the rest. Labor costs were: secretarial—$1,800, editor of the A.R.—$1,600 ($400 per issue).
> As has been the case for the past several years, the society realized a gain, although it was smaller this year than usual. Cash balance for the year was about $6,000.

Of the above figures the most significant by far are the modest expenditures for labor. . . . I feel that members who are not satisfied with the content of this magazine should not confine their efforts only to offering criticisms, or even suggestions as to what should be done (by someone else!). No one gets paid for the work they do on behalf of the magazine, with the exception of the Editor who is clearly underpaid. How about a little work from our critics?

In the next issue I will discuss the administrative problems which confront the Society (or 'Getting Blood from Turnips for Making Silk Purses from Sow's Ears').

It was time for another savior. Letter to Erich Katz from Rhoda Weber (8/26/72):

> [Our new secretary] almost wrecked the ARS (single-handed!) and dragged us all down with her. But now all is well. Ken has hired a fine man named Bill Leatham, an experienced secretary, who has everything well in hand.

We had decided a retired person with some experience (like Clara Whittaker) was what we needed to be secretary of the ARS. William H. Leatham, a pianist and organist, was, at the time we met him, running an outfit called the "40-plus club." Ken had applied to him to put an ad in the club's *Newsletter*. Bill thought about it and decided he wanted the job himself; he was appointed secretary-treasurer of the ARS on September 7, 1972. At that point we had even somehow lost the passbook to one of our bank accounts. But Bill coped with this situation and immediately started pulling the Society together financially. Sour note from me to Erich: "At least we do have a decent secretary at the moment. The big question is whether he will stay on . . . long enough to totally clean up the mess he inherited. At least the Directory got out." I need not have worried, then. Bill Leatham took upon himself all the usual secretarial duties as well as those of treasurer and proceeded to run the Society. He also started publishing an informal *Newsletter* (I presume he found an inexpensive way to mail it) and kept up a lively individual correspondence with many members. An affable and intelligent man, he was an excellent banner-carrier for the ARS during the years of his tenure. He tried, albeit unsuccessfully, to organize ARS trips by chartered plane or boat (Cunard Line, no less!) to various exotic places. One of his money-saving ideas was to get the children of a "Retarded Children's Home" to mail copies of the magazine to members and subscribers (a dubious enterprise, in the end). It also occurred to him that reducing the number of copies printed of AR would save us money. We actually came out of the financial woods long enough to make a very small loan to the Providence chapter in order to help them pay for a concert by a visiting German artist, Sebastian Kelber. In 1974 we had 2,800 members. Our budget climbed to $28,870 and we doubled the dues to $10.

The price of the magazine was raised, for the first time since 1960, from $1.00 to $1.25 (November 1973) then to $1.50 (February, 1974). John Koch had had just as hard a time as editor of the magazine as his predecessor Elloyd Hanson. In the days before e-mail and when long-distance telephoning was an expensive luxury, his physical distance from New York City (he lived in Vermont) made communication difficult, and he had seemingly insurmountable problems dealing with his contributors, with the printer, and especially with Bill Leatham, who was always trying to get him to adopt some economy measures. The magazine was, again, always "late, late, late," to quote Ken's later memo to his detractors.

Ken finally let John Koch go and appointed New Yorker Daniel Shapiro editor of AR in July of 1974. Danny improved the looks of the magazine, changing the printing from letterpress to offset, which was a cheaper way of producing it, at the same time improving the quality of the paper. He also began designing jazzier covers. And he upgraded the content. Tui St. George Tucker's "Prelude and Blue for Erich," an interesting piece involving unusual fingerings and special dynamic effects, was printed in the November 1974 magazine. A quartet by David Loeb was printed in May, 1975. The February, 1975 AR, a special education issue, was devoted to "The Recorder in the Classroom." It was hoped this would be the beginning of more involvement of the ARS with recorders in the schools. This issue of the magazine was a good start; there were interesting articles in it on teaching the recorder in school programs and in normal schools (teachers' colleges).

Although I did not have as much to do with the Society during the years of my "reprieve" from the Board, I do know that Board meetings became much more infrequent in 1974 and '75. Many of the Board members were living outside of New York by that time, and there was no thought of paying their way to meetings. Bill Leatham took an occasional "poll" of the Board. But things were going so well no one seemed to notice the lack of activity from the ARS administration. Summer workshops were still flourishing. In the summer of 1974 there were three sponsored by the ARS: Mideast, 7/28–8/3 at St. Vincent College, Latrobe, Pennsylvania—Marilyn Carlson, Director; Midwest, 6/30–7/7 at Lawrence University in Appleton, Wisconsin—Louise Austin, Director; and Salve Regina, 8/17–8/24 at Salve Regina College in Newport, Rhode Island—Kay Jaffee, Director. The workshops were still tightly controlled by the ARS. Directors were appointed by the ARS president acting on behalf of the Board of Directors. Brochures for the workshops were mailed by the ARS. Each workshop director was asked to submit a budget to the administration and to keep within it. Tuition was $90 per week. Directors of the workshops received salaries of up to $475, and the faculty $200 per week plus 10 cents per mile transportation. Most important, the ARS participated in any profits made by the workshops and guaranteed against loss.

A notable development in the structure of the ARS workshops was begun by Kenneth Wollitz when he directed the workshop at Goddard College in 1971. He decided on a "theme" for the workshop—in this

ARS faculty at Goddard College, July, 1971. Left to right: Shelley Gruskin, Arnold Grayson, Valerie Horst, Elloyd Hanson, Friedrich von Huene, Ken Wollitz, Judith Davidoff (viol), Marleen Forsberg Montgomery, Robert Kuehn (voice), Paul John Skrobela, Martha Bixler.

case music of the Italian early Baroque—and early music workshops have been doing this ever since. In 1972, at Salve Regina College in Newport, RI, we bravely decided on medieval music. In the amazing "cathedral" we used for classes and the concert, with the resident nuns in the top stories leaning over the inside balcony railing to listen to our rather weird rendition of the Machaut mass, it worked! LaNoue Davenport brought the Machaut mass to Idyllwild in 1975.

ARS chapters were flourishing as well. There were 60 in 1975, including three in Canada. By 1974 Bill was calling himself the "executive secretary" of the ARS.

Dr. Erich Katz died July 30, 1973. To the regret of those of us who had known him well, he and his contributions to the American Recorder Society were already being forgotten by its younger members. Those of us who knew him set about making sure his memory would be preserved and honored in a practical way. The Society published a special memorial issue of The American Recorder, with letters of remembrance from friends and colleagues. The Erich Katz Memorial Fund of the Society was conceived and created by the Board of Directors of the ARS to:

> . . . honor and perpetuate his memory and to keep alive his impact by providing scholarships, grants or commissions to deserving applicants. . . . As soon as the Fund has reached $10,000, its income will be disbursed at regular intervals in a manner which we are certain would have pleased Erich Katz." [Letter to the membership of ARS from Frank Plachte, chairman of the Erich Katz Memorial Fund, early in 1974.]

The words of Ken Wollitz in a magazine editorial (February, '74) gracefully state the objectives of the Society:

> By establishing and developing the Fund, the Society wishes to honor the memory of a man whose generous spirit and inspired teaching touched and enriched all who knew him. . . . [Interest from the Fund] will be used to offer scholarships for workshops or other studies and projects of worthy candidates.

In varying forms, the Katz Fund has been a source of income to be used for worthy causes by the Society, particularly in the areas of music education and music publishing, from that day to this. Though its growth was not as quick as its founders had hoped, the Fund had raised $1,000 by March 18, 1974, $2,000 by July, 1974, and $3,000 by October 1975.

Some things were being neglected—in fact in administrative matters we were running on empty. Board elections were due but not held in 1974. The publishing contract with Galaxy had lapsed. A lot of administrative time at what few Board meetings were held was wasted discussing whether or not the American Recorder Society should change its name to cover an increased range of activity, and to include other instruments.

There were, as always, complaints about the lateness of the magazine and no replies to correspondence with the editor. Danny Shapiro was a good editor and competent designer, but he was already having the usual troubles with lack of time and a very small budget. The November 1975 issue of the magazine was not published at all! I have a nightmarish memory of sitting in a restaurant at around this time with other members of the ARS leadership, and deciding to throw out an entire printed issue of AR rather than distribute it to the membership, because it was so full of terrible mistakes—probably it was this November issue. In any event, Volume XVII of AR, which should have ended in 1975, was carried over to the February issue of 1976, which is Volume XVII, No. 4. (The volume numbers of AR did not get straightened out until 1981, when the May magazine was issued as Volume XXII, Nos. 1&2.) A report from Danny to the Board in early 1976 gives his excuses: he is paid too little; trying to keep costs down means hiring typesetters who are not up to snuff. He protests that lateness of the magazine will *not* bring forth suits from advertisers (evidently one of our fears) since the advertisers are not billed until the ads are published. It will also *not* mean a loss of our permit for the bulk-mailing rate from the post office as long as no volume numbers were skipped!

The February and May issues of the magazine were each made fatter by half to compensate for the lack of a November issue. In an effort to help Danny out, Sigrid Nagle was appointed assistant editor of AR. The August, 1976 issue contains his *apologia*: he *did* re-design the magazine, increase advertising, and publish a lot of music, but somehow Danny became one of the scapegoats, along with Ken Wollitz, for all that continued to ail the Society.

"Après moi . . ."

Bill Leatham, who had been almost single-handedly holding the administration of the ARS together since he came to work for us, died of cancer on September 25, 1976. His fatal illness had begun much earlier, and things had begun to unravel then. The ARS membership gradually became aware that despite Bill's heroic efforts as a one-man administration there was a distinct lack of communication with the ARS brass. Besides the obvious problems with the magazine, at least half the "Board" with names printed on the masthead was illegal, Ken's presidency was really "illegal" also because he had been re-elected by phone rather than by ballot, and his re-appointed presidency had never been announced to the membership.

. . . le déluge."

The ARS was ripe for a *coup d'état*, and there were several of us who thought of it, including Andrew Acs, a young Columbia graduate student, already a fine recorder player and teacher, who had been assisting in the ARS office, and myself. But steps had already been taken by a group of mid-western members of the ARS, something of a cabal, we provincial Easterners thought at the time, led by Louise Austin, a "legal" Board member. At the time we were a bit disdainful of their efforts, but they did a tremendous service to the Society, which really was in trouble. They may well be numbered among the various "saviors" of the ARS at different times. It had become evident to this group that Louise's term and those of other members of the Board were about to expire without any provision for a new Board election. Jan Custer Bryan, Beverly Inman, and Roberta Sweet, members of the Executive Board of the ARS as chapter representatives from Chicago, Madison, Wisconsin, and North Shore (Chicago), Illinois, respectively, blew the whistle. At this time chapter representatives were still considered *ipso facto* members of the Board of Directors of ARS. This group was very much alarmed by what they perceived to be a terrible situation in New York: "All vital services" had ceased; "various violations of our by-laws" meant that the whole organization might cease to exist; the terms of office of all members of the Board of Directors were about to expire; there were no "officially appointed" officers (or at least no public record of same); "no financial accounting

[had] been made to the board or to the members since 1974;" there might be "no money in the treasury;" and worst of all, when these Board members "attempted to check the legal status of the ARS with the counsel listed on the masthead of the last issue of the magazine," they had been unable to do so because said counsel had been "dead for some time." Furthermore, there had been:

> . . . no annual meeting [required by the bylaws] since 1972, no Board meeting since 1974; no communication for almost a year from the new york [sic] office to the board or to the members about the state of the affairs of the ARS; inquiries from board members and others have gone unanswered; the annual directory . . . has been so late as to practically negate its usefulness; there has been no issue of *The American Recorder* for 1975–76 and only three issues in 1974–75. . . . In short the membership cannot point to a single service it has received from the national office this year.

This situation was delineated in a May, 1976 letter to all members of the Executive Board, that is, the Board of Directors, administrative officers and chapter representatives, also to the trustees of the Erich Katz fund, former administrative officers of the ARS, and examiners and certified teachers, for their information. An accompanying letter from Louise Austin indicated that she was also very angry with Ken about the firing of John Koch two years before, a fact she had only discovered when John wrote to her himself to tell her he was no longer editor of the magazine. The "Chicago group" (although they were not all from Chicago they were all colleagues of Chicagoan Louise Austin, and their expenses were borne by the Chicago chapter) did, very much to their credit, make some concrete proposals. As stated in their letter, there was certainly "no provision in the bylaws of the ARS for dealing with such an irregular situation"; nevertheless they tried to think of ways to remedy it in a way that would "conform to the bylaws."

They had decided that the Executive Board, such as there was of it remaining in legal existence, should immediately appoint Jan Bryan and Roberta Sweet acting co-chairmen of the Executive Board "for the purpose of overseeing the results of this meeting and overseeing the election of the Board." "This meeting" was the letter itself. "The election of the Board" was a "legal" Board election to be conducted as soon as possible, with five members of the Chicago chapter to act as a nominating committee. Before the Board election could take place, however, the "Chicago group" had created a ballot that they sent to the other members of the Executive Board with their letter, containing the following proposals for temporary appointments of officers: for temporary secretary, Philip Levin; for treasurer, Martha Bixler; and for ARS Ed. and *AR* editors, Joel Newman and Danny Shapiro, respectively. (Joel and Danny were already acting in these capacities.) Since the "Chicago group" maintained that all activities of the Executive Board must be conducted publicly, the members of the Board and chapter representatives to whom the letter was sent were provided with a ballot, which was not secret, on which they could approve or disapprove of all of these appointees, including the co-chairmen of the executive committee, and the results of the vote would be publicized to the membership. The duties of all of us "temporary appointees" were spelled out: co-chairmen Bryan and Sweet were to goad the rest of us into action, the various editors to continue with what they were already doing, and Phil and I (if approved) were to "obtain the services of a competent lawyer," an accountant to give us audits for the fiscal years 1974–75 and '75–76, and "report to the board any and all information relative to the control and management of all affairs and business of the ARS as the Executive Board may request of them."

   My reprieve from the administration of the ARS was over. An "ad hoc" committee was formed to meet at my apartment in New York on May 13th, 1976. Members of this committee were: Andrew Acs, Louise Austin (nationally known as a workshop teacher and director as well as being a "legal" Board member at the time),

Martha Bixler, Marilyn Carlson, Ben Dunham, Joan Munkacsi and Hannah Rose (the last two were active members of the New York chapter), Bernard Krainis, Phoebe Larkey, Phil Levin, Pat Petersen, Dale Taylor (who had been assisting Bill Leatham in the office along with Andrew Acs), Doris Van Pelt (one of the Chicago movers and shakers), Daniel Waitzman, a professional recorder player and flutist who had been active in the New York chapter, Rhoda Weber, and Ken Wollitz.

The "ad hoc committee" drafted and sent out a letter to all the members of the Society, asking for ideas about what to do with the ARS, now rudderless, practically leaderless, and certainly clueless. As might have been expected, there were many suggestions as to the wonderful things the ARS might do, such as hold "Renaissance dance" parties as money-raisers; hire a paid executive director; start a national lending library; give more help to chapters, teachers, juniors, high school students, college students; put out the magazine on time; send "pros" to the hinterlands; raise/lower dues; keep the same dues. An interesting and elaborate plan presented by Bernard Krainis that he entitled "The Pursuit of Excellence" represented, once again, Bernie's attempt to get the American Recorder Society to shake loose what he perceived to be its aura of amateurism and mediocrity and insist that its members, in order to stay members, keep improving their playing.

A "National Business Meeting" was held in Chicago in December 1976 to formalize some of the procedures that had been drifting along for some time by themselves. First, Valerie Horst Citkowitz was appointed director of the "original" ARS summer workshop, started at Interlochen, Michigan, and then being held at Hampshire College in Amherst, Massachusetts. Sigrid Nagle was recognized as assistant editor of AR, and Andrew Acs, who had been assisting in the ARS office, was made temporary office manager. These were all significant appointments. Sigrid Nagle became editor-in-chief of the magazine a little later, and remained at that post until 1990; Andrew eventually became chief administrative officer of the ARS, staying until 1979.

Most important, the "Chicago group" took it upon themselves to organize a national election. In fairness to Kenneth Wollitz, who was very much the scapegoat here, it should be said that he hadn't simply ignored elections. It was just that our system was terribly cumbersome, with yearly elections that had to be managed by first class mail. The then- vice president of the Society had also been chair of the nominating committee, and when she presented a slate that included one of the members of the nominating committee she drew so much criticism from our national "gadfly," Frank Plachte, that she threw up her hands and decided, on her own, that there would be no elections that year. (The attentive reader will note that this was not the first time it had happened that a member of the nominating committee ended up on the slate of candidates, but somehow this time it was noted and criticized.)

The Chicago group, needless to say, was alarmed by the fact that the ARS had no legal Board. They sent out ballots to the membership and a surprising 1225 ballots were cast. The ballots were counted at the December "business meeting" and the following "new" and legal Board of Directors was elected: Louise Austin, Martha Bixler, Gerald Burakoff, Valerie Horst Citkowitz, LaNoue Davenport, Bernard Hopkins, Philip Levin, Arthur Nitka, Peter Seibert, and Colin Sterne.

The new legal Board got busy immediately, holding three meetings in calendar year 1977. All were held in my apartment in New York. Peter Seibert, who later became vice president, could not understand why we didn't meet in the ARS office. We had to explain to him (he lived in Seattle and had never seen our headquarters) that our office, still at Bob Rhodes's American Name Printing Company on 20th Street, was about the size of a large closet, not the spacious suite Peter (and no doubt everyone west of the Hudson River) expected it to be. Our office remained at Bob Rhodes's shop until late 1978. My apartment was the only available place large enough for the 10 members of the Board to sit in one room.

At our first meeting, in late January, 1977, we immediately appointed

Andrew Acs, who had been working assiduously in the office to try to put things to rights, as administrative assistant, for a small salary. Fortunately, in spite of the chaos that had reigned for so long in the office, our finances were not in bad shape. At that January meeting Andrew reported that we had $4,000 in our checking account, $3,215 in the Katz Memorial Fund and $16,500 in savings. And we still had over 2,000 members, although dues payment checks from mid-September had yet to be recorded. We had lost approximately 450 members. Andrew suggested a budget of $1,000 a month for the ARS, including his own wages, to cover the costs of running the organization. I can't resist reporting a story Andrew told me at about that time. After Dale Taylor left the ARS office Andrew's new assistant (who must remain nameless here) proved to be somewhat less than competent. According to Andrew, he (Andrew) narrowly prevented a bunch of membership renewal forms in window envelopes from being dropped into the mail with the addresses facing in, not out. Needless to say, this assistant was fired. Andrew was an exceedingly good administrator for one so young. He was also one of our many saviors.

We heard a report from Danny Shapiro, asking for a higher budget, higher advertising rates—and a 100% salary increase for himself, from $500 per issue to $1,000 per issue—and decided to give him the axe instead of a raise, appointing Sigrid Nagle, who was willing to take the $500, the acting editor of AR. Sigrid was a splendid editor, and she managed to put out the next issue of the magazine, the February, 1977 issue, on time. Peter Seibert was asked to take on the ticklish job of letting Danny go, which he did, rather nobly.

Ken Wollitz, who though no longer a member of the Board was invited to this meeting, lobbied hard for a paid executive director of the ARS. We were not lacking in candidates, and we certainly needed one, but we were simply not able, financially, to hire one at this time. From the minutes of that Board meeting:

> The problem has been that the ARS is too large an organization for volunteer labor, and too small to afford full time professional help. [Where had we heard that before, and since?] He [Wollitz] also suggested that election procedures be improved.

That they were, but again it was volunteer labor that did the job.

We were careful in our appointments: Phil Levin and I continued as acting secretary and treasurer, but we still had no president. We made official the appointments of directors of the summer workshops in 1977: Paul Skrobela for Telluride III (a lovely workshop in the high mountains of Colorado, which had to be canceled that year for lack of enough enrollment); Peter Seibert for the Northwest Workshop, Louise Austin for the Midwest Workshop at Lawrence University in Appleton, Wisconsin; Marilyn Carlson for the Mideast Workshop at Latrobe, Pennsylvania; and Valerie Horst Citkowitz (already named by the "Chicago group") for the East Coast workshop at Hampshire College in Amherst, Massachusetts. There was obviously much to be done, so we held another Board meeting in April. By now membership was at 2,450, down 400 from a year before. The financial situation was a little precarious, but we decided we could afford a telephone answering machine and a postage meter!

We discussed the faltering education program. We needed some changes. For some time the only person willing and able to keep revising the teachers' exam was myself, and there had been so much criticism of the exam and the way it was administered (admittedly not at the best time and place—at the summer workshops) that we decided, as a Board, to suspend the Teachers' Certification Program until such time as we could figure out something to take its place. All of those teachers who had successfully passed the exam and received a teacher's certificate from the ARS were, of course, permitted to keep their credentials, as did the ARS Examiners. Peter Seibert took care of writing to all of the ARS Examiners to apprise them of this development.

Bernard Krainis, ever hopeful, presented his proposal once again for a restructured ARS, with a "chief executive of the organization with a staff to implement the various projects. First among those projects would be a really excellent magazine. Next would be a bibliography of recorder music and a well-organized and understandable teaching manual." Bernie proposed a radical re-structuring of the ARS involving a shift in power to a paid education director (himself) and/or a paid executive director. Ben Dunham reported on bylaws changes he was working on, with a view to putting an executive director (himself, I feared) in charge of the organization. He also "suggested possibilities for raising money to further the educational work of the ARS." (Quotes are from the minutes of the Board meeting April 9, 1977.)

Although we were respectful, we had no use for either of these suggestions. In fact we really fought them off. I was dead set against the $50 individual membership dues required to set Bernie's plan in motion. Never a visionary, I saw the goals of the ARS as immediate ones: mounting a legal election, appointing officers, getting the magazine out on time and, most essential, getting things straightened out in the office, as once again we were very much in arrears in processing membership, answering letters, paying bills, and generally behaving like a responsible organization. I was determined that the ARS should not be an oligarchy in the hands of two people, talented though they might be. In a long letter to Bernie, I tried to tell him that the ARS, with its education program and its workshops, was not devoted to mediocrity, but really very much interested in raising the standards of recorder playing in this country. In a long letter back, he sorrowfully told me of how very much disappointed he was in my lack of vision and understanding of his goals. But always a gentleman, he then gave up the battle, and although he never really forgave me, he did not try to make things more difficult for me.

Joel Newman also had big plans for the ARS Editions. He wanted to start a pedagogical series and an easy "flauto acerbo" series, as well as publishing ornamentation models from Ganassi and Ortiz. These were all good ideas, but there was no possibility that they would ever be carried out, particularly since Joel was having a hard enough time keeping up with the current publishing schedule.

We had to select a president, and I was it. Peter Seibert from Seattle became vice president—we had our first bi-coastal administration! Colin Sterne, a college professor, professional flute and recorder player, and composer living in Pittsburgh, though originally from the New York area, was our secretary. Louise Austin was made assistant secretary. Partly as a result of this appointment, Louise took upon herself the job of making a badly needed revision of the bylaws of the ARS. Philip Levin, who had lived in Miami but was now firmly ensconced in New York as a professional bassoonist and recorder player, instrument repairman, and budding instrument maker, was treasurer. Arty Nitka was named assistant treasurer. Father Bernard Hopkins was made coordinator of chapter representatives. Andrew Acs was given a boost up the administrative ladder and named administrative officer. Andrew was busy working on a membership directory and brochures for the summer workshops. Sigrid Nagle was hard at work on the next issue of AR, getting things back on schedule and trying to get more advertising. Among the problems she had inherited was the fact that the mailing of the August, '76 issue of AR (which had been printed in September) was incomplete, so we had to send a general notice to all the membership asking them whether or not they had received their August issue.

It was agreed at this meeting "to discontinue publishing music in The American Recorder until policy concerning the direction and the content of this feature can be determined by the board." In other words we were in disagreement as to what music should be printed.

After the April meeting, I took upon myself the task of keeping the Board members informed about what was happening between meetings. My first letter (there were 12 in all during the four years of my first presidency) to the Board was sent June 25, 1977. There was a great deal to do! I was already heavily involved in every aspect of ARS administration, including running the office and editing the magazine, keeping track of the bylaws changes everyone was suggesting, and coping with increasing problems of advertising in the magazine. Arty Nitka, our esteemed Board member, had started running advertising inserts that had been objected to on several grounds: they were often thought to be in poor taste and they were "discount advertising" that very much annoyed our other advertisers. We floundered a bit, tried having a loose insert in the magazine that did not work, and then we tried, unsuccessfully, to get Arty to stop putting the ads in altogether. We tried to establish a policy of refusing discount advertising, then found we would be in a lot of legal trouble if we did so. It took a lot of time and patience to untangle ourselves from this situation.

Although the number of paid memberships in the ARS by June was up to 2,600 it was still 200 lower than the year before. For the first time we were really worried about finances, and in the end we had to borrow from our own savings.

Peter Seibert, a good and conscientious vice president and member of the Board, decided that as a West Coast member he should take us "chauvinistic Easterners" to task for the way we were doing things. In a letter written to the other members of the Board on August 13, 1977 entitled "RUMBLINGS FROM SEATTLE" he says: "In order to assure the national character of the ARS, I would like to see a system of nominations and elections that brings a more balanced board. The presence of six New York area people on the board certainly means no lack of integrity or of energy. But it does mean that the traditional blindnesses caused by the Big-Applecentric mind will continue, and it assures that the ARS will always be a provincial organization. I am struck by the attitude shown in some of the conversation at meetings, and I wonder if I'm really attending the meeting of a national organization or merely another administrative body of the New York Recorder Guild. . . .

"Having our office in New York symbolizes domination of the ARS by New Yorkers. It arouses suspicion and distrust in people elsewhere. I therefore propose that we move the office to a city that is emotionally a neutral city."

Well, yes, this was a good suggestion, and we were finally able to follow it many years later. In the meantime we were busy putting the Society back together. Peter himself was helpful in the area of education. After we had been scratching our heads for some time as to what we should do about the education program, I asked Peter to come up with a plan, which he did, and what he called a Level of Achievement program became the basis of our educational system for many years.

LaNoue Davenport resigned from the ARS Board before the September 1977 meeting, and Arty Nitka soon after. LaNoue had perceived that he never was going to have the time to come to Board meetings, much less do any work for the Society. Arty felt he had too much conflict of interest as a recorder merchant and advertiser. The ARS Board appointed, by internal mail ballot, two new members to take the places of LaNoue and Arty: Jim Barker from Minneapolis, and Constance (Connie) M. Primus from Denver. Jim was an entertaining fellow, and as an airline pilot he received free travel from his airline, so it did not cost the ARS any money to bring him to Board meetings, but Connie Primus was a gift from the gods. An accomplished flutist and recorder player, teacher, and chapter leader, she soon became an invaluable Board member, committee member and chair, and, later, president of the American Recorder Society. An extremely able administrator and organizer, she was and is devoted to the causes of the ARS, scrupulously honest, meticulously fair, and absolutely steadfast. I had met Connie in the summer of 1975 at an ARS workshop in Telluride, Colorado, but I had no idea then or when she first come to the Board of the many supporting and leadership roles she was to play in the life of the ARS and in my life as well.

The late '70s were an extremely busy time for the ARS and for me as president. We managed to squeeze in two Board meetings a year—three in 1977—of our far-flung Board. We were very proud of ourselves for pulling the ARS back from the brink and saving it from disaster. By August, 1977 we had put out a new directory, and Sigrid Nagle was promoted to the position of editor-in-chief of AR. After publishing three issues in very close succession Sigrid achieved the much-needed goal of putting the magazine back on schedule. This was important as a sign to the membership that the ARS was up and running again. Sigrid did have a few bumps along the way. Unaccountably, the November 1977 issue was labeled Volume XVIII instead of Volume XVII. But that tiny mess was soon straightened out. By the fall of 1977 the price of an individual copy of AR had been raised to $2.00. Sigrid's salary was raised to $800 per issue, or $3,200 per year. In the spring of '78 Andrew Acs was made administrative director and his salary raised to $7,000 per annum. Sigrid, whose initial modesty was short-lived, was raised to $1,000 per issue, or $4,000 a year. There was beginning to be some real money in working for the ARS!

In 1978, with the help of our new, energetic counsel, Benjamin Feldman, we finally finished writing and putting through, on February 15, 1979, the new bylaws, which changed the structure of the ARS substantially. It was to be run by the Board of Directors, not the Executive Board. The Board would choose all of its administrative officers—president, vice president, secretary, treasurer, assistant secretary and assistant treasurer—from its own ranks. All administrative officers would, therefore, be members of the Board of Directors. The Board of Directors would no longer have such specific duties as planning concerts and musical meetings (how provincial this now seems!) but they would retain responsibility for both the musical and business affairs of the Society. Chapter representatives would no longer be members of the Executive Board, but they would get a special new

Andrew Acs leading a class in New Orleans, 1980s.

task: the nominating committee for the Board elections would be selected from among their ranks. Elections were to be held every four years.

The American Recorder Society was moved from Bob Rhodes's office to 12 East 16th Street, into a room we shared first with our typographer, Letter Space, and later with the New York Recorder Guild. The president and her husband painted the floor of the new office.

In 1979 Andrew Acs resigned as administrative director of the American Recorder Society and moved to New Orleans. We as a Board wasted a lot of time at the February Board meeting interviewing candidates for his position of administrative director before deciding upon Mary Ann Fleming, who had been assisting Andy in the office. She was given the less imposing title of office manager. Mary Ann was bright and creative, but after a promising beginning she was no match for the work that began piling up. She became pregnant, and decided she could not keep her two cats and her baby in the same apartment, so her cats moved into the ARS office; the officers of New York Recorder Guild were so much displeased by this that they refused to pay their share of the rent for a time.

By 1979 we were beginning to be aware that the ARS Editions were in jeopardy. It was becoming increasingly difficult for Joel Newman, a college professor, recorder teacher, and professional performer, to keep up with the publishing schedule and, unfortunately, the more promises he made the more he was unable to keep. One of the most difficult tasks I ever undertook as president of the American Recorder Society was to take the subway trip to Joel's office at Columbia to ask him to resign as editor of the ARS Editions. Actually, it was more complicated than that. I reneged on my promise to the Board to "fire" Joel, and on his request granted him "one more chance" to prove he could shape up. What he said he would do was to write a letter to the Board stating his plans for revitalizing the series. Unfortunately he broke his promise once again, and I had no choice but to ask him to resign. He took it well, as there was no denying that he simply was not doing his (volunteer) job, but it was a sad moment for us both, nevertheless. Years later Bernie Krainis claimed, in an interview for this history, that Joel Newman had been the one person who had "kept things spinning" at the ARS, the only faithful one (forget the magazine, forget the workshops), whose editions always came out on time, and that he had been tossed out without a word of thanks. Of course that wasn't the case at all. It was only with the greatest reluctance that we let him go, and he was thanked, publicly, over and over again for all that he *had* done for the ARS, which was considerable.

This really meant the end of the ARS Editions. Joel had a few more editions on the fire that were published in the early '80s. For a time we pursued the idea of having a board of four editors on four separate tracks, "pre-Baroque," "Baroque," "new music," and "education," with four series of publications. The editors of the separate series were to be Jennifer Lehmann, Michael Lynn, Pete Rose, and me. In my "Letter from the President" in the February, 1980 issue of *AR* I state, optimistically, that "it is hoped that one or more editions in each of the new series will be published in the fall of 1980. . . . Editions will be scholarly, with . . . background historical and musicological information." We even printed, a little too optimistically, the names of the editors of each series in the magazine. However, after many meetings, music read-throughs, letters, and a lot of talk, very little came of this idea for expansion. We had a few more editions that had been prepared by Joel, and a set of five canzonas by Giovanni Cavaccio (ARS 93) edited by Robert Lynn, the father of flutist and recorder player Michael Lynn. But nobody (with the notable exception of Connie

Primus, who immediately got busy and produced about a dozen items for the educational series) really had the time or the will to pursue this dream. Then Donald Waxman resigned from Galaxy Music, our publisher, and Galaxy was sold to E.C. Schirmer in Boston. We finally realized that the ARS Editions, so necessary in the early days, had run their course; there were so many other publishers—London Pro Musica, for instance— now putting out recorder music at a tremendous rate, that our task in the area of the music-publishing world was really done.

Since we had so badly botched our elections of 1974 (they didn't happen) and 1976 (it took the "Chicago group" to get them going), I took upon myself the task of supervising the 1980 elections and even saw to it that the new bylaws stated that future presidents would do the same. We had set up a system that turned out to be even more cumbersome than the previous one of holding elections every two years. We wanted to change the terms of directors (members of the Board) to four years, but with staggered terms; we found to our dismay that the Not-For-Profit Corporation Laws of New York State prevented us from doing so. In reading Section 704 of the NFPCL, Ben Feldman discovered that "if directors are classified for voting purposes so as to stagger terms, the terms of office of the directors shall not exceed in years the number of classes." This meant that if we had two classes of directors (Class A's term would begin in 1980, say, and Class B's term would begin two years later) the terms of the directors could last for only two years, not four, or not be staggered at all, and the system would be no different from what we already had. Being anxious to extend terms to four years, we decided to hold elections every four years and hope, for continuity's sake, that some members of the Board of Directors would be willing to run for a second term.

Another factor was expense. We decided that the only way to hold elections, even every four years, in anything like an economical way (the special elections of 1976 had cost us $3000—a fortune at the time) and at the same time make sure we did not disenfranchise anybody with the slowness of bulk mailings, was to use the magazine as a vehicle. It was necessary, therefore, to start two years in advance with the appointment of a nominating committee from among the chapter representatives as provided for by our new bylaws, choose one of them as chair, announce the committee panel, call for suggestions for candidates from the membership, print names and biographies of candidates, call for petitions "from the floor," distribute ballots to the membership with instructions for their use, and, finally, to publish the results. Every step of this process had to be done via *The American Recorder*, much to the disgust of its editor, who had metamorphosed from a shy and extremely conscientious assistant editor, grateful for all the editorial and business help she received from the rest of us, into a rather proud editor-in-chief, who thought of the *AR* as "her" magazine. She had even begun, without any authorization from the Board, printing the words "A Journal for Early Music" on the front cover of the magazine. And she absolutely refused to put the words "Important—ballot inside" on the cover of the February, 1980 issue as I asked her to.

In spite of the obstacles, however, 323 ballots were counted, and 10 members were elected to the Board of Directors of the ARS to take office on June 30, 1980 for a term of four years. They were: Philip Levin, Peter Seibert, Andrew Acs, Shelley Gruskin, Connie Primus, Bernard Hopkins, Valerie Horst (Citkowitz), Patricia Petersen, Susan Prior, and Suzanne Ferguson. We had three alternates: James Barker, Benjamin Dunham, and Helen Jenner. The geographical distribution was good (only two from New York, and one from Canada, making us "international.") Half were repeats, as we had hoped they would be for continuity. The Board meetings of September 19, 20, and 21, 1980 were held once again at my apartment in New York City. Shelley Gruskin was chosen to be president of the new Board; Connie Primus, vice president; Philip Levin, treasurer; Valerie Horst, assistant treasurer; Suzanne Ferguson, secretary; Patricia Petersen, assistant secretary. I was off the hook!

So what happened on my watch? We had plenty of slippage, sometimes teetering on the edge of extinction, then pulling ourselves back with the help of our several "saviors": Arty Nitka, Bill Leatham, "the Chicago group," Sigrid Nagle and Andrew Acs, and then, finally, perhaps myself—at least I was told I was. This was, also, the period when Valerie Horst began her valuable service to the ARS, both on and off the Board, as a thinker, planner, organizer, administrator, and editor. Her nimble intellect and extraordinary command of the English language became more and more evident to me in the decade that followed, when she and I made up the "home team" of those trying to keep the ARS literate and functioning.

During my watch the ARS was saved from its predators when it was up for grabs, its debts were paid, The American Recorder was rescued, the
ARS administration was put to rights, and the bylaws revised. The "old" education program including the teachers exam was scrapped, and a new one begun. The ARS began to get a little wiser financially and we put $5,000 into a Dreyfus Liquid Assets Fund. We held orderly elections and a new Board was elected with excellent geographical representation. Most important, faith in the organization as a viable body was restored. Now it was time, I hoped, for a much-needed rest from the ARS.

I was living in a dream world.

CHAPTER SIX

Expansion in the '80s

One way the history of the American Recorder Society might be examined would be in terms of periods of stability and unrest, or calm and tumult. I have chosen to write this history in terms of decades, and sometimes this arbitrary division into time periods doesn't quite fit the scheme. Nevertheless, the '80s decade (most of it) could be called a time of calm, and at the same time a period of heady expansion. This was in large part due to the efforts of our wonderful new executive director, Waddy Thompson. The '80s might be called, in fact, the "age of Waddy."

Executive Director Waddy Thompson at his desk in the SoHo office, late 1980s.

Waddy Thompson (the interesting first name is Scottish) was "found" by Andrew Acs. He was an extremely talented and creative person: an artist, a musician/composer with a BM degree with distinction, also a writer and a natural-born administrator. His previous experience had included work with a publicist for several dance companies, work with a music publisher, and coordinating the chamber music program for the Spoleto Festival USA. One of his most admirable traits was/is that he was/is able to work alone, organize his own time, see what needed to be done and do it, without ever getting into the frenzy that the office staff of the ARS had been in the habit of before and for a while after Waddy left.

Waddy was appointed Office Manager of the ARS in early 1982 and soon re-appointed Administrative Director, then Executive Director. In the fall Board Minutes of that year the Board takes note of "the superb way he has re-organized the office in his short tenure." Probably Waddy's most important achievement as administrative/executive director was to "computerize" the ARS. He started looking around for a computer immediately after coming to work for us. We had been in despair because the cost of a computer ($8,000) was prohibitive. But Waddy managed to find the money. From the Spring, 1983 *Newsletter*: "On November 16 a computer was installed in the ARS office, thus ending slow, manual maintenance of our records and ushering in a new era of efficiency. Our computer is a TeleVideo 802H system with hard disc capacity of 10 kilobytes as well as floppy discs. It manages all of our membership and subscription records and has a word processing program as well. The 1983 Directory [this was the one proofread so painstakingly by Valerie and me] will be out soon. [It] will be printed by the computer (as was this *Newsletter*). The benefit to the Society of the computer cannot be overstated; at the very least it is like having another full-time employee.

> The purchase of the computer was made possible by several benefactors to whom we owe a great debt of thanks: Generous contributions from Michael Zumoff and Neil Ivory were supplemented by very low interest two-year loans from Céline Karraker, Martha Bixler, Suzanne Ferguson, Geoffrey Naylor, Gary Porter, Richard Sacksteder, and Elizabeth Wauchope. Some ARS savings were also used.

Waddy Thompson immediately set about teaching himself how to use the computer. The entire appearance of everything emanating from the ARS office changed, and the work of running the Society was greatly enhanced. At the time of his resignation, in October, 1988, Waddy prepared a statement concerning his activities from which follows an extensive quote:

> When I took over the [ARS] office from Mary Ann Fleming [in 1982] income was at a very low ebb, members' correspondence with the Society went largely unanswered, records were in disarray, nothing went out on time, and no Directory had been published for over two years. Within eight months, I increased income by 30% through more efficient management, published a Directory, organized the Society's membership, subscription, and financial records, and put the Society back on an even keel.
>
> A few months later we purchased our first computer equipment and I coordinated not only the purchase of the equipment, but also the solicitation of donations and loans to cover the purchase. Within six weeks, I had entered all the membership and subscription records into the computer and was able to use the new data files for mailing and finance. I was now able to send detailed quarterly financial reports to the Board, something which had never happened before.
>
> In my second year, I instigated and ran the first annual [President's] appeal, preparing the first draft of the appeal letter and taking sole responsibility for production of all materials needed for a direct mail solicitation. The funds from this appeal allowed us to increase our reserve funds and to initiate new projects. I have been largely responsible for the subsequent four appeals as well.
>
> I have taken an active role with many committees. For the Education Committee, I administered the Teaching Seminar, assisted in the preparation of the second revised edition of the Study Guides (which I also typeset and did the layout for) and worked on the Level I-Classroom Study Guide.
>
> I have also been the watchdog who kept track of which

committees needed to accomplish which projects and have prodded them until the product was produced, e.g., the Workshop Committee's massive revision of the Workshop Directors' Booklet and the Teacher Listing; the Membership Committee's two revisions of the membership brochure; and the Chapter Relations Committee's production of the Chapter Circular. I have also run two Board Elections and I oversaw the revision of our By-Laws four years ago.

The Directory has improved through my efforts. I programmed the computer to produce all the listings along with the indications for teacher, playing level, and chapter affiliation. I added the alphabetical and teacher indices. All paste-up and layout has been done by me, saving the Society the $1,000 that a graphic artist would have charged. I have published the Directory on schedule each year.

I have improved Society publicity, initiating the annual workshop poster mailed to schools and libraries, preparing advertisements for periodicals, designing exhibitions for the Boston Early Music and Nakamichi Baroque Music Festivals, writing and mailing press releases, etc. It was at my recommendation that the Society established the Distinguished Achievement Award.

Other projects I initiated were the ARS 50 celebration, the cumulative index for AR, and the commissioning of a composition by Conrad Susa.

Last, but not least, the annual budget has grown enormously during my administration. It is now almost two and a half times what it was in 1982. It has gone from $60,000 then to $148,000 next year.

I was there, and it is all true.

Things looked good for the ARS at the first Board meeting of the '80s: September 19–21. We were solvent and had $5,000 in money market funds. There were 74 chapters of the ARS; the 1980 budget was $46,000. Martha Bixler and Joel Newman were made life members.

Negotiations were under way with the committee planning the first Boston Early Music Festival for some support from the ARS, probably in the form of a loan. Financial changes were under way. At the first Board meeting of 1980, at her request, Sigrid Nagle was made an independent contractor rather than an employee of the ARS, and this change in the status of the editor of *AR* has been maintained ever since. Sigrid was then hired by the ARS to edit the next five issues of AR. The price of a single issue was still $2.00. Mary Ann Fleming's salary was raised to $7,000 for the fiscal year 1980–81 and $8,000 the next year. The proposed raises for staff, rising office rent, production costs for the magazine, and new programs were seen to require raising dues for members of the ARS. Individual U.S.A. membership dues were raised to $12.50 in May of 1980 and to $15.00 in fiscal year 1981–82. By 1989 individual dues had been raised to $25.00.

At the September Board meeting of the ARS Shelley Gruskin was selected to be president of the Society. I was not only no longer president—I was no longer even on the Board of Directors. I continued, however, to attend Board meetings, out of force of habit, I suppose, and I remained very much involved in Board affairs during the time I was supposedly "off." The other "off-again-on-again" member of the Board who did this was Valerie Horst. She was on the Board from '80–84 and off again from '84–88. (I was off from '80–84 and on from '84–88. These gaps were, of course, due to temporary term limits for Directors.) She continued, however, to attend every Board meeting during that period, as I did. I think it would be fair to say that Shelley was an excellent leader and an inspiring President of the ARS, but he was pretty much an absentee president, and during the '80s it was a triumvirate of Valerie, Waddy, and Martha who looked after the store.

At the same time, although Board meetings took place only once a year, the number of committees formed and committee work undertaken by members of the Board proliferated during this decade. Besides being the "age of Waddy," the expansive '80s might also be called the "age of the committee." The work of the Society began to be distributed more equally among the Board members. As nature has always abhorred a vacuum in the ARS, the amount of work began to proliferate to keep up with the number of people involved.

At this first Board meeting of the new decade, a number of projects were set in motion. The **education committee**, which was already hard at work re-vamping the education program of the ARS, was made a **standing committee** of the Board, with Connie Primus as its chairman. A workshop committee, chaired by Phil Levin, was formed to

> . . . examine and develop policies to govern ARS relationships with summer and weekend workshops, ranging from financial assistance to possible supervision of curriculum, faculty selection, contracts, tuition and fees, and planning [Board of Directors meeting minutes, September 1980].

Other new committees were: a **chapter relations committee**, Andrew Acs, chairman; a **membership development committee**, Patricia Petersen, chairman; and a **publications committee**, Shelley Gruskin, chairman. The chapter relations committee, which changed in personnel and purpose over the years, was originally formed to help chapters plan their activities and to make them feel the ARS was doing something for them. The membership development committee was launched with the hopeful premise of building membership in the Society by means of contact with other early music groups, like college collegia and Renaissance Festival groups. The publications committee had as its main task at first the promotion of ARS publications with Galaxy Music, especially the promotion of the projected new series. Later it became involved with all of the ARS publications, including *AR*, the ARS *Newsletter*, and the Members' Library Editions.

The workshop and membership development committees were eventually disbanded; the other committees (with small changes in names) have remained vital Board committees with active participation by the Board members in their activities. And now there are more: In the year 2000 there were 12 standing committees and task forces of the ARS Board, some more active than others, including an **executive committee; compensation fund/development review; chapters and consorts; education; Junior Recorder Society; publications; scholarship; special events and professional outreach; Berkeley and Boston Festival task force; seniors task force; fund-raising task force; special membership representatives; and an ARS/AOSA joint advisory task force.**

For better communication with the membership by and large, the old ARS *Newsletter* was revived to appear semi-annually with a new format and a new editor, Father Bernard Hopkins. Although I was not on the Board, I soon became tangled up in the committee work, particularly on the education, workshop, and publications committees, and after a few issues I also became editor of the *Newsletter*. The current editor is Gail Nickless and the *Newsletter* is published four times a year.

Education program

The very first ARS Teachers' Certificates awarded by the American Recorder Society were distributed at the ARS Seminar held at the National Music Camps in Interlochen, Michigan, in the summer of 1961. The first exams required performing, sight-reading, and conducting on the part of the applicants, plus a written section that included naming reference works, notating scales, chords, and recorder trill fingerings, planning a recital, and arranging a piece for recorders. The point of the exam was to give some kind of accreditation to teachers by the ARS, thus raising the standards of both teaching and playing in the U.S., rather than simply putting an asterisk beside their names in the ARS Directory, as we had been doing. Joel Newman was made chairman of the education committee (we called it "Educational Director" then) in 1964. Initial members of the committee were

LaNoue Davenport, Bernie Krainis, and Martha Bixler. Colin Sterne joined in 1964. Morris Newman and Eric Leber joined in 1965, and Bernard Krainis resigned. Eric Leber was chairman for a time.

As a committee we tried to keep standards high by periodically revising the exam (we thoughtfully drew up a list of 17 "examiners" and tried to get more by making people take an even more rigorous exam—only Daniel Waitzman ever did) and making sure those who passed were really entitled to pass. There was a $10 examination fee, $5 of which was retained by the examiner. Successful applicants received an ARS Teacher's Certificate. The examiners were told: "The Teacher's Certificate does not require virtuoso playing or professional interpretations. The applicant should, however, demonstrate a correct approach to, and a reasonably expert execution of recorder technique. The applicant must be observed by the examiner conducting a class or giving a lesson. He should be able to hear mistakes, both musical and technical, and should know how to correct them effectively." (From the "Report from the Education Committee, AR IV, No. 3, August, 1963.) Examiners listed in the report were Bernard Krainis, Eric Leber, Martha Bixler, Morris Newman, Joel Newman, Erich Katz, Kenneth Wollitz, Colin Sterne, Hugh Orr, Arnold Grayson, Gloria Ramsey, Carolyn Wilhoyte, George Vollmer, Leo Christiansen, Robert Clements, LaNoue Davenport, and Friedrich von Huene.

By 1971 I was the only active person left on the committee, and I continued to revise the exam and try to see that it was administered fairly at ARS workshops and other places. But there were many difficulties and many hard feelings. The exam retained its main features for more than a decade. Examiners, or a group of them, tested an individual's knowledge and also did their best to observe him/her in a teaching situation. The exam was difficult to administer and sometimes quite traumatic to take, often on the morning after a sizzling faculty concert at a workshop, by a quivering applicant who had been up most of the night and then found that same faculty glaring at him as he tried to impress them with his teaching skills. A lot of people passed who probably shouldn't have, and on the other hand there were plenty of people who either should have passed or would have passed if they had ever bothered to take the exam. In addition, sometimes classes in recorder pedagogy being taught at workshops turned into question and answer sessions on the exam to be given at the end of the workshop.

In the spring of 1977 I, as President of the ARS, asked Peter Seibert to re-form the education committee and take on the project of revamping our education program and, specifically, figuring out how we could certify teachers for our members. Nobody was satisfied with the old teachers' exam and we had suspended the program utterly for a couple of years. After studying our programs of previous years and current programs in other countries and holding many discussions with the Board and in particular with Gerald Burakoff and Connie Primus, Peter came up with a plan for "Levels of Achievement." Once again we abandoned the idea of teacher certification and concentrated on a plan whereby we could help our members educate themselves, with or without the help of a teacher, in order to improve their playing and add to their enjoyment of the recorder. It was to be a students' program, rather than one of teacher certification.

There were to be five Levels of Achievement. The basic plan for these levels was worked out by Peter Seibert and Connie Primus. Each level consisted of a Study Guide to be given free to anyone who was interested, and an examination to be given, at first for only the higher Levels, III and IV. Levels Ia (for child beginners), Ib (adults), and II (intermediates) were intended to be guides for study. When the demand for exams for these two levels increased, exams were devised. The exams for Levels I (the division into a and b was soon discontinued) and II could be given by a member of the applicant's chapter or virtually anyone willing to do it. (In 1984 Mary Scott, a student of Connie Primus, was appointed to grade exams for individuals who were not near a chapter.) Examinations for Level III, advanced amateurs, could be taken privately, with the approval of the education committee, or at a workshop. Level III exams were taped, and were judged not by the examiner (although he or she could make a recommendation), but by a committee of three chosen by the education committee, who either met at a Board meeting or sent the tape (with tremendous inefficiency) around to each other. When a candidate passed the exam, a Level III certificate, signed by the president of the ARS and the chairman of the education committee, was presented to him or her. The Level III exam was tough, and many people failed. As of this writing (August, 2003) 30 people have passed the Level III exam.

The Study Guides for Levels II and III were published in the November 1980 AR and Levels Ia and Ib, put together under the supervision of Gerald Burakoff, in May, 1981. Later a booklet with Study Guides for all three levels was printed for the ARS by Sweet Pipes, Gerald Burakoff's publishing company. Although the booklets cost the ARS $1.50 apiece, they were distributed free to new members of the ARS. Each Guide contained a list of possible goals for the applicant, a structured program in technique, theory, sight-reading and performance practice, a list of repertoire, resource materials (books and articles), and a description of the requirements of the examination at that level. Level I focused on basic technique; Level II on ensemble skills, and Level III on solo repertoire. Any individual, (or consort, in the case of Level II) who passed the examination at a particular level was certified as having passed that level; his/her name was printed in the ARS *Newsletter* and he/she was given a certificate. From the outset it was emphasized that the program was to be an *educational* program, to be used with a teacher or for self-study; the examination was optional. The goals were set for well-rounded amateur recorder players.
The first person to pass the Level III exam, in September 1981, was a student of mine, Paul Jacobson, a talented flutist, recorder and keyboard player, and college professor of music, who was willing to be

a "guinea pig" for the new exam and take it for free. (Later applicants initially paid $50, then $100). Paul Jacobson is pictured with Connie Primus, chairman of the ARS education committee, in the February, 1982 issue of The American Recorder, as she presents him with the Level III Certificate.

Level III exams were offered at all ARS workshops but one in the summer of 1981 (President Shelley Gruskin appointed the examiners) and at all in 1982. Some of the classes at the workshops were directed toward helping candidates pass the exam. In the late '80s we offered "Level III prep" classes at some of the ARS workshops. Following the Study Guide for Level III, we attempted to give students an idea of what they needed to know to pass each section of the exam—theory, sight reading, performance repertoire, performance practice, reading from early notation, etc.

The education program was developed, much discussed among the committee members, modified, re-formatted and re-thought during the next two decades. Under the committee's subsequent chairmen in the '80s, Susan Prior, Kenneth Andresen, Jennifer Lehmann, Judith Whaley, and Carolyn Peskin, it remained essentially the same, although there was more emphasis on the exams than on the self-study and self-evaluation. Study Guides and exams were rewritten; and experiments were made with other levels, like I-C, for example, for classroom teachers, Level III-A, for those between Level I and Level III (this turned out to be useful as a practice exam) and Levels IV (for professional teachers) and V (for professional performers), but these modifications were, for one reason or another, abandoned. Another modification in the program in 1985 made it possible to take portions of the Level III exam separately, and to re-take a portion that might have been failed the first time. Names of those passing any one of the three exams were listed in the ARS *Newsletter*.

On February 5–7 of 1983 a subcommittee of the education committee, consisting of Martha Bixler, Connie Primus, Peter Seibert, and Mary Scott, met at the home of Connie Primus in Denver, to work on a revision of Levels II–III. We also talked about the frequently requested "teachers' supplement" to Level III in order once again to tackle the problem of teacher certification. We made small changes in the Level I repertory in the Study Guide, changed wording in parts of Level II, and made some additions to the repertoire. The most significant changes we made were in Level III. The section on *Ear Training* was completely revised. We also made an attempt to divide Level III into easier and more difficult parts, in order to lessen the large gap between Levels II and III. *Scales and Arpeggios* was divided by marking those up to four flats or sharps with an asterisk, leaving the remaining scales listed without an asterisk, indicating that they were more difficult. We marked the pieces in the *Prepared Repertoire* section similarly. On May 27 of that year another subcommittee (Susan Prior, Philip Levin, Michael Lynn, Jerome Kohl, and Connie Primus) met in Boston to discuss possibilities for a Level IV (professional) Study Guide and Examination. A level IV program did in fact eventually evolve, but it was never used very much. The first Revised Version of the Education Program was published in 1984, the second in 1987, the third in 1991.

Connie Primus was chairwoman of the education committee until she resigned at the 1985 Board meeting. This was a very great loss to the committee and to the Society. Three chairwomen since: Jennifer Lehmann and Judith Whaley in the '90s and Carolyn Peskin in the "noughts" have risen to the task. And Mark Davenport (beginning with his term in 2004) has been exemplary.

In the fall of 1985, after the Teaching Seminar sponsored by the American Recorder Society had taken place (see under ARS summer workshops, page 114), a modification of the program was developed whereby candidates who wanted to work toward a Teacher's Certificate (our ever-present, ever-elusive goal) could take 25 hours of courses at one of the ARS Workshops in pedagogy, ensemble techniques, and performance practice. They would then write summaries of the courses to be submitted to the education committee, along with a personal assessment from the teacher of each course. The content was to be approved by the education committee ahead of time. Candidates would also submit a résumé of their teaching experience with professional and student references. Finally, candidates needed to pass, or have passed, the Level III exam. This program was in place during the seven remaining years of ARS workshops, with a small amount of success. Among those actually completing the requirements for Level III Teacher certification in the years following the Teaching Seminar were Marie Blankenship, Nisargo Eck, David Fischer, Laura Hagen, Andrea MacIntosh-Lee, Donna Messer, Gerald Moore, Carole Rogentine, and Marie-Louise Smith. The program, beset with administrative difficulties, was scrapped in 1990. From the minutes of the committee meeting February 23, 1990: "The committee decided to drop the program for Level III teachers' certification and will suggest that passing Level III be used as 'certification' for those who may need credentials."

In the late '80s, two new projects came under discussion by the education committee. Our then-secretary Scott Paterson, a Canadian member of the Board, an educator, recorder player, and writer, started developing information packets for ARS chapters—booklets that could be used by chapters for meetings and the education of their individual members.

The price of these packets (which are still being sold) to the members (or chapter) buying them was, first $5 for members, then $10, later $13 including postage. I was sorry that there had to be any charge, but it was clear that the ARS could not afford to give them away. In total, seven information packets were developed and published between 1990 and 1991:

- Packet No. 1: Scott Paterson's "Recorder Care" provides a lucid compilation of facts and opinions about recorder use and care from many sources, with an excellent reading list, mainly from articles in *American Recorder*, the English *Recorder and Music Magazine*, and information sheets from the recorder maker and repairer Philip Levin. In his introduction Scott states: "This information packet is intended to provide ideas for discussion and group activity at ARS meetings and workshops. The packet is organized into discussions of different common problem areas encountered by recorder players." Under discussion are topics like whether or not to use a thumb rest and what kind to use, breaking in an instrument, oiling, voicing, and tuning.

- Packet No. 2: Connie Primus's "American Recorder Music" offers a comprehensive list and discussion of American music suitable for the recorder, including early American sacred and secular music, music composed for events celebrated by the American Recorder Society, such as the Fiftieth Anniversary, traditional popular American music, and other music by American composers. Intending this booklet for use primarily by chapters, Connie assigns difficulty levels to each piece of music listed and/or discussed, using the Roman numerals I–IV assigned to the different levels of the ARS Program.

- Packet No. 3: Jennifer Lehmann's "Music for Mixed Ensembles" lists and discusses a large quantity of music that can be played by recorders combined with other instruments, and provides many valuable tips for orchestration. Although necessarily dated, this packet is still a valuable resource.

- Packet No. 4: Susan Prior's "Improve Your Consort Skills."

- Packet No. 5: Louise Austin's "Playing Music for the Dance."

- Packet No. 6: Judith Whaley's "The Burgundian Court and its Music" comprises a superb booklet, put together by members of the Kalamazoo Chapter of the ARS with Judy Whaley. The publication includes maps of Burgundy along with its neighbors in the fifteenth century, a map of Burgundy within modern Europe, a family tree of the dukes of Valois and their relationship to the kings of France, a history of musicians and music-making in the Burgundian court, a selected list of Burgundian composers of the fifteenth century plus biographies of the most important composers, suggestions for ways to perform the music, and a bibliography. This packet, a true labor of love, is a shining example of the way the efforts of a few, promoted by the American Recorder Society on behalf of its members, can benefit the many.

- Packet No. 7: Peggy Monroe's "Adding Percussion to a Recorder Consort."

All in all the production of these packets, although labor-intensive on everyone's part, was a very good idea.

The other project, long advocated by chapters, individual members of the ARS, and the Board, was for a videotape, preferably a teaching videotape, or a series of videotapes, that could be lent or rented to chapters, schools, and individual members of the ARS as a pedagogical tool. What a good idea! Ken Andresen, appointed chairman of the education committee in 1988, offered to pursue the plan and struggled with it through the two years of his tenure. Ken tried very hard to get a grant ($10,000 was envisioned) for this project, and he also tried to enlist the services of several well-known recorder luminaries as teachers. The grant never materialized, and the "participating teachers," although pleased to be asked to participate (who doesn't want to appear in a video?) were unable to come up with concrete plans for what they would actually do on the tape. So this project failed, but I think the main reason it did was that like so many other ideas floated at meetings of the Board, it got blown up too much. From my idea of its being a simple home video with a stationary camera giving one or two angles of teacher and students, the projected videotape bloomed into an MTV-type affair, with ARS "ads," voice-over, fancy camera-work, the whole commercial treatment (At this writing—2006—the idea has actually achieved fruition. A teaching videotape called "Recorder Power" was released by the ARS in late 2002 with the help of a matching grant from the National Endowment for the Arts. The artist is John Tyson.)

Workshops

ARS summer workshops continued to proliferate and prosper during the '80s. This was the hey-day of the ARS Workshops. Most were small—with a faculty of five, six or seven—and well-run; those who ran them made a serious effort to structure the workshops so as to promote the skills of the participants as well as to give them a good time. All except New Orleans (1980 was its third year) and Colorado had been happening each summer (or winter) for five or six years at least, and there had been a workshop at the beautiful mining town of Telluride in the high mountains of Colorado in 1975 and 1976. The workshops were printing their own brochures, but the ARS sent them, giving the workshops free "ads" in The American Recorder. A rotating group (by the 1980s, there was not so much "rotating") of workshop directors was appointed yearly by the ARS Board.

In 1980 there were six ARS summer workshops: a new one under the directorship of Connie Primus at the University of Colorado, Boulder; the Long Island Recorder Festival, called LIRF, directed by Eugene Reichenthal; the Midwest Workshop, directed by Louise Austin at Lawrence University in Appleton, Wisconsin; one at Tulane University in New Orleans directed by Andrew Acs; the Mideast Workshop at St. Vincent College, Latrobe, Pennsylvania, directed by Marilyn Carlson; and at Hampshire College in Amherst, Massachusetts under the directorship of Valerie Horst. The ARS was also sponsoring a very successful "Mid-winter Workshop" in Miami, directed by Arnold Grayson.

The Hampshire College workshop was special. I always think of it and the following Amherst College Workshop as descendants of the first ARS week-long workshop, the ARS post-season "seminar" held at the National Music Camp in Interlochen, Michigan, in 1961, perhaps because I was there every year until the summer of 2000. The workshop had migrated from Interlochen (although there were smaller repeats at Interlochen in 1964, 1968 and 1970) to Goddard College, in Vermont, 1963–1971; to Salve Regina College in Newport, Rhode Island, 1972–1974; to Hampshire College in Amherst in 1975, chiefly because it was getting too big for each campus in turn. While still at Goddard the workshop had been expanded to two weeks because of the large number of registrants. By 1980 it boasted a faculty of 33 and a registration of 183 students (counting both weeks). The Hampshire College Workshop was certainly the leading ARS Workshop, not only because of the size of the faculty but because of its quality, and the variety of offerings to students that were possible because of its size. Viol lessons had always been offered at ARS Workshops, but instrumental classes at Hampshire now included Renaissance flute, cornetto, sackbut, double reeds, lute, vielle, rebec, early harp, pipe and tabor, percussion, and voice. There were also classes in historical dance. Special features in 1980 included classes in original notation, improvisation, Renaissance ornamentation, editing, and the study of historical woodwind design.

Still, the smaller workshops had their advantages, and they all stressed the high caliber of the teaching, if not of the students! From the beginning the ARS Workshops were open to all, not just experienced or talented players, as were some of the English ones. The chief difference between those of the two countries was the ratio of faculty to students, which was much higher in America. This ratio plus the ever-higher salaries (although never high enough!) offered to faculty by the American workshops made them much more expensive for the students than those in England or European countries. Tuition scholarships for less affluent students became absolutely necessary. The ARS sought to provide these, but its resources were always too small for more than a "drop in the bucket." The workshops had to begin providing work-study scholarships on their own as well.

Seven ARS summer workshops were held in 1981. The Colorado Workshop was moved to Colorado College in Colorado Springs, a much more congenial locale, with its integrated small college campus, than Boulder. Two new workshops in 1981, in addition to those already named, were those at Rider College in Lawrenceville, New Jersey, directed by Gerald and Sonya Burakoff, and the Smoky Mountain Workshop at Warren Wilson College in Swannanoa, North Carolina, directed by Andrew Acs and Martha Bixler. The life of the latter was short. We had horrible financial troubles, although we were in a really beautiful location and had a terrific faculty, including Martha Bishop (viols), Jack Ashworth, and the incomparable David Hart. North Carolina in the summer was really much too hot. There was no such thing as air-conditioning in the Blue Ridge Mountains then! Registration was low. We took a financial beating and called it quits.

David Hart, workshop concert, Asheville, NC, 1978.

In 1982 the Hampshire College Workshop was moved to Amherst College. This was an inspired move, not just because of the more accessible campus in a town of the same name. The new location gave this workshop the

Workshop concert, Asheville, NC, 1978. Left to right: Martha Bishop, Andrew Acs, Martha Bixler.

cachet of association with an elite Ivy League college that has remained to this day, even though neither the summer workshop (since moved to Connecticut College in New London, Connecticut) nor the weekend workshops under its incorporated sponsorship have anything whatsoever to do with Amherst College. The five other summer workshops were Rider, Colorado, LIRF, Mideast, and Midwest, making six ARS workshops in all.

Although "early music" had been well established on the West Coast of the United States since the '60s, in 1980 there was no direct link between the West Coast and the ARS as far as ARS Workshops were concerned. Following LaNoue Davenport's tenure as director of the first ARS Workshop (1964 and '65) at the Mendocino Art Center in Mendocino, California, were those of Peter Ballinger and Kenneth Wollitz in 1966 and '67. ARS Workshops were held at the Idyllwild School of Music and Art at the University of Southern California in Idyllwild from 1968 to 1975, but after that the "California connection" was broken. In the meantime the San Francisco Early Music Society was well established. Since 1977 summer early music workshops (actually four separate workshops) have been held at Dominican College in San Rafael, and in

1988 Canto Antiguo, formerly the Idyllwild Workshop, moved to a beautiful setting at the Thacher School in Ojai, California. The cast was stellar, including LaNoue Davenport, Shirley Marcus, Shirley Robbins, and Gloria Ramsey. But none of these was an "ARS Workshop."

1984 was a big year for ARS summer workshops. There were eight. New was the Chesapeake ARS Seminar at Notre Dame College in Baltimore, Maryland, directed by Gwendolyn Skeens, and a revived New Orleans "World's Fair Workshop," directed by Andrew Acs, who was living there at the time. Andrew planned for a very large faculty at this workshop, but some had to be let go before the workshop started. I was one of these! All of the workshops were increasing the number and variety of their offerings. There was less and less emphasis on the recorder, and more and more emphasis on "related instruments." The eras being explored kept pace. In 1985 the entire Colorado workshop was devoted to Baroque music. Almost from the beginning, English Country Dance was offered for recreation, it being a favorite form of exercise (after we got too long in the tooth for volley ball) of many of the faculty and later the students at these summer workshops.

In the summer of 1985 the ARS experimented with a workshop for teachers run entirely by the ARS, a "teaching seminar" at Southwest Texas State University (LBJ's alma mater) in San Marcos, Texas under the direction of Martha Reynolds, a professor at the University. The purpose of the seminar, as originally planned by Connie Primus, chairman of the committee, was "to offer pedagogical instruction based on the ARS Education Program to ARS members who currently teach recorder and to those who are interested in teaching." The workshop was intended as a supplement to the Level III program and was another attempt by the American Recorder Society to find a way to certify teachers. An ARS "Teachers' Certificate" was to be awarded to those who attended the seminar and completed all assignments, passed the Level III exam (not necessarily before the Seminar) and submitted a résumé of teaching experience and references to the committee.

Several plans were submitted to the education committee chairman by those of us who were interested in directing this seminar, and the proposal of Dr. Martha Reynolds, an associate professor of music education at Southwest Texas University, was chosen by the committee. Dr. Reynolds's plan was as follows: "The subject matter of classes, lectures, and discussions should address the variety of musical, educational, administrative, and social [!] skills which the effective teacher must develop." There were to be two lecturers in musicology (it ended up as one); the faculty of five (it ended up as four), at least for the first seminar, were to be drawn from among the members of the committee.

The plan, therefore, was for a strictly ARS venture, with financial backing, publicity, clerical and bookkeeping services to be provided by the ARS. The main purpose of the workshop under the aegis of the committee, some of whom (myself, for example) were not such wonderful pedagogues, was to give instruction in pedagogy, without much emphasis on the subject matter. In-service credit was offered for teachers.

Later the plan of the workshop was modified to include a "distinguished person." We did manage to get Edgar Hunt, an already legendary figure, a former head of the Department of Renaissance and Baroque Music at Trinity College, London, and a founding member of the English Society of Recorder Players, as a distinguished guest teacher. While he gave some excellent instruction in conducting, arranging, and editing, his lectures consisted mainly, so I was told, of reminiscences of the recorder movement in England. The rest of the faculty consisted of Martha Bixler, Shelley Gruskin, then president of the ARS and also a distinguished player and teacher, Connie Primus, teacher of recorder and flute, director of education for the ARS, and exvice president, and Martha Reynolds, the director of the workshop. It sounded good, but it was not at all what I had wanted. I did not think our faculty, myself included, was distinguished enough in the fields of recorder performance, music history, or music education. I had wanted to see the Swiss recorder performer/educator Hans-Martin Linde on the faculty, or even the sensational Dutchman Frans Brüggen or his student Marion Verbruggen at the seminar to teach technique, repertoire (including the avant-garde), and performance practice; Bernard Krainis to give a big baroque master class; LaNoue Davenport to teach arranging and conducting; and Lucy Cross to teach medieval music. I had wanted us to have classes in score reading, writing and arranging for recorders, ornamentation, early notation, and musicology. And a "collegium colloquium"—with discussions of literature, instruments, and how to conduct an early music group. We got none of these things, and there was just too much pedagogy to suit me.

The workshop for teachers was a noble experiment, but it was not totally successful. In the end there were fewer instructors than we had wished to have, and those few had to take salary cuts due to severe budgetary problems. Waddy Thompson, who as ARS executive director was the administrator of the workshop, was not even able to attend. In order not to compete with other ARS Workshops, the seminar was held too early in the summer (June 16–22) for many teachers, so enrollment was low (21 students) and there were attendees without the remotest interest in teaching who went to the workshop simply to support it and the ARS and for the fun of it. It was extremely hot in southwestern Texas, but the temperature in the air-conditioned dormitory was kept at a frigid 60 degrees. The walks across campus in the hot sun to meals and classes were long and rather arduous. In the end the

Martha Reynolds at ARS Teaching Seminar, 1985.

American Recorder Society lost money and although the original plan had been for the seminar to be biennial, there was little incentive to continue with it another year. The workshop did, however, inspire the committee to plan a course of study whereby students could take courses at ARS workshops leading toward a Level III Teachers' Certificate. This plan was implemented and carried out with some success at later ARS workshops.

In addition to the Teachers Seminar seven other summer workshops, the usual suspects minus New Orleans, were held in the summer of 1985. In 1986 Rider was canceled, and so there were six. Likewise in 1987. In 1988 there were eight, with the addition of the Yellow Springs Workshop of the Early Music Center in Yellow Springs, Ohio, which was actually held at Wright State University in Dayton, and the Southern Utah Early Music Workshop in Cedar City, Utah, developed by Jeffrey Snedeker from a weekend of early instrument instruction for attendees at the Utah Shakespearean Festival.

The ARS administration of the '50s, '60s, and even the '70s has often been accused of geographical myopia for its inability to establish its influence on the West Coast of the United States until the late '80s. We were always waiting for the people on the West Coast to join us, and they were always waiting for us to ask them. It was not until 1989 that the workshop at Canto Antiguo, in Ojai, California sought ARS "endorsement," as it was by then being called. At the same time, after a lot of heavy persuasion in our 50th birthday year, we finally succeeded in getting two "SFEMS" workshops in California—the recorder workshop and the baroque music workshop—to join us as well. The big Vancouver "Early Music Program & Festival," despite ardent wooing, never joined the roster of ARS workshops in early music. But in 1989 there were 13 "ARS-endorsed" summer workshops, just as we were about to lose the summer ARS Workshops altogether.

Workshop Committee

I haven't been able to ascertain whether a workshop committee existed prior to 1979, but, backtracking a bit, I should say that in the '70s the ARS administration was feeling it necessary to tug a bit at the reins with which it held its summer schools. From the beginning the ARS Workshops were the jewels in the ARS's crown. But from the beginning they were difficult to manage, especially at long distance. And oddly, the more the summer workshops tried to extricate themselves from under the control of the ARS office, the more the ARS administration tried to control them. A letter of December 23, 1965, from then president Howard Brown to Sue Erlenkotter, one of the organizers of the ARS Summer Seminar in Mendocino, California, states that "although we [the Executive Board of the ARS] were delighted to confirm [Peter Ballinger's] appointment as co-director, we were disturbed by the fact that the principle of selection by the national Executive Board seemed to have been violated." It seems that the local folks had approached Peter Ballinger before the national ARS had had a chance to do so. Howard Brown stated that:

> . . . it has always been ARS policy that the Executive Board appoints directors for these nationally sponsored summer seminars. The principal reason for establishing the policy is to ensure a modicum of control by the national organization, since it is financially responsible for the entire operation.

As the years went by and more and more workshops came into being, the ARS administration began publishing manifestos and forming committees in an effort to control their creation, their financial affairs, their way of operating and, increasingly, the quality of the teaching. On January 27, 1976, the ARS had published a set of "Guidelines for the Organization of ARS Workshops," signed by the president, Ken Wollitz. In it the responsibility for appointing directors was stated to rest with the president, acting on behalf of the Board of Directors. The director of the workshop was to submit an estimated budget in advance, and the Society was to guarantee the workshop against financial loss and participate in any profit. The ARS recommended the amount of salaries to be paid the Director ($475 per week) and faculty ($325) plus transportation at 10 cents a mile. The ARS even dictated tuition fees, $90 for members of the ARS and $100 for non-members, who could apply the extra $10 toward a one-year membership in the ARS. The workshops would produce their own brochures (the size was stipulated), as they were already beginning to do, but the ARS would mail them for free. The ARS reserved the right to cancel a workshop if it was not going to be financially viable (this happened to "Telluride III" in 1977) and, most unrealistically, the ARS demanded financial liquidation of each workshop within four weeks after the event.

Needless to say, some of these guidelines, particularly the financial constraints, did not sit well with the workshop heads. The ARS administration began backtracking almost immediately. From the minutes of the January, 1977 Board meeting: "The financial guidelines originally set up by the ARS will not be used this summer. Each director will decide the fees to be charged and the salaries to be paid. No percentage of profits will be returned to the ARS. Directors will be responsible for all advertising of the workshops with the exception of free advertising in The American Recorder. The ARS will also provide address labels, and will donate $100 in scholarship money to each director. In other words, though our "children" were growing up and gaining more independence, we were still giving them a lot of financial support.

The minutes of the September Board meeting in 1979 state that the Board of Directors of the ARS re-formed the workshop committee with Valerie Horst as its chairman. Members were Philip Levin, Gerald Burakoff, Louise Austin, Peter Seibert, vice president of the ARS, *exofficio*, and Martha Bixler, *ex-officio* (I was still president of the ARS). On

March 8, 1980 I mailed another "agreement" to the workshop heads assuring them that they would keep their autonomy concerning place, dates, and faculty at their individual workshops, that they would make their own financial arrangements with the faculty and the institution involved but that the ARS would assume financial responsibility for individual workshops that might be canceled (up to the magnificent sum of $200), that brochures would still be mailed by the ARS office, and that scholarship aid ($100 per workshop week from the Erich Katz Memorial Fund) would be continued. I also reiterated the stricture that all participants at ARS workshops should be members of the ARS. This gave the workshops the onerous task of collecting dues for the ARS from those who had not yet joined. Workshop heads were asked to sign and return this agreement.

At the September, 1980 Board meeting, when new committees were being formed and old ones re-formed, it was realized and accepted that Valerie, who had taken the post of chairman provisionally (and who had done a fine job, taking responsibility, for instance, for getting ad copy from the various workshop heads for the magazine in a timely fashion), was not suitable, as a workshop director, to be chairman of the committee, and new ARS President Shelley Gruskin appointed Philip Levin to this office. Members were Patricia Petersen, Andrew Acs, Valerie Horst, and, ex-officio, vice-president Connie Primus. The committee was formed to

> . . . take up policies on tuition and salaries for ARS-sponsored workshops, curriculum, teacher-pupil ratios, policy on cancellations, certification of teachers, coordination of the education program with the workshops, and financial relations of workshops with ARS" [Board Meeting minutes, September 1980].

In the summer of 1981 the workshop committee asked in its agreement with the workshops that "all students at the workshops be members of the ARS" and "all recorder-playing faculty be members also." It was also requested that "where possible, the workshop make an additional surcharge of $5.00 per person in return for [ARS] support." The ARS hoped that workshops would make use of the new education program. The Society continued to be responsible for publicity and mailing brochures, but scholarship money was not forthcoming that year. Through the efforts of Gerald Burakoff, who was always helpful in educational matters, particularly public school education, the ARS began offering in-service credit to teachers at its workshops in 1981.

Ruth Bossler was appointed chairman of the workshop committee early in 1982. Members of the committee were Martha Bixler, Valerie Horst, and Andrew Acs. The mandate from the 1981 Board meeting was to "set up criteria for ARS-sponsored workshops, inform directors of the criteria, and coordinate the announcements." The committee met seven times during fiscal year 1981–82, mostly dealing with communications with summer workshop directors. In the 1982 agreement the workshop directors were given instructions as to the size of their brochures (for ease of mailing), and reminded of the $5 fee. (The fee was rescinded at the October 1982 Board meeting.) They were also asked to make comments on the implementation of the education program, and to fill out a financial report. We published a planning packet for ARS summer workshop directors. In 1982 Ruth Bossler anounced that a new "Workshop Scholarship Fund" was being inaugurated in hopes of applying scholarship money to participants at ARS workshops.

The Board of Directors of the ARS decided at their October 1982 Board meeting that beginning in the summer of 1983 membership meetings should be held at each ARS summer workshop. These meetings were perhaps not just the idea of the workshop committee, but it was the workshop committee that made sure they took place, sometimes with only the lukewarm consent of the workshop director. They were part of the attempt being made to keep the ARS workshops in line as *ARS* workshops, even as they were slipping away. Another of our endeavors was to put together a teachers list—names of those who would teach at workshops or lead chapter meetings—which was distributed to all chapters and summer workshop directors. In 1986 there were 286 private teachers and 79 "workshop teachers" on the ARS list.

Polly Ellerbe joined the committee in 1982. In that year we inaugurated "ARS Weekend Workshops." There was lots and lots of paperwork involved on both sides. An ARS weekend workshop was defined as lasting two days or more; classes were to be offered in the ARS curriculum or aspects thereof; all students and faculty who were not ARS members had to join; use of the Society name was authorized contingent upon approval by the ARS Workshop Committee after receiving application. Benefits to the workshop included 1,000 free address labels of ARS members, use of the ARS bulk mail permit, free national publicity in the ARS *Newsletter*, and a guarantee of up to $50 to cover expenses in the event of cancellation. In the spring of 1983 we published a "workshop planning booklet" with "information, suggestions, and advice from several chapters and individuals who have planned successful workshops. This booklet is intended primarily to help chapters and other groups plan their first one-day workshop." (ARS *Newsletter* No. 6, Spring 1983). We were full of advice on everything from planning dates ("be sure to avoid holidays") to materials to have on hand ("magic markers, pens, pencils") to choosing faculty to showing how to write a registration form.

We continued backing and filling, trying to decide what our role was vis-a-vis the workshops. A letter from me written on December 10, 1982 and addressed to the other members of the committee complains as follows:

> What are we here for, or what is the function of the workshop committee? I was somewhat startled to find a Puerto Rican Workshop very solidly in the works for this March that I knew absolutely nothing about. Then, too, there is the cancellation of the

> Miami Workshop. Do I have to be in a position where I must guess at what is going on? Polly had thought we would be involved with policy rather than paperwork. What control do we have, if any? Several people have told me they were horrified to learn that ARS Workshops were in fact ARS workshops in name only, that they were not run by the ARS. [It seems clear] that the workshops have gotten farther and farther away from the ARS.

Unfortunately, there was considerable internal strife among members of the committee, with suspicion on all sides. It seemed to some of us that the committee was operating mainly for the benefit of some workshops over others. In 1983 we had begun requesting, then insisting, that directors send their workshop evaluations or copies of them to the workshop committee to see. We had started demanding the individual workshop evaluation forms, or copies of them, first of the education program, then those written by the students concerning their classes. This last evaluation, originally conceived as a way of judging the teachers at the workshops, became in time a way for the committee to evaluate the workshops themselves. The request was not welcome. Not only was it a nuisance for the workshop heads, but some of them felt, perhaps rightly, that it was unreasonable for the workshop committee to take so much interest in what was in fact their internal business. The evaluations were tedious reading, but they became a *cause célèbre*. They were perceived to be more important as directors of some of the larger workshops dragged their feet about producing them. This made some of the committee members more suspicious. At a meeting of the committee during the Thanksgiving weekend in 1985, there was a terrible blow-up between two members of the workshop committee. I was of course caught in the middle—as I so often am—and at the end of it a member of the committee left my apartment in tears and a friendship was destroyed forever.

President Shelley Gruskin, far away in Duluth, Minnesota, was in the unenviable position of having to "do something" to end the impasse. His letter of February 4, 1986 to the "wounded" member reads in part: "What I've decided to do does not pretend to demonstrate justice or due course. The situation of incompatibility is a recognized human phenomenon, and in human terms is exempt from judgements. Hoping that you sense my strong belief in this principle, I have to continue by saying that I feel the only way to restore the workshop committee to full working order is to remove you from the committee and this letter is to tell you of that decision."

Shelley was eloquent, even on paper, but it did not make his judgement any less unpleasant to the committee member involved. The reaction was instant rage, coupled with a serious attempt to destroy the American Recorder Society by getting members to withhold their dues, and to form another, alternative Society. Fortunately for all concerned, the attempt was not successful.

We always had a limited amount of scholarship money. The ARS had been giving scholarships or money for scholarships to the summer workshops since the '70s, first from its operating funds, then from the Erich Katz Memorial Fund. We started setting aside funds for weekend and even one-day workshops in the form of loans at first, then of cash grants of one tuition fee per 15 participants, and in 1982, the year we inaugurated "official" ARS weekend workshops, we began giving $100 grants toward teacher expense for new weekend workshops. We also began giving partial scholarships to a member of a chapter, to be chosen by that chapter, toward tuition for a summer workshop.

In 1987, as the result of a successful President's Appeal, we inaugurated seven new full-tuition scholarships to members of the ARS for summer workshops:

> Scholarships will be awarded for any combination of the following criteria: 1) financial need, 2) musical merit and promise on recorder, 3) possible benefit to other members as a result of the scholarship. All

else being equal, preference will be given to those who have not already attended a week-long workshop." [*Newsletter* 16, Winter 1987.]

We had finally come up with a real benefit to our members, a perk for membership, available to only a chosen few, of course, but we were actually "doing something" for the membership. After the death of Andrew Acs in 1987 the Board of Directors of the ARS established an Andrew Acs Scholarship Fund, using funds originally obtained from the sale of Andrew's instruments, but supplemented by hundreds of dollars contributed by Andrew's family, in particular his parents, and friends. There have been many grateful students whose workshop tuition has been paid by the Andrew Acs Fund. The ARS was now awarding three kinds of scholarship: the President's Scholarship, Andrew Acs Scholarships, and chapter/collegium scholarships. In 1988 the ARS awarded seven full-tuition President's Scholarships and five Andrew Acs Scholarships (one of the five recipients was Roxane Layton, who had been a student of Andrew's). Also in 1988 the ARS endowed the Margaret DeMarsh Scholarship for a weekend workshop in honor of one of its prominent members. Margaret DeMarsh was a performer and conductor of early music in the Glens Falls (NY) area. The first recipient was Rotem Greitser at the Hudson Guild Columbus Day Weekend Workshop in the fall of 1989.

In 1985 Mary Maarbjerg, a graduate (MBA) of the Wharton School of the University of Pennsylvania, a vice president and treasurer at Pitney-Bowes Credit Corp., and an amateur player who wanted to do something for the ARS, joined the workshop committee with the understanding that she would take over as chairman from Ruth. Mary described herself in a letter to the chapter representatives as "an amateur recorder player and a self-confessed workshop addict." Thus began Mary's short but influential career in the administration of the ARS. She was appointed a member of the Board in 1986, then re-elected and made treasurer in 1988. Mary immediately started "earning her keep" as a member of the workshop committee by getting to work with

Valerie in preparing workshop "ads" for *AR*. These were the free notices the ARS had been giving workshops in the magazine besides sending out brochures. We finally gave up the practice in 1989.

More important, Mary kept the committee running at full tilt for five years. The committee met six times during the year 1985–1986. In her first report to the Board Mary states:

> The committee defined and documented two workshop assistance programs for weekend one-day workshops. Program I provides a $100 grant to chapters who would like to launch a new workshop program, and Program II provides scholarships and other benefits to chapters and other groups seeking ARS weekend workshop designation and endorsement. The committee decided that it would no longer assemble and compile all the evaluation questionnaires from participants in ARS summer workshops. The committee felt the need for a wider variety of suggestions and opinions from a wider geographic area. It therefore set up a workshop advisory panel made up of amateur and professional members country-wide. The committee, on listening to ARS members from around the country, sensed a need for the ARS to take the issue of recorder instructor qualification more seriously.

The ARS workshop committee was in continuous existence throughout the decade. Under Mary's management it became increasingly active. With varying personnel as members (at one point I tried to resign but didn't succeed) it sought to define and re-define the relationship of the ARS to "its" workshops, in the above-mentioned and many other matters. We wrote and re-wrote information booklets, guides to becoming a workshop, guides to getting grants, "how to be a good workshop teacher," etc. We even become involved (although we changed our minds once again and soon took steps to become uninvolved) in matters such as which dealers were to be present at workshops as either faculty members or vendors or both, and which were to be kept away.

As photocopying of music became ever more popular and ever more illegal, we asked President Shelley Gruskin to send out a "statement of compliance" to the workshop directors, which they were to sign and return to the ARS office, stating that they would "promulgate, at any American Recorder Society workshop directed by the undersigned, such procedures and policies as may be reasonably required in order to prevent violations of the copyright laws at that workshop."

In 1986 we began serious attempts to control teaching standards at the workshops. We stopped demanding copies of workshop evaluations from individual students but started concentrating on requirements for teachers. At a meeting in May, 1986, the committee decided to write to the current and recent past summer workshop directors soliciting their comments and suggestions on a set of proposed standards to take effect for summer workshops in 1988. The proposed standards would be that those who teach recorder would have either a performance degree in music at the graduate or undergraduate level, or will have passed the Level III ARS exam. At this time we had just set up an advisory panel to the committee, consisting of people interested in education but not necessarily workshop directors or even workshop teachers. Their opinions were asked on the question of standards for teachers as well. The committee letter occasioned many thoughtful replies but in the end it became obvious that neither requirement could be fulfilled. A letter from Peter Seibert dated July 19, 1986, is quoted here in part:

> Each ARS workshop is a private business rather than a franchise. Private businesses themselves must respond to any displeasure with the product they offer or suffer the consequences. If the ARS connection is limited to use of the logo, some free publicity and a small amount of scholarship money without any assumption of financial risk, how far can it go in establishing standards before its help will be unwanted?

> The ARS Level III was intended only as an optional exam for amateur players who felt they needed a goal to work toward.

As always it was ascertained that there is no way to judge objectively whether a teacher is "good" or not, whether he/she will relate to the students, and whether he/she possesses that peculiarly necessary skill needed for ensemble coaching of a small group meeting together daily for a week, and accomplishing anything at all!

The committee met five times in 1987–88, twice in 1988–89. Members of the committee were now Martha Bixler, Valerie Horst, Mary Maarbjerg, and Connie Primus. Connie was put on the committee at her own request, as she felt, rightly, that sometimes the needs of workshops other than those directly under the eye of the members of the committee (she was the director of the Colorado Workshop) were not being met. For the summer of 1989 we asked that ARS meetings at workshops that year be treated like parties, celebrating the 50th anniversary of the ARS. This was a successful move; many people, including the chairwoman of the committee herself, felt that we had won more friends and influenced more people with this event than at any of the meetings held previously.

At the fall 1989 Board meeting Mary Maarbjerg (who was by then a member of the Board of Directors of the ARS and its treasurer, and involved with several other committees) resigned as chairman, and new Board member Neil Seely took over as chairman of what was renamed the workshop advisory committee. Neil, who up to then had not been a particularly active member of the new (since 1988) Board of Directors, took firm hold of the chairmanship. One of his first tasks was dealing with a complaint from an attendee at the newly-endorsed Canto Antiguo Workshop (mostly about the lack of air-conditioning) and letting the director of the Yellow Springs workshop know that her workshop was not being endorsed for the summer of 1990.

The ARS workshop committee under its new name continued meeting, endorsing workshops, awarding scholarships, sponsoring weekend workshops, putting free "ads" in the magazine, asking for (and not getting) financial statements, through 1991. In April, 1990 we put together a nifty new Workshop Directors Agreement and Information Booklet, worked on by all members of the committee: Martha Bixler (*ex-officio*), Valerie Horst, Patricia Petersen, Connie Primus and Neil Seely. Here is the Table of Contents:

1. Important Deadlines for notices and reports in AR and the *Newsletter*, and the date by which a proposal for a new workshop should be submitted to the WAC [workshop advisory committee]

2. How to Apply for Endorsement [for those previously endorsed this was a rubber stamp; for workshops new to the ARS—albeit having already operated for one or more years—a description of proposed faculty, schedule, and courses had to be supplied]

3. Benefits of being an ARS-Endorsed Workshop [scholarships, in service credits for teachers, free display ads in AR and notices in the *Newsletter*, free mailing labels, financial assistance in the event of a cancellation]

4. Obligations of an ARS-Endorsed Workshop [acknowledgment of ARS endorsement in all—sometimes this was done in exceedingly small print; distribution of evaluation forms to students; membership meetings; providing all recorder-playing attendees "with an easy means of joining ARS"; tuition discounts to ARS members; permission for an administrator to give the ARS Level III exam at the workshop]

5. ARS Scholarships [descriptions of four types of scholarships]: Collegium Scholarship; President's Scholarship [funds from the President's Appeal]; Acs Scholarship [funds from the Andrew Acs Memorial Fund]; and Chapter Scholarships [initiated by chapters—grant from ARS provides one-third tuition]

6. Preparing your Brochure
7. Ordering ARS Labels
8. Bulk mailing through the ARS
9. Mailing Lists [names of organizations from which lists could be obtained, e.g., the Viola da Gamba Society]
10. Copyright Compliance [keeping within the law while using photocopied music]

Appendices included a workshop announcement form to send to the editor of *American Recorder*, a label order, a workshop evaluation form, "What makes a good workshop teacher?," a scholarship application, and a workshop agreement, to be signed by the workshop heads, now called "sponsors."

Other areas in which we became involved

There are only something like 10 weeks during a summer, and, increasingly, workshop dates began to conflict. And there were always other workshops like the Viola da Gamba Society Conclave, and Early Music Week at Pinewoods. The workshop committee found itself trying to assign dates, even to those who didn't want to have them assigned. We also found ourselves trying to decide whether a new workshop was in competition with another workshop nearby either geographically or chronologically, and acting as policemen for the crowded calendar.

We kept insisting that all participants, teachers as well as students, be members of the ARS, or some other early music society, like the Lute Society, or the Viola da Gamba Society of America, but the workshops became more and more rebellious and more and more disobedient. One large workshop simply did not send financial statements for six years.

However, the workshop committee continued with its instructor guidelines, collecting ads for the magazine, and approving and endorsing new workshops. We also kept in the business of publishing teachers lists. In the "Workshop Agreement" sent to workshop heads in the spring of 1988 the word "endorsement" was used for the first time to describe the relationship of the ARS to one of its workshops. The ARS agreed to "endorse" the workshop "and to make all students attending the workshop eligible for all grants, scholarships, tuition assistance, fellowships or similar programs offered by ARS."

The ARS was still responsible for the free ads in the magazine and the mailing of brochures provided by the workshop. The "sponsor" (workshop director) agreed "to make all financial and physical arrangements for the conduct of the workshop, to submit a detailed financial report" and to submit the evaluation forms "or a summary of comments to the ARS Workshop Committee no later than September 15."

Everything sounds normal in this agreement except for the word "endorsement." We had faced the fact that the workshops could not be called "ARS workshops" any longer. It was the beginning of the end. The ARS clung to the "ARS-endorsed" description of the workshops in the summers of 1989, 1990, and 1991, but by 1992 there was clearly no longer any such thing as an ARS workshop, and the word "ARS" began to leave the vocabulary of participants at the summer schools. At its September 1991 meeting the ARS Board decided to replace workshop endorsement with a program of benefits for "workshop members" of ARS. A $10 membership fee enabled a workshop to order mailing labels at a 25% discount. *American Recorder* still lists summer workshops (originally for a small fee, now for free) in March of each year in a clever grid originally designed by Neil Seely, along with descriptive paragraphs containing information gleaned from a questionnaire sent to the workshop heads. The workshop directors are encouraged to buy ads, full-page or smaller, in the magazine as well.

The ARS continues to give scholarships through its various scholarship funds, but the "children" have left home, and the end of the relationship was salutary all around. For years the ARS had had less and less to say about what happened at workshops while continuing to worry about them. For a long time many of the participants, both faculty and students, were not recorder players and had scarcely heard of the ARS. The workshops became incorporated on their own and did not wish to be even associated with the ARS. Nor we, any longer, with them. For decades whatever happened at a workshop was, in the public mind, the responsibility of the ARS. Once when I was president of the ARS I walked, resentfully, 10 blocks to the post office in Manhattan in the pouring rain to pick up a registered letter from one of the participants at the Hampshire College workshop blasting me because he had not yet received the audiotape of a concert that he had ordered the previous summer.

For the historically-minded, here are the 1991 ARS-endorsed workshops: five under the auspices of "SFEMS," the San Francisco Early Music Society (the instrument-building workshop had been added to the Baroque, Renaissance, medieval, and recorder workshops in 1990), at Dominican College, San Rafael, California; the Long Island Recorder Festival ("LIRF") at the New York Institute of Technology, Central Islip, Long Island, NY; the Chesapeake Workshop, at Mt. Vernon College in Washington, D.C.; the Southern Utah Early Music and Dance Workshop at Southern Utah State College in Cedar City, Utah; the Mideast Workshop at LaRoche College, Pittsburgh, Pennsylvania; the Midwest Recorder Workshop at Carthage College, Kenosha, Wisconsin; Canto Antiguo Early Music and Dance Workshop at the Thacher School, Ojai, California; and the Amherst Early Music Festival/Institute (two weeks) at Amherst College, Amherst, Massachusetts. There were 12 in all, 13 if you count Amherst as two separate weeks, which the administration of that workshop was beginning to do.

1991 was the last year of the ARS-endorsed workshops. A letter from Connie Primus to Neil Seely dated April 26, 1991, gives some of the reasons for giving up ARS endorsement.

1. The word "endorse" causes problems because the ARS is not fully able to evaluate workshops and because we acknowledge that there are other excellent workshops which choose not to be "ARS endorsed." 2. Instead, our present "endorsement" plan is actually a business relationship—we give selected workshops certain benefits in return for specific services. 3. Our present "endorsement" plan is not working—the ARS has not received the required services from some workshops, but we continue to "endorse" these workshops.

4. The ARS "endorsement" plan does not, and cannot, support new workshops, which need support more than existing workshops.

5. As more and more workshops become "ARS endorsed," the costs to the ARS increase and, due to limited funds, the benefits (such as scholarships) to each workshop decrease.

So, we decided to endorse no longer. At the September 1991 meeting the ARS Board decided to replace workshop endorsement with a program of benefits for "workshop members" of ARS. A $10 membership fee entitled a workshop to order mailing labels at a 25% discount, and to be listed in *American Recorder*. The workshop advisory committee went out of existence when Neil Seely finished his term on the Board in 1992.

Chapters and Membership

Among the new committees formed at the ARS Board meeting of September 19–21, 1980 were the chapter relations committee chaired by Andrew Acs, with members Bernard Hopkins, Patricia Petersen, Susan Prior, and a membership development committee with Pat Petersen as chair and members Suzanne Ferguson, Gerald Burakoff, and Shelley Gruskin. Throughout the '80s the ARS leadership tried to increase the number of both chapters and membership, and the activities of these committees were intertwined.

74 chapters were listed in the August, 1980 issue of *The American Recorder* and just under 90 in 1989. (During this time there had been, of course, some fluctuation, with new chapters coming in and out—at one time there were 95 ARS chapters altogether.) Chapter representatives had had a part in the national elections since the passage of a set of ARS bylaws in 1979 providing that members of the nominating committee for each new Board be selected from among them. At the fall 1981 Board meeting the chapter relations committee was re-organized under the chairmanship of Suzanne Ferguson. The original aims of this committee had been obvious: to help chapters get started and to plan activities. We on the Board were always trying to find ways to increase the number of chapters, to make chapters be an important part of the ARS, and to keep their officers, at least, fully informed as to what was going on at "national." The chapter relations committee did a survey in 1982 of all of our chapters and discovered, from those who responded, that the average age of an ARS chapter was 11-1/2 years, its average size 39. 80 percent of ARS chapter members (from responding chapters) were amateurs. The average chapter dues were $8 annually. There were few beginners.

In the fall of 1982 the ARS started publishing a *Chapter Circular* to give the chapters a shot in the arm. Valerie Horst was editor and Martha Bixler was the associate editor. The Circular was produced by Waddy Thompson. At that time we had a total chapter membership of well over 1600 and 82 chapters. By November 1983 we had a total of 1728 chapter members and 94 chapters. On meeting with a "most positive response" [ARS *Newsletter*, Fall 1983], publication of the *Chapter Circular* was increased from three to four issues per year. In 1987 Suzanne Ferguson took over as editor. CC was sent to all Chapter representatives and all members of the Board of Directors. It was one of our many attempts to get chapter members interested in national activities, such as the formation of the education program, the summer and weekend workshops, the membership meetings held at summer workshops (begun in the summer of 1983), elections, and the like. We were "teaching" the representatives their duties (like collecting dues), helping workshops to get tax-exempt status, giving them information on copyright laws and scholarships, and how to get a list of teachers from the national office, and giving them ideas for meetings, urging them to publicize and get more members for the ARS, and, increasingly, urging that all chapter members be or become members of the ARS.

The ARS ceased publication of the *Chapter Circular* in October 1988 and published nothing especially written for chapters until the appearance of *Leader Link*, in February, 1997, under the editorship of then Board member Israel Stein. This publication continued intermittently (twice a year) until March, 2005, when it was replaced by a column, "Chapter Check up" in the ARS *Newsletter*. Subject matter was the same (e.g., how to get and keep members, what to do at chapter meetings, notification of meetings and elections) and new and different (e.g., chapters and the internet, chapter hosting of Board meetings, the ARS 60th birthday in 1998, the Junior Recorder Society and news of the Boston and Berkeley Music Festivals).

In 1984 Suzanne became interested in setting up a program of regional groups or chapters "for the purpose of stimulating chapter activities and cooperation around the nation." [Letter to chapter representatives, December 6, 1984.] Suzanne, now called the ARS Coordinator of Chapter Representatives, envisioned a coordinating committee for each region who would plan regional meetings of chapter representatives for the obvious purpose of coordinating activities such as: weekend workshops, teacher tours, a "jamboree," regional *Newsletters* etc. What a great idea! Suzanne even made lists and drew up maps of the projected regions. Unfortunately, as in so many of our grand designs, not too much came of it.

In March of 1985 the Board of Directors learned through another survey that we had only 27 chapters with 100% ARS membership. We had been worrying about the problem in all of our Board meetings since 1980, even before. The nefarious practice of accepting non-ARS members as "adjunct" members or even full members of the chapters had been happening from the beginning, but nobody knew how many of these "pseudo-members" there were, and nobody knew how flagrant were the violations until the ARS Board, the chapter relations committee, and Suzanne began to investigate. We were horrified. The ARS membership requirement was stated clearly in the charter sent to every chapter as it was formed, but the requirement was being ignored. There were many reasons for this. As chapters and their activities flourished, their dues increased, as did those of the ARS; many people were not interested in the ARS magazine or the *Newsletter* or what was going on at "national," and did not see why they should support the activities of what they considered an elite and self-serving few operating in New York. Also, many people thought they were members of the "national" when they joined the chapter. And the chapters became tired of collecting dues for both themselves and the ARS. When ARS started sending out separate dues notices so chapters would not have to do the collecting, there was confusion all around as to who was paying what dues to whom.

The ARS Board embarked on something of a crusade for 100% national membership in the ARS for chapters. On March 25, 1985 Suzanne Ferguson sent a letter to all of the chapter officers making a strong case for insisting that all chapter members be members of the ARS.

> According to the charter issued to you by the ARS, all members of an ARS chapter must "be or immediately become" members of the ARS upon the acceptance of the charter by your chapter. In common-sense terms, you could say that a chapter, by definition, is in fact composed of members of an organization; if a group has members who do not belong to the organization, it's not, properly speaking, a chapter of the organization. A chapter enjoys a privileged status with respect to the national organization. It receives information

from the Society; it can avail itself of programs such as the Education Program and the workshop assistance programs; it may send members to ARS workshops on scholarship; it can call upon the Society for assistance. The chapter in turn helps support the national organization.

In her letter Suzanne went on to outline the ways in which the chapters can accept "responsibility" and "achieve compliance with their charter." They could make sure all of their members were or would immediately become members of the ARS. They could have a kind of dual membership within their chapter, with those who have full ARS membership being able to call themselves members of the ARS, and those without it having a complete understanding that they cannot. They should make sure that their chapter officers were all members of the ARS, and that only full ARS members participated in ARS elections.

Going on, Suzanne requested that the chapter officers write her telling her what means of compliance they were planning to use, and told them that she depends upon their "cooperation in spreading the word on the values of ARS membership."

Reasonable people might agree that though perhaps a bit stern Suzanne's letter is not offensive, and that the ARS was right in finally attempting to lay down the law. But in fact an enormous firestorm was raised, which took years to die down. Patricia Petersen, who as membership committee chairman had visited six ARS chapters in California in June of 1984, had been met with many complaints (and perhaps some abuse!) about their relationship with the ARS. High on their list was the issue of "compulsory" membership in the ARS for members of a chapter. Suzanne's letter only exacerbated the hostility we were feeling from the chapters. Members of the Boston chapter in particular, our firstborn "child," were overcome with fury that we had dared to tell them what to do, that we were trying to extract money from them, and that we did not "do anything" for them. Again Pat Petersen bore the brunt of some hostility when she visited the Boston chapter in April of 1985. According to her report she tried in a completely reasonable manner to point out the reasons the ARS should receive "compliance" from its chapters. She was met with complaints that the ARS had "done nothing" for the Boston chapter, that Bostonians were not invited to teach at summer workshops, that the ARS was trying to "punish" the chapter for non-compliance by not giving Boston chapter members scholarships to summer workshops, that we were discriminating against poorer members by requiring them to pay double dues, that we were disenfranchising them by not allowing non-ARS members to vote in our national elections. Every bit of this was nonsense, of course.

Pat pointed out, in her well thought-out and reasonable report to the Board of May 3, 1985, that at least part of the problem had long been semantic. The Boston chapter of the American Recorder Society often abbreviates its name to Boston/ARS. Their members tend to think of themselves, therefore, as members of the ARS, whether they are or not. It comes as an unpleasant shock when they find that even after paying fairly steep dues ($35 in 1985) to their chapter they still may not have the "rights and privileges" of belonging to the ARS.

Pat concluded in her report:

> It will do us no good to impose restrictions on them (or any other chapter, for that matter); in doing so we run the risk of generating ill will that will be extremely difficult to overcome. The hostility between Boston and the ARS feeds on itself, and has come from both sides. I feel we must handle these situations even more carefully, avoiding an "us-them" situation and mollifying people as much as possible. We must be very careful about the tone of our communications, and avoid scolding; if something can be taken wrongly, it will be.

Unfortunately, not everyone in the ARS administration was as diplomatic, and I remember a very unpleasant shouting match with members of the Boston chapter and some of its officers at the Boston Early Music Festival that year.

Suzanne continued the "crusade," though she was one of the diplomatic ones. In a letter dated June 25, 1985 to Executive Director Waddy Thompson, President Shelley Gruskin, Counsel Ron Cook and me, Suzanne writes that she is

> . . . really astonished that everyone seems to be surprised and frightened by the flack [sic] we're taking over the compliance letter. We've been talking about getting after the errant chapters ever since I was elected to the Board in 1980. The only logical, legal, sensible, defensible position is the one we've taken: a chapter consists of members of the ARS and only of members of the ARS.

However, the chapters continued not to see eye-to-eye with the Board on this matter. The history of this period in the relationship of the Board to its chapters is dreary, and does not need to be pursued further. After many meetings, between brass and brass, "little guys" with little guys, and friends with potential enemies, the issue died down, and everything remained more or less as it was; having a chapter representative be a member of the national organization is just about the only requirement the ARS makes of its chapters. Suzanne did succeed in getting us to the point of understanding that we would never resolve the issue of "chapter compliance" so we might just as well leave it alone.

Suzanne was always interested in trying to help chapters to exchange information with each other and with the ARS. She did many good things for the chapters. With the ARS workshop committee she worked out a system of ARS-sponsored weekend workshops for chapters with financial and other support (free mailing labels, free publicity) from the ARS, and also chapter scholarships for ARS summer workshops. She proposed a new membership category, Consort Affiliates, for small groups with not enough members to become a chapter. 24 Consort Affiliate groups were listed in the ARS Directory of 1986. She ran chapter officers' meetings at the Boston Early Music Festival. The purpose of these meetings, which were held annually at one of the bi-coastal annual music festivals, was to stimulate chapter representatives into finding and keeping new members for themselves and for the ARS, as well as supplying them with ideas for meetings, money-raising, etc.

From February, 1985 to May, 1989 Suzanne was editor of "Chapter News" in The American Recorder. In the November, 1985 issue of the *Chapter Circular* she wrote a "Message of Hope" for faltering chapters, suggesting activities for smaller chapters and giving a general pep talk to "hang in there." In 1987 and 1988 she was the editor of the *Chapter Circular*. In a thoughtful article in the November, 1987 issue of the *Circular* she outlined, once again, the benefits for both members and chapters of becoming members of the ARS. By the time she retired as chairman of the chapter relations committee, in 1988, Suzanne had overseen eight publications available to chapters on such matters as tax-exempt status, copyrights, "What is a Chapter Representative?," "How to Run a Weekend Workshop," and "Making a Chapter Brochure." She was also responsible for starting a teachers' directory that was to be distributed to all chapters as well as summer workshop directors.

At the 1988 September Board meeting Ken Andresen, a new member of the Board of Directors, was named chairman of the chapter relations committee. At this meeting also each Board member was assigned several chapter representatives to keep in touch with by phone, in another attempt to keep the chapters and chapter reps feeling that they were part of the ARS family. There were immediate problems with slowness, busyness, and just plain laziness on the part of some of the Board members. At one point it was thought that perhaps only members of the chapter relations committee should be doing the calling. This program began to slacken after the February Board meeting in 1990, when it was decided that only chapters who had no chapter newsletter would be called.

Connie Primus took over the chapter relations committee at the February Board meeting in 1989. As in everything she did for the ARS, Connie applied herself immediately to the work at hand. Connie was responsible for the development of a new category of ARS financial aid to chapters—Chapter Development Grants. Chapters were encouraged to use tiny ($100 each) grants from the ARS to promote both their own growth and that of the ARS by means other than putting on workshops. A total of $1,300 was budgeted for the year 1988–89. Some suggested possible uses of a Chapter Development Grant were: to purchase music for the chapter, to purchase an instrument, to print brochures, sponsor a concert, pay for a conductor, or rent a booth at a Renaissance fair. The grants, representing something tangible the ARS was doing for its chapters, were immediately very popular. Many of the chapter grants awarded that first year were used by chapters in celebration of their "ARS 50" events.

Some interesting projects (besides those suggested by us) included making period costumes for chapter performing groups, buying an electronic tuner for the chapter, a "consort leadership" retreat, and the production of a "Level II workbook" to enable chapter members to prepare for the Level II exam. 13 Chapter Development Grants were awarded the first year. In 1990 the "Chapter Workshop Start-up Program" ($100 granted to chapters starting a new workshop) was included in the "Development Grant" program.

Board members of the three committees—education, workshop, and membership development—worked diligently during the decade, both during and between Board meetings. In those days most Board and committee business was carried on by mail; the mountains of papers generated by their activities are ample evidence. The aim, always, besides keeping track of and "doing something" (the constant request) for our members, was to increase the membership, but despite great effort the growth of membership was never as fast or as permanent as we hoped it would be.

In 1982 the chairwoman of the membership committee, Patricia Petersen, launched a membership drive. Among her ideas was a plan whereby chapters could take ARS brochures, print or write the name of their chapter on them, and distribute the brochures locally to schools, music stores, festivals, and concerts. Another idea entertained by the Board from time to time was to try to get celebrities like John Updike and James Earl Jones who were recorder players to record radio spots that, on audiotape cassettes, could be distributed by ARS chapter members to their local radio stations. As previously stated, in the summer of 1983, in an effort to get people to voice their opinions, and to help us in recruiting new members, we instituted "membership meetings" at ARS summer workshops. At the end of the 1982–83 fiscal year we had 3,833 members. In November 1983 the ARS had 94 chapters and 3,672 members, of whom 1728 (about half) were members of chapters. On January 1, 1984 the ARS was reported to have 4,127 members, but in the Fall 1984 issue of The American Recorder it was stated

as 3,659! Of course the amount of fluctuation was so wide, particularly at certain times of the year, and the confusion so great, with family memberships and collegium memberships being multiple memberships but counting only as one, that no one can say exactly what our membership was at any given time. One can only guess with a fair amount of certainty that it hovered around 4,000 in the early '80s. Our goal was to increase the number of members to 5,000 by the time of our 50th anniversary in 1989, but this goal was never reached.

At the fall Board Meeting in 1984 Pat Petersen acknowledged to the Directors that the membership drive had been disappointing so far. Her efforts, including articles (ARS *Newsletter*, *Chapter Circular*), journal advertisements (MENC *Journal*, MTNA *Journal*, Orff *Echo*), direct solicitation (letters to lapsed and non-ARS chapter members), and the distribution of some 14,000 brochures, did not prevent a net loss of members. Collegium directors, teachers and merchants throughout the U.S. had been solicited. Future generations should never think we hadn't tried! In 1984 we established a category of business membership for those merchants who would carry instruments and publications for recorders. These merchants paid $100 apiece and received a listing in the annual Directory, all of our publications, and rental of the mailing list at a reduced cost. Collegium memberships were started in 1984; for $50 a year a collegium director and all of the student members of his collegium would be entitled to attend ARS-sponsored workshops without paying a further membership fee, would be eligible for one partial scholarship to an ARS week-long workshop, and would receive three copies of all ARS publications and a listing in the ARS Directory for the collegium and its director. Some of the early institutions with collegia to join were Swarthmore College, the College of St. Scholastica, Florida State University, the Cincinnati College Conservatory of Music, and Wake Forest University.

Pat continued her efforts to increase the Society's membership the next year and at the fall Board meeting in 1985 she was able to point to a net increase of 150 new and returned members. Another membership survey was mailed in 1985 to 3,605 members of the Society and 1,804 surveys were returned. There had been talk of changing the name of the American Recorder Society to the American Early Music Society or some similar title, in order to become more of an umbrella organization, but only a third of those answering the survey were interested in this idea. Most liked the magazine—then, as now, our biggest, most visible benefit to members—and expressed interest in articles on performance practice and technique, interviews, consort playing, recorder care and recorder making. A quarter of those replying said they were using the education program. They wanted more music (sheet music was printed off and on in the magazine, but anthologies were wanted). One third of the respondents were interested in more weekend workshops.

In 1986 there were 4,071 members of the ARS, 4,514 if you count two for each family membership. This is the highest number ever recorded for the American Recorder Society, and it has dropped since then. Although we have continued, strenuously, to try to get new members since that golden year we seem to have reached our limit then. Minutes of the Board meeting of 1986 report that 10,000 brochures were being sent annually to music stores, libraries, community music schools, teachers, and chapters; advertisements continued to be placed in music magazines.

In the fall of 1987 our membership started inching down, to 3,916 (individual membership) and 4,368 (family membership), a discouraging loss of 155 individual members for that year. The 1988 Fall *Newsletter* reported a slightly higher total of 4,010.

After the Board elections of 1988 the new Board decided, among other ambitious projects, on yet another membership campaign. Pat Petersen had resigned as chairman of the membership committee after six years of struggle. The new membership chairman, David Barton, and his wife Susan designed and prepared a new, somewhat jazzier shiny maroon brochure, with pictures, to send out with all new memberships, to non-members, and to be distributed as widely as possible. We sent a special letter to all the professional players we knew who were not members of the Society, informing them of the benefits of joining and urging them to join. ARS meetings at the summer workshops were to take the form of ARS celebrations (there was a particularly gala reception at Amherst) and due emphasis was to be given at these meetings to the many positive steps recently taken by the Society. Waddy Thompson prepared a workshop advertisement, a large poster with pictures of old and young players, again to be distributed as widely as possible.

Two members of the Virginia chapter, Deborah Roudebush and Linda Waller, calling themselves the Moribund Membership committee, came to the May 14, 1989 meeting of the ARS 50 committee, to help with the ARS membership drive. Membership continued to drop, however.

Publications in the '80s

I have called the '80s the "age of Waddy," but have not mentioned him much heretofore. During the time he was with us, however, Waddy was the glue that held the Society together. At the Board meeting of October 2–3 1982 he was made our full time Administrative Director. In the minutes of that meeting the Board noted "the superb way he has reorganized the office in his short tenure." It was Waddy who thought of making a cumulative index for the magazine. It was he who kept the lines of communication open among the members of the various committees, the office, and each other. It was Waddy who kept track of deadlines and made sure meetings got met, letters got written, checks got signed, and clerical things got done. It was Waddy who thought of the booklet for workshop directors, Waddy who kept all the records, collected members' dues, paid the office rent, and prodded all of us into keeping our promises. It was Waddy who thought of commissioning Conrad Susa to write a piece especially for us during the celebration of our 50th Anniversary (see page 162). And of course it was Waddy who found and installed our very first computer.

Waddy's talents as a graphic designer became particularly obvious in the production of our various publications: the ARS *Newsletter*, the Directory, and the *Chapter Circular*, first doing beautiful paste-up jobs and photo-copying, then printing them in-house with the new ARS computer. He was also involved in the production of the revised Education Study Guides, the Workshop Directors' Booklet, the Teacher Listing and the membership brochure, the mailing labels, and many other documents. One of Waddy's many innovations was the regular posting of news releases announcing ARS activities like the Erich Katz Competition (*see* page 150).

The ARS *Newsletter* was first published in January, 1950. The *Newsletter* had disappeared with the advent of The American Recorder, but in the late '70s it became obvious that we needed a *Newsletter* once again, in order to give our members topical news that might not appear in the increasingly scholarly AR. At the September 1980 Board Meeting Father Bernard J. Hopkins, a second-term member of the Board, was made editor of the new *Newsletter*, free to members, which was to appear twice a year, in October and April. In 1983 I became editor, with Valerie Horst as co-editor. At the 1984 Board meeting we decided to make the *Newsletter* a thrice-yearly publication. It now appears four times a year. Over the years it has been a useful vehicle for announcements, dates and current events, including reports on Board meetings, festivals, concerts, and workshops. Valerie and I worked very hard at our two publications, the *Newsletter* and the *Chapter Circular*, as editors and writers during the '80s, with Waddy as production manager. We often felt that we three were running the store.

Another printing project we were all three heavily involved in was a new, magnificent Members' Directory, put together after the purchase of our first office computer in 1982. We certainly needed one. Problems in the ARS office discussed at the 1981 Board meeting included the fact that our computerized mailing service was not doing well, letters were not being answered, an issue of the ARS *Newsletter* was lost, and

Valerie Horst, 1988.

the annual Directory was late. What we needed most at that time, obviously, was a thorough revision of our membership lists and the publication of a complete, up-to-date Directory. Waddy was a whiz at production, but proofreading was not his forte, so Valerie and I found ourselves picking up the slack. We each took half of the 3,500 names and addresses in the Directory and proofread every single one, congratulating ourselves all the way. But of course we never could have done it without Waddy and the computer.

The most important of our publications was The American Recorder. Sigrid Nagle became editor-in-chief in 1977, after serving a short apprenticeship as assistant editor. From that moment on we never had to worry about the appearance of the magazine, either what it would look like or whether it would come out on time. By 1982 the price had risen to $3.00 per copy. For a time everything was rosy. Sigrid was ultra-conscientious in her duties. Like any good editor she was always on the lookout for material. Gradually the magazine became not only more sophisticated but more scholarly. For every article on "Tips for Classroom Teachers" there was one on "Developing Baroque Ornamentation Skills." Tributes to celebrities of the recorder world were cheek-by-jowl with "Furniture and Recorders: The Problems with Making Copies." We got into the habit of interviewing recorder celebrities of the time, and these interviews were fascinating; not so interesting were articles like "Checklists of Historic Recorders in American Private and Public Collections." Chapter news and (increasingly grudgingly) Board meeting minutes continued to be published in the magazine, but the print became smaller and smaller.

A real coup for The American Recorder was the publication of several historical treatises in translation. These included (among others) William Hettrick's translations of those portions of Sebastian Virdung's *Musica getutscht* and Martin Agricola's *Musica instrumentalis deudsch* dealing with the recorder, and Catherine P. Smith's translation of J.P. Freillon Poncein's *La Veritable Maniere d'apprendre a jouer en perfection*.

Book and music reviews, letters to the editor, articles on ensemble playing, instrument care and making instruments, stage fright and how to manage it were included as all these were of interest to everyone. But then along would come a description of the "Detroit Recorder Manuscript," and yawns could be heard from our member/readers throughout the land. It is not that the articles weren't good, or timely, or well written. They were just too "scholarly" for our readers, or so we began to think. With the May, 1979 issue Sigrid even began to print "A Journal for Early Music" under the title The American Recorder, but this was stopped by the Board at its 1984 meeting.

Perhaps the worst "mistake" Sigrid made as editor of AR was to publish three long, dreary articles on "The Motets of Orlandus Lassus; their sources and stylistic idiom," by Paul Echols in three issues of the magazine. The motets of Lassus are gorgeous; many can be essayed by recorder players. But nobody, especially not amateur recorder players, wants to read about them at this length. Furthermore, the articles were equipped with an enormous number of footnotes. Sigrid had by this time met the editor of the new English journal, *Early Music*, and she was trying to make our in-house magazine into something like his. This was frowned upon by our "music publications committee," which had appointed itself as a "super-editor" of AR. At the same time Sigrid was, at each and every board meeting, lobbying hard for a raise in salary. In 1981 her salary was raised to $7,000; in 1985 it was $8,500, but she continued to ask for, and get, more. This certainly does not seem like much now, but in those days, to me at least, it seemed like a great deal. I had myself, after all, edited the magazine for nothing. We had only started paying our editor after it became evident that all of our clerical positions, as they became vacant, had to become paid positions. The job of editor of the AR had never been intended to be a full time job, but Sigrid thought of it as that, and did a lot of complaining that we weren't giving her a "living wage." She continued to irritate me a great deal throughout her editorship, although if I had foreseen the sad way in

Sigrid Nagle, Connie Primus, Bob Primus, Edgar Hunt, 1991.

which her tenure was to be terminated I might have been more patient.

This demand for more money and her well-meant but ill-advised attempts to make our magazine scholarly eventually led to Sigrid's downfall.

Music Publications

During the '80s the ARS got well into the business of publishing music. The ARS Editions were moribund, but the Board was anxious to keep them alive. The goal was to publish an anthology of music for intermediates. This was actually accomplished. Galaxy Music published, in December 1986, A Recorder Sampler, a collection for intermediate players of 25 trios and quartets previously published as separate editions in the 1960s. These were excerpts from ARS Editions 41–69. Jennifer Lehmann and Joel Newman were the editors. Another anthology, Recorder Sampler No. 2, which included some of the solos, was published in 1989. These anthologies, like the ARS Editions they contained, were published by Galaxy Music Corporation, not the ARS, and were not free to members. The cost was $7.95 each. Their publication was a part of the effort to make music available inexpensively to our members. Another anthology taken from previously published ARS Editions was *Renaissance Songs and Dances*, edited by Erich Katz and published by Associated Music in 1967.

The ARS had been publishing music in the magazine for its members since the Fall 1970 issue (two dances, handwritten, by David Goldstein). Colin Sterne (music editor of *AR* 1978–82), published free music for members in virtually every issue of his tenure, and this tradition was continued into the '90s. All of the music in the magazine of the '80s was handwritten, sometimes by the composers or arrangers themselves. We published all kinds of music, much of it beautifully autographed by Wendy Keaton or Jennifer Lehmann. I once estimated that by December 1996 we had published about 65 editions of "free music" in the magazine. The first piece of computer-generated music published in AR was our 50th anniversary piece, *The ARS Night Watch*, with music by Holborne, lyrics by Lucy Cross, and typesetting by Richard Sacksteder. This was an insert in the February, 1989 issue of *AR*.

The ARS made an actual start on publishing in 1986 when the Erich Katz Memorial Fund Committee announced its first annual composition contest. From the Winter, 1986 *Newsletter*: "The Trustees of the Dr. Erich Katz Memorial Fund of the ARS will award a prize of $400 for an original, unpublished composition of 4–10 minutes duration for recorder consort (3–6 recorders). Technical difficulty should fall within the intermediate to high intermediate range." The purpose of the competition contest was not only to encourage composers to write for the recorder but to raise money for the Fund through sales of the music. Jenny Lehmann, as chairwoman of the music publications committee (since 1984) ran the competition, which we called the Erich Katz Competition. Originally the judges of the competition were the trustees of the Katz Fund themselves. There were 35 pieces submitted that first year. The first contest winner was Frederic R. Palmer of Belmont, California with his recorder quartet, *Entrevista*.

The music was beautifully typeset by the composer himself, and was duly published by the ARS. The next year there were four Honorable Mentions and none published.

Executive Director Waddy Thompson was himself a composer, and the success of our very first "real" publication stimulated him to put forward the "Erich Katz Contemporary Music Series," which was also funded by the Katz Fund. The aim for these publications was a little different from those of the competition. From Waddy's news release of 10/26/88:

> The series will make available the finest contemporary recorder music at affordable prices. Special attention will be given to works which, because of their technical demands or their non-traditional idioms would not be published by most commercial publishers.

In 1987 the Erich Katz Memorial Fund committee announced the imminent appearance of four new publications in this series: *Aphorisms* for solo alto recorder by Robert Strizich ($10), *Entrevista* for recorder quartet by Frederic Palmer ($6—now $8 for members), Fantasia for recorder quartet by Robert Strizich ($16), and *Sonatine* for three alto recorders by Lee Gannon ($12—now $14). Gannon was asked at first to bear the cost of typesetting his piece—$450—himself, but was later paid back by the Erich Katz Fund. The Frederic Palmer piece was, as stated, winner of the Erich Katz Competition for 1986, and Lee Gannon's piece was an Honorable Mention in 1987. The two Strizich pieces were difficult to play, and never sold very well. Strizich later took back his copyright.

There were 28 entries in the 1988 Katz Competition. The Katz Fund trustees began to think they needed a more professional judge than themselves, so they asked the eminent Austrian composer Hans Ulrich Staeps to be the final judge, and he obligingly said he would. The winner was Stanley Osborn's Kyrie and Vocalise for soprano voice and recorder quartet. Osborn received the $400 prize for winning the contest and his piece was published as part of the Katz Contemporary Series. All subsequent winners of the Katz Competition were published as part of the series.

The 1989 contest was for a recorder duet. There were over 40 entries but no winner. Suzanne Angevine's "Across Distance," a duet for two bass recorders, won Honorable Mention and was also published as part of the Erich Katz Contemporary Series.

In 1990, when Jennifer Lehmann became seriously ill, I took over the competition. The contest that year, the fifth, was for a piece for a double choir of recorders, and Peter Ballinger won the prize and $400. Peter Ballinger was/is a distinguished musician and composer and music publisher, and was for a short time the president of the American Recorder Society. It was gratifying to see this fine piece of his win the prize. Once again, it was included as part of the Erich Katz Contemporary Series.

In 1991 the contest was for "recorder trios, quartets, or quintets." Judges were Pete Rose, Shelley Gruskin, and Board member Phillip Stiles. There was no winner but we gave Honorable Mention to Sally Price's *Dorian Mood*, which was eventually published. (We only "promised" to publish actual winners.) I think the ARS made her pay for the typesetting herself.

In 1991 the ARS published, as part of the series, Cecil Effinger's *Dialogue and Dance*, not a prize winner, but one which had been commissioned by the Denver Chapter. Typesetting and printing were paid for by contributions from members of the Denver chapter. Another addition to the Erich Katz Contemporary Series was also published in the '90s—Vaclav Nelhybel's *Six Short Pieces* for three recorders.

In 1992 we specified that the competition should be for music to be used at ARS chapter meetings and we raised the amount of prize money to $500. The winner that year was Jeffrey Quick, with *Picnic Music*. We stopped publishing both the Katz Competition music and the Katz Contemporary Music Series in 1992. They were just too expensive for the ARS to keep producing.

The ARS started publishing another series, its Members' Library Series, in 1987. These were/are short four-page editions, either arrangements or original music, supplied free to members of the Society. They were begun by the indefatigable Jennifer Lehmann, who had held various editorial music positions on the ARS Board since the late '70s. Jennifer was a very talented woman, a mathematician and musician possessed of a fine musical hand, who loved to browse in the Princeton Library, make transcriptions of unpublished early music arranged for recorders, and give them away to her friends.

Jenny was also for a time editor of the "Renaissance series" of the ARS Editions—part of an abortive attempt we made, in the early '80s, to flog the dying ARS Editions back to life. Nothing ever came of that.

But in 1987 she started the Members' Library Editions. The Series was launched with money from the President's Appeal. The ARS Board decided in 1990 to use Katz funds to publish the series and to send the Members' Library music as an insert with the magazine, which was a great money-saver. Music from the series was and still is (2010) sent to members along with copies of *AR*. Issues appeared once a year at first, later, twice.

Left to right: Bernard Krainis, Philip Levin, Jennifer Lehmann, 1983.

The first Members' Library Edition was *Elizabethan Delights* (January, 1987), with music selected and edited by Jennifer Lehmann and commercially typeset. It included music by Morley, Ford and Ravenscroft. Number 2 (1988) was *Vintage Burgundy*, which included the marvelous Du Fay *Gloria ad modum tubae*. Number 3 (1989) was Colin Sterne's *Slow Dance with Doubles*. This was the first of two pieces that comprise a set, *Two Antiphonal Dances*, which had been commissioned by the Pittsburgh chapter of the ARS in celebration of its 25th anniversary. With the publication of this piece Jennifer modestly announced her own typesetting by stating simply on her music publications committee report that it was done on a MAC using Professional Composer. She also typeset Stanley W. Osborn's *Kyrie and Vocalise* for the Katz Contemporary Series. It was fitting that Jennifer be one of the first among us to get involved in desktop publishing. She had always been interested in copying music to make it accessible to amateur early music players. She figured that she saved the ARS $225 per issue for publishing these pieces.

Looking ahead, No. 4 (1990), David Goldstein's *Sentimental Songs*, appeared in 1991. Number 5 (1991) is Virginia Ebinger's arrangements of three little songs from a Spanish Christmas play from the American Southwest.

From this issue on, the Members' Library editions were enclosed with copies of *American Recorder* and called a supplement to it. Postal regulations would not allow issues of the magazine and issues of the series to have different numbers. So we have only copyright dates for series identification—a pity.

Jennifer Lehmann died of lung cancer on September 6, 1992. Her death was a terrible loss to her family, friends, and the ARS. What would have been No. 6 in the Members' Library Series was her own arrangement of Anton Bruckner's *Ave Maria*. It had been played and sung at her funeral, and was published in the series as a memorial to her. The arrangement is beautiful, not very difficult, and successful on recorders.

I was appointed editor of the Members' Library Editions at the Board meeting in January, 1993. At the same meeting the Board decided we needed to publish two editions a year. My first assignment (also decided upon by the Board) was a reprint of some of Erich Katz's *New Rounds on Old Rhymes*, a collection of nursery rhymes set to music and made into rounds by Katz when he was teaching at a girls' school in England in 1942. These little songs are quite charming and they fit well on recorders. This would have been No. 7. It and subsequent editions were typeset by Ken Andresen, publisher of *Polyphonic Publications* (and a musician and former ARS Board member). Ken agreed to typeset for us gratis in return for payment in kind—that is—ads in *AR*.

At first the publications of the Members' Library were paid for out of the ARS general operating fund, but the executive committee decided in August of 1994 that the money should come from the Katz Fund. This was continued until the fund was nearly depleted. A very generous grant from an ARS member keeps the Library going today.

I continued as editor of the Members' Library until 2001. I tried to maintain a balance between arrangements and original pieces at first but began favoring original compositions in the last few years on the grounds that they are not as likely to be published by other publishers, and there are so many arrangements of early music being published today. Among my favorites are Nos. 9 and 10 (May and November 1994), by Stephan Chandler. These are original compositions titled "Different Quips" and "Other Quips." Although Chandler was already a published composer, and a very good one, he seemed to be delighted to get his pieces published for no royalties by the ARS. The music is witty, well written for recorders, fun to play and to listen to. He typeset them himself.

Number 13, March, 1996, is Laurie Alberts's "Poinciana Rag." This is a real charmer, a well-written original rag composed by a woman who was influenced by Stan Davis's publications of piano rags composed by American women in the late 19th century.

With No. 20 we went all-out, reprinting Erich Katz's *Santa Barbara Suite* in a gala centennial edition, celebrating the 100th birthday of Erich Katz and the end of the second millennium. The *Santa Barbara Suite* was first published in 1955 by Associated Music Publishers, Inc., as No. 18 of the American Recorder Society Editions. Page-turns and following the "route" in the early edition had always been tricky, actually impossible, and it was the great wish of Erich's companion, Winifred Jaeger, that the piece be re-published in honor of his birthday in the year 2000. The gala edition also included a biographical piece by Mark Davenport, pictures, a tribute by me, and a list of all of the available music by Erich Katz.

After the publication of another fine piece by Laurie Alberts, *Imitations*, in 2002, I gladly relinquished the editorship of the Members' Library Editions to Glen Shannon.

Back to the '80s: Significant Events (in the ARS and elsewhere)

One of Waddy Thompson's many bright ideas was to institute the **President's Appeal**. We were always strapped for funds, and a begging letter sent to all members each fall was one way to go about getting donations. The first annual President's Appeal was inaugurated at the 1983 Fall Board meeting. President Shelley Gruskin sent a direct mail solicitation to all the members of the American Recorder Society. The goal was $10,000; we made $10,511.24. There were responses from 264 of our members, representing 8% of our membership. Funds were used, as President Gruskin reported at the 1984 board meeting, for the workshop scholarship program, the membership survey, new membership brochures, first-class postage for the board elections, and the addition of an alphabetical index to the Directory. Additional projects planned were an anthology of recorder music and commissioning compositions for the recorder. The goal for the next year was $15,000. That goal was not reached, but with 264 members responding, we did receive $10,915. Donors were listed in both the *Newsletter* and The American Recorder. The goal for the next year was again $15,000. We received $11,508, of which $2,594 was designated for the Katz Memorial Fund. "Unrestricted funds . . . [were] used to enhance ARS programs and to expand activities into new areas." In the third appeal, ended in 1986, we received $12,015.13. In the fourth appeal we received $13, 516.

Appeal funds were used for chapter workshop grants, president's scholarships and chapter scholarships (half-tuition) to the summer workshops, scholarships to weekend workshops, and honoraria for articles in AR. $1,653 was transferred to the Erich Katz Memorial Fund. In the fifth Appeal we received $14,922.60. The 1989 appeal collected $15,000. The goal for 1990 was $16,000. We continued, for a while, to cite the achievements of the increased funding: the formation of the Members' Library, the addition of a winter *Newsletter*, an increase in the number of scholarships including the President's scholarship (covering full tuition at a summer workshop), higher honoraria for authors of articles for The American Recorder, and the sponsorship of the Katz competition for new music for the recorder were all mentioned in my letter as president in December, 1988. We had also started sending slightly more personal letters to those who had donated in the past, thanking them for their generosity and calling them by their first names. There was a separate list for chapter members. Of course all of the letters needed to be signed by the president and later a letter of thanks sent to everyone who contributed. One of the last acts performed by Waddy Thompson before he resigned as executive director was to help—using a still rather unfamiliar computer—with this arduous job.

The annual President's Appeal has continued to the present day. Donations are used now for general operating expenses instead of special projects and a direct mailing is no longer sent to the entire membership, only to those who have given in the past.

A significant event, the **Boston Early Music Festival**, a.k.a BEMF, began in June, 1981. When I was still president of the ARS I received a letter from Friedrich von Huene asking for aid from the ARS in the form of a loan (of course that was out of the question!), to help put together this festival. The festival was the inspiration of Friedrich and his wife Ingeborg and their friend Scott Kosofsky. It was fitting that the "Boston Early Music Festival & Exhibition," as its full name eventually became, be held in Boston, the biggest center of early music, of both makers and performers, in the United States. The initial aim of the festival was to exhibit the wares of the makers of historical instruments of all kinds and to present some concerts. From the beginning it was a truly international affair, attracting performers, scholars, instrument makers, and just plain enthusiasts of early music from this country and abroad. The exhibition filled two halls and contained about 80 booths belonging to various early music organizations, including the American Recorder Society. There were lectures, including a very interesting one given by harpsichordist Ralph Kirkpatrick (it sounds pretty antiquated now, but he stated that he had "made his peace" with the French style!), panel discussions, and demonstrations of instruments at the Museum of Fine Arts in Boston. The finals of the 14th Erwin Bodky International Competition were part of the program. At this first festival there was not as much emphasis on performance as later (it became a biennial event) but two stunning concerts took place, one with the Belgian viola da gamba player Wieland Kuijken and harpsichordist John Gibbons, and a solo concert (played from memory, as he was by then completely blind) by the legendary Kirkpatrick.

A Boston Early Music Festival has been held in the Boston area in odd-numbered years every other year since the first took place.

A new national organization, Early Music America (EMA), was formed in 1986. Its aim was to serve "the whole field" of early music, to promote "historically-informed performance of early music" and to assist professionals in this field. It is a highly successful organization, at least as seen from the outside. The first president was Ben Peck, a sackbut player and musicologist. EMA started a scholarly journal, *Historical Performance*, in 1987. The first editor of the journal was the distinguished musicologist Stewart Carter, who was also a fine sackbut player. The magazine has since been yuppified and made trendy, with pictures, livelier articles, and the modern use of mixed fonts, as has *American Recorder*. This was probably a good thing to do in both cases. Both magazines are more readable and of greater interest to the amateur musician.

Distinguished Achievement Award.

At the fall 1985 Board Meeting the motion was made that we establish an ARS award for distinguished achievement in the field of recorder playing. The first award was presented to Friedrich von Huene, the pioneering recorder maker, at a joint EMA/ARS reception held at the 1987 Boston Early Music Festival. In many ways this first presentation was the most gala and the most fun. Friedrich, a truly gifted recorder maker who had with his instruments vastly influenced recorder playing in the U.S, was suggested as a recipient by Michael and Kay Jaffee, and the ARS Board of Directors concurred fully with their suggestion. The choice was kept a secret from the ARS membership until the actual day of the presentation. We ordered a beautiful engraved silver Revere bowl for President Shelley Gruskin to present to Friedrich. Waddy purchased it and I brought it up from New York to the Boston Early Music Festival and nervously kept it hidden in my room at a B&B during the days preceding the presentation. Shelley made a very gracious speech at the reception, and Friedrich (who had, of course, been notified) gave one that was equally gracious. His wife Ingeborg spoke also. It was a truly gala event. The reception and presentation, along with the annual meeting of the Society, rancorous though it was, helped to enhance ARS presence at the Festival.

Two years later, at the suggestion of Marilyn Boenau, the Board decided to give the award to Bernard Krainis. I will have to say that I was somewhat against this; Bernard had been so anti-ARS in so many ways, but I was outvoted. In 1989 I was again president of the ARS, and I presented the award to him at a reception, jointly sponsored by Early Music America and the American Recorder Society at BEMF on Friday, June 2, 1989. This time the name of the recipient was announced in advance. There were some comic aspects to this presentation: There were some who wasted no time in pointing out (privately, of course) that the bowl was somewhat smaller than the one Friedrich received. My speech (unwritten) took note of the many things Bernard had done for the Society and for recorder playing in this country (he was, indeed, a virtuoso player and teacher), and Bernie, in his acceptance, took the opportunity to blast the ARS for what he called its "support and encouragement" of "recreational noodling." The ARS should "employ the latest technology and exploit the talents of our finest professionals" in order to "change the American musical landscape." Poor Bernie! He was never able to give up the idea that, if it were offered, American recorder players would flock to a very expensive school made up of illustrious teachers like himself, and that somehow, by acquiring more skills, American amateur recorder players would improve the employment scene for professional recorder players. He never seemed to take notice of all of our efforts in the fields of education and instruction—the teachers' exams, achievement levels, the workshops

Friederich von Huene, 1989.

with our (admittedly somewhat strife-ridden) attempts at overseeing them, the chapter development grants, even the publication of difficult pieces for the recorder. The very *raison d'etre* of our existence, going way back to Suzanne Bloch, was to make teachers teach better and players play better. And we had been increasingly trying to do more for our professional members in the way of financial aid. Always a gentleman, Bernie did couch his speech in elegant terms. It is printed in the November, 1989 issue of AR.

Another dive into the future: the third Distinguished Achievement Award was presented to Shelley Gruskin by then-President Connie Primus at the Boston Early Music Festival of 1991. The fourth, in 1994, went to Nobuo Toyama, inventor of the Aulos plastic recorders; the fifth, in 1995, to LaNoue Davenport; the sixth, in 1996, to Martha Bixler; the seventh, in 1997, to Edgar Hunt; the eighth, in 1999, to Eugene Reichenthal; the ninth, in 2001, to Frans Brüggen; the tenth, in 2002, to Valerie Horst; the eleventh, in 2005, to Pete Rose; the twelfth, in 2006, to Marion Verbruggen, the thirteenth, in 2007, to Joel Newman; the fourteenth, in 2009, to Kenneth Wollitz.

Connie Primus presents the ARS Distinguished Achievement Award to Shelley Gruskin at the Boston Early Music Festival, 1991. Left to right: Shelley Gruskin, Friedrich von Huene, Connie Primus.

At its fall, 1986 meeting the Board of Directors of the ARS created a new committee, a **special events committee**, with Valerie Horst as temporary chair. (She was not at that time on the Board of Directors of the ARS.) The original purpose of this committee was to help to plan ARS events at the Boston Early Music Festival in 1987 and subsequent music festivals, but it soon became involved in a general project of helping professional recorder players in ways we had not heretofore, i.e. with grants, particularly recording grants (we started doing this in 1991), and subsidizing personal ads in *Musical America* (1992). The committee later (1997) started a "disco club" helping to sell recordings, and took the responsibility for putting on "recorder relays," short performances by budding recorder professional performers, at both the Boston and Berkeley exhibitions. In 1987 the ARS awarded a grant to the San Francisco Early Music Society for its recorder festival, which included concerts as well as master classes. We also started lobbying rather heavily to get professional performers to join the Society. The election of Marilyn Boenau, a very much respected recorder and bassoon player, first to the ARS Board of Directors in 1988, and then to vice president of the Board was a big plus. Marilyn's presence on the Board lent credence to our efforts to get professional players to join the Society.

One of the biggest undertakings of the special events committee was **ARS 50**. "Everyone knew" that the American Recorder Society was founded in 1939 by Suzanne Bloch. This made the year 1989 the fiftieth anniversary of its founding. It was Waddy's idea to make a really big deal of this, with a year-long celebration of the ARS's birthday in 1989. This would give an impetus to money-raising and publicity for the organization, and it would of course gain new members. One of our goals was to reach a membership of 5,000 by the time of our 50th birthday. Another was to have chapters in all 50 states. We did not reach either of these goals.

But we did a lot of other things. Valerie Horst, by this time a re-elected member of the Board of Directors, slipped easily into the full-time chairmanship of ARS 50. She did an amount of work that can only be described as phenomenal in getting the celebration up and running. Another member of the committee was Waddy Thompson, whose idea it had been at least partly in the first place. He made a very large contribution as well. I was a member at first but wisely dropped out after a couple of breathlessly ambitious meetings. (The reader must remember that at this time just about everything having to do with the Society still took place in New York!) A "professional commemorator," Alfred Stern, came to our first meeting (undoubtedly for a high fee!) and gave us lots of advice, most of which we didn't take, as we had plenty of ideas of our own. One of the first projects was to run a competition for an ARS 50 logo. To our surprise and delight there were 16 entries. The winning logo was a handsome design by Dan Reiken, a recorder and viol player whose day-job was, not surprisingly, working as a commercial artist and letterer. The logo "ARS 50," a gracefully lettered "ARS" over the "50," white on a blue or black background with the words "American Recorder Society, 1939–1989" beside it, was immediately put on our ARS stationery, envelopes, publications, and all announcements of ARS events.

Good-looking stickers were made from the logo, with a gold ARS 50 on a dark blue background. Also a piece of thin cardboard with the logo printed in different sizes on it. The gold sticker was to be used on new charters for chapters. One of the many projects of the ARS 50 celebration was the re-numbering and issuing of new charters for chapters that did not have them; this actually happened. The black and white logos were included in a very elaborate press kit intended to be sent, along with a "package of incentives" to early-music presenters all over the U.S. and Canada, to the press, to chapters, and anyone else who wanted or could use it.

In the kit, as well as copies of the logo, were a short history of the ARS, a description of the planned ARS 50 celebration, an exhortation to name all events involving the recorder "ARS 50" events and to use the logo, and public relations guidelines for presenters. All of this, and much else, was handsomely produced by Waddy Thompson. Since Waddy resigned as executive director in the fall of 1988, much of what was planned for ARS 50, including sending out these press kits, simply did not happen.

However, much did, including a listing of 150 "ARS events" in the *Newsletter* and The American Recorder, Vol. XXX, No. 1 (February, 1989). These included classes, concerts, workshops, feasts, and parties involving recorders from October 1988 through March, 1989, all of which could be considered ARS 50 events. Another listing was planned for the November issue of *AR* but it does not appear there, I suppose partly because of deteriorating relations between the ARS 50 committee and the editor of *AR*. Additions and corrections to the ARS 50 calendar were printed in the Winter 1989 *Newsletter*.

Other projects included a contest for photographs to be used in the ARS 50 membership drive, the promotion of an exhibition of the 200 recorders in the Dayton C. Miller Flute Collection at the Library of Congress, and a discography, with an index, of recorder recordings. To my knowledge none of these ever took place.

One ambitious project of the celebration that did see fruition was the commission of "a new work for recorder and standard chamber ensemble that could be used by recorder players to get themselves and the recorder beyond the usual early-music milieu," (from Waddy Thompson's Report to the ARS Board of Directors, September, 1988) "to be performed by leading recorder players throughout the United States in 1989" (press release). Waddy and Colin Sterne chose Conrad Susa, a San Francisco Bay area composer, to carry out this commission. Susa was/is a writer of chamber music, opera, theater music, and television scores. From Waddy's Report to the Board of Directors, February 8, 1988: "Susa's music is best described as eclectic, combining elements of contemporary concert music with some jazz and traditional concert music." He seemed ideal.

What followed next was in some ways a comedy of errors. Susa gladly accepted an advance of $2,500, half of the fee agreed upon. He agreed to deliver the finished manuscript by January 1, 1989. Marilyn Boenau, who lived in the Bay area, was to be his "recorder consultant," although he had written for recorders before. The January 1 deadline came and went. The minutes of the February, 1989 Board meeting report that "although composer Conrad Susa missed the deadline for delivery of his piece, it is now nearing completion and should be ready in time for its scheduled premiere." In the Spring 1989 *Newsletter* we confidently announced that Nina Stern would give the premiere of the new work by Susa with the Classical Quartet and harpsichordist Arthur Haas on September 19 in New York City, and Scott Reiss would give the Washington, D.C. premiere on November 19 at the Kennedy Center. Both concerts came and went, but there were no performances of a notas-yet existent Susa work. We gamely designated Scott's concert a "birthday bash," even though we had no new piece to present. He performed six concertos for recorders and strings by Vivaldi, Telemann, Naudot, and Graupner with his group Hesperus at the Terrace Theater in the Kennedy Center. I called the performance "sizzling" in my "Message from the President" in the March, 1990 *American Recorder*, and there was a black-tie reception afterward hosted by the ARS and the early-music Hesperus. On view at the reception was a display of some of the flutes and recorders from the Dayton C. Miller Collection of the Library of Congress.

Marilyn Boenau dropped in on Susa sporadically in the spring of 1989, and reported that the piece was all "still in his head." I nearly met him at a brunch party held at the home of Board member Ken Johnson in San Francisco, but a freak accident kept Conrad away. In the early summer I made an attempt, during a visit with relatives in the San Diego area, to meet Conrad Susa at the Old Globe Theater in San Diego, where he was resident composer, but he managed to avoid me, and it was now evident that something was amiss. In the meantime we had tried hard to get grants from Meet the Composer and the

Nakamichi Foundation for Susa's fee, but with no success. Who among us has not written a grant proposal? It's so much work, and so discouraging when it doesn't come through! But it has happened many times to the ARS. We took the money for Susa from our own cash reserves. It seemed like a fortune then.

I don't remember exactly when it became clear that Susa was not going to deliver, in fact had not written a note, but sometime in the summer of 1989 Ben Dunham got in touch with Ezra Laderman, who had been on the first short list, to ask him to write a new piece for the ARS. Laderman, a noted composer who was then Dean of the Yale University School of Music, delivered a three-movement piece for recorder and string quartet, *Talkin'-Lovin'-Leavin,*' in record time. Michala Petri performed the piece with the New World String Quartet at an already scheduled concert at the Grace Rainey Rogers Auditorium at the Metropolitan Museum of Art in New York on March 9, 1990. Michala was especially gracious about changing her planned program and performing the piece on rather short notice. Later, regional premieres were given by Judith Linsenberg (December 6, 1990) with the Stanford String Quartet at Stanford University, by John Tyson with the Boston Composers' String Quartet, by Natalie Michaud (May 13, 1991) with the McGill University Faculty String Quartet in Montreal, and by Eva Legêne at Indiana University in Bloomington. Funds to support these concerts were obtained from the President's Appeal. Although it was a rather inconsequential piece, Talkin,'-Lovin,'-Leavin' brought substantial notice to the American Recorder Society in its 50th birthday celebration.

In the meantime, then-Treasurer Mary Maarbjerg set about getting our $2500 back from Conrad Susa. She and Marilyn Boenau, on a surprise visit to Susa, had managed to get a check for part of the money on the spot. The beleaguered composer promised us a check for the remaining amount, but the weeks went by and it never came. Mary then decided on a sort of "Chinese water-torture" means of persuasion.

I don't know for how long she did this, but it was quite a long time. Every Monday morning, promptly at 7:30 (his time), she telephoned Susa to chat and to inform him gently that we had not yet received the money, and that we would like to. She was never unpleasant, but her persistence won the day. He finally gave in, and returned the money after what I think were months of owing us. It was quite a triumph, both for Mary and for the ARS.

Capital Campaign

At the September, 1988 Board meeting new Board member Phillip Stiles was appointed to chair a **development committee**, which was to oversee all of the Society's fund-raising efforts, including the Katz Fund and the President's Appeal. At a "special" February, 1989 meeting the Board decided we needed a capital campaign as part of our ARS 50 celebration. Stiles was to head the campaign for what we called the "ARS Endowment Fund for the Second Fifty Years." The goal set was $100,000, $50,000 from the membership and $50,000 from businesses, corporations and foundations, to be raised over three years' time. This was in addition to continuing to ask members for money in the President's Appeal. Some of our aims were to broaden the recorder repertoire through commissions and publishing, to support professional performers and teachers in the U.S. and Canada, to produce instructional videotapes, to encourage American and Canadian recorder players, to help in the funding of recorder concerts and recordings, "and much more!" From the Spring 1989 *Newsletter*:

> The Board has come to the conviction that its single most important job in its four-year tenure will be to put the Society in a strong financial position so that it can fulfill its larger mission. The Endowment Fund, and the strength and security it will bring, will speed the course of the ARS as nothing else can.

> Board members themselves have already pledged an unprecedented $15,700; they have stretched considerably [there was a lot of talk about "stretching"] because of their belief in the goals of the society. Do give serious consideration to a pledge that is significant for you. We will all benefit from such choices.

$46,000 was pledged by the spring of 1990 and $52,000 by June, 1992, although I believe not all was collected.

In a report from the ARS president to the executive committee on March 19, 1997 Gene Murrow wrote: "While the 1989 Capital Campaign did not achieve its goals from corporate contributors, the individual contributions almost reached the goal. This enabled the Society to pay some outstanding debts and to set up the Capital Fund." This is an optimistic final report on the Capital Campaign of 1989.

Probably the most exciting and entertaining event of the ARS 50 celebration was the worldwide play-in that took place on April 1, 1989, the designated birthday of the American Recorder Society. Because of the discovery of a letter from Suzanne Bloch "to whom it may concern" announcing the founding of the ARS on March 30, 1939, the date of April 1 was chosen to be the official 50th birthday, allowing two days for the delivery of the letter anywhere in the United States. Also, April 1 happened to be a Saturday in 1989. The "Great Simultaneous Worldwide Recorder Play-in" was masterminded by Valerie Horst. She planned for recorder players around the globe to play and sing a birthday song to the ARS simultaneously, hopefully with radio or television hook-ups between New York and various other American cities. Colin Sterne was approached, to see if he would write something for "3 to 10 recorders" for various groups to play. He declined, but the ARS 50 committee finally decided upon Antony Holborne's *The Night Watch*, for the music, a five-part instrumental piece "on the grounds that it is useful under many playing conditions; the top part is melodic and suitable for a member who must play alone; none of it is too hard to play; the concept of the Nightwatchman (sic) announcing that all is well and the ARS is 50 is appropriate." (ARS 50 Committee Meeting Minutes, December 3, 1988.)

Lucy Cross was asked to write appropriate lyrics. She promised, but like so many promisers, she failed to deliver until she was brow-beaten into doing so by Valerie at the very last minute, so that Richard Sacksteder could add them to his setting of Holborne's piece (using a microfilm from the British Library provided by Joel Newman, we avoided breaking any copyright laws). An insert with both words and music to The ARS *Night Watch* was delivered to ARS members with the February, 1989 (XXX, 1) AR. On the bright red cover was the ARS 50 logo and a picture of "The Triumph of Maximilian's" shawm-players on horseback. These are the words she wrote:

> The night watch lamps are burning, the night to daytime turning,
> and by their light ten thousand pipers tune and start to play.
> The ARS is fifty, and tootling still is nifty,
> we know no joy surpassing ours to celebrate this day.
> Hark! I hear the great bass hooting out harmony
> while the sopranino ornaments with graceful loops and bends.
> Altos, tenors give the inner voice liberty.
> Goodness sakes knows what we'd do without out little four-foot friends!
> Schütz, Schein and Scheidt, and Schmelzer, Valentin Haussmann, too:
> ARS, ARS, sing Happy Birthday to you!
> Brade, Van Eyck, Praetorius, come join in Holborne's song:
> ARS, ARS, bring music our whole life long!

55 members of the New York chapter of the ARS performed at 5:00 p.m. Eastern Standard Time on Saturday, April 1 on the stage of the Symphony Space in Manhattan under my baton. Valerie had actually figured out the times for places all over the world to perform simultaneously, not only in the 50 United States but in Argentina—7:00 p.m., Norway—11:00 p.m., Israel and Zimbabwe—12:00 midnight,

and Japan—7:00 a.m. *Sunday*, and many, many more. Valerie also managed to get a telephone hook-up (in lieu of any radio or television) to Paul Leenhouts and six other players in Amsterdam so that we could in fact play simultaneously, with Valerie listening to Paul on a speaker phone while conducting me, and me looking at Valerie while conducting the New York group. The audience could hear both groups.

More than half of all ARS members participated in this event. Members played in 45 states and five Canadian provinces as well as Australia, Austria, Belize, England, France, Germany, Mexico, Nepal, the Netherlands, St. Barthelemy, Scotland, and Tobago. The largest group—in Princeton, New Jersey—had 100 players.

One "event" planned for the ARS 50 celebration at the 1988 board meeting was the writing of this *History of the ARS*, as it was then expected to be. It was expected that I would spend a couple of years on this project. It has taken many more than that!

Junior Recorder Society

From its beginning the American Recorder Society was an organization for adults. Children learned the recorder in school, and sometimes came to ARS meetings with their parents. There were also student memberships in the Society. Occasionally someone would mention a program for children, but the first official suggestion came from Ken Wollitz, one of our more visionary presidents. From "Message from the President," *AR* XI, 2, Spring, 1970:

> Many of us who teach children feel that the recorder is an ideal means of introducing music to the young. It is an easy instrument for children to learn. With so many recorders being placed in so many small hands would we not as a society do well to involve ourselves in this musical renaissance? A number of people involved in teaching children have urged that the ARS take a guiding role in

this field. Should we instigate a program of advice and instruction in the use of the recorder in schools? There have been several suggestions: more school-oriented material in The American Recorder, ARS sponsored workshops for school teachers, and it has even been suggested that we form a Junior American Recorder Society.

Then, as now, members of the ARS were of the opinion that most teaching of children, especially in public schools, was inferior. President Wollitz tried to interest the New York City Board of Education in starting pilot programs teaching public school music teachers how to teach the recorder, with ARS members as faculty. This was a wonderful idea, but there were no funds to pay our teachers. We did publish articles of interest to recorder teachers over the years. The index of Volumes I through XXXIII (Winter, 1960 through December 1992) lists 30 articles under "Recorder in Education," having to do specifically with teaching children. Some of the distinguished pedagogues writing these articles were Gertrud Bamberger, Gerald Burakoff, Johanna Kulbach, and Eugene Reichenthal. There has been no dearth of "tips for teachers," as Gene Reichenthal liked to call it. But then many of these articles were preaching to the choir.

Finally, at the fall 1991 ARS Board meeting in Chicago, the first steps were taken in the formation of a Junior Recorder Society. Peggy Monroe, a newly appointed member of the Board, announced a pilot program at the February, 1992 Board meeting to begin the following September. Initially the program was to be called the "American Recorder Club." Plans were under way for a brochure, a *Newsletter*, a logo, stickers for the children, a teachers' handbook by Gerald Burakoff and a music list to be compiled by Ken Andresen and Eugene Reichenthal. The program was soon re-named the **Junior Recorder Society**, and split into two programs, a Club Program and a Class Program.

Two booklets were printed, both with the JRS logo of the wizard

Peggy Munroe, 1993.

Merlin on the cover. The Club booklet contained a welcome letter from the ARS President, Connie Primus, a letter to parents, lists of music and reference materials, suggestions on how to start a JRS Club, articles, some reprinted from AR, and suggestions for meeting activities. The Class Program booklet, intended as a resource for classroom teachers, included, as well as the welcome from the ARS president, articles on introducing recorder teaching into the classroom, worksheets for children, and class award certificates. Although the Club Program was intended for after-school activities and the Class Program as an aid to classroom teachers, the two programs were not mutually exclusive, and were eventually thought of as one Junior Recorder Society.

Gerald and Sonya Burakoff's fine Introducing the Recorder; Information and guidelines for teachers was published by the ARS in 1993 and became part of the program. Volume I, No. 1 of the *Newsletter* of the Junior Recorder Society Club (carefully kept dateless) was published in the early '90s, and there was a Volume II as well. By 1995 there were 12 Junior Recorder Society

Sonya and Gerald Burakoff, 1984.

Clubs in existence, with members paying $5 dues annually, but because of illnesses, office problems, inattention, and lack of interest by other Board members, the Junior Recorder Society sputtered and nearly died before it was fully taken over and brought to life by Virginia Ebinger in the fall of 1997. But that is a story for the '90s.

Milestones

It is perhaps appropriate here to record a few milestones. Although the "father" of the American Recorder Society, **Erich Katz**, died on July 30, 1973, our "mother," **Suzanne Bloch**, outlived him by many years, living into her '90s. **LaNoue Davenport** and **Bernard Krainis** lived well into their '70s and the century's '90s. But it was inevitable that in the '70s and '80s we would begin to lose some of the important people in the history of the ARS and the recorder movement in this country. Some of the milestones of the late '70s and '80s follow:

Josef Marx, "oboist and musician extraordinaire," as he was called in AR XX, 1, May, 1979, died on December 21, 1978. Josef was indeed an extraordinary musician, known to the early music community of New York not only for his virtuoso playing, his publishing company McGinnis & Marx, and his management of the Group for Contemporary Music at Columbia University, but for his amazing store, tucked in the courtyard of a rundown apartment building on Second Avenue in New York. I worked as a clerk and bookkeeper there for several years. Josef's wife Angie worked there, too, bringing her toddler, Debbie, with her; for years the story was repeated about how I rescued a wandering Debbie who had fallen head-first into a waste basket. Somehow in that cluttered space Josef kept and was able to find on demand treasures of chamber music, particularly wind music, early and late, some of it available nowhere else. The store was a great gathering place for the early musicians of the city. Josef knew everyone in the ARS, extended credit to all, and was a fount of information for everybody.

Theodore (Ted) Mix, founder and president of Magnamusic Distributors of Sharon, Connecticut, died in January, 1979. Ted was one of the first importers and distributors of recorders in the U.S. The recorder method that headed his catalog, the Trapp family's *Enjoy Your Recorder*, must be one of the biggest sellers ever in the recorder world. Besides founding and running Magnamusic, one of the principal American sources of music and instruments for early music enthusiasts for 40 years, Ted was a great friend to ARS. Some of the earliest meetings of the American Recorder Society were held at his first retail store on West 57th Street in New York. Ted and his wife Alice and later their daughter Madeline were the most honest, most conscientious, and generous business people I have ever known. Ever ready with a suggestion or an aid to the ARS, they have helped us out in countless ways, sending brochures, giving endless time to checking publication information for the education program, and making sure we receive review copies of new publications. In his obituary of Ted in *AR* XX, 2, August, 1979, Maurice Whitney wrote that the traditions of Magnamusic "are based on customer service and the application of the golden rule, guided by people of dedication, understanding, and the highest ethical standards."

Arthur Nitka, known as Art or often Arty, died in the fall of 1981. The beloved proprietor of Terminal Music, on West 48th Street in Manhattan, Arty wore many hats. In his day job he was a salesman, and a very good one, but he was also a recorder player and teacher, a onetime member of the Board, and friend to many recorder players. He had started as a clerk in Terminal Music, but when he took over the ownership he made it into a retail store for recorder players *nonpareil*. He was extremely supportive of the American Recorder Society at a time when most of what was happening took place in New York. His death created a void that was never filled. Even now an out-of-town visitor to this city who comes expecting as a matter of course to find many outlets for recorders and recorder music must be told no, no, there is nothing much here since Arty died. His death prompted a flurry of admiring and sorrowful letters in AR XXIII, 1, February, 1982.

Dr. Maurice C. Whitney, a recorder player, music educator, chapter leader, performer, reviewer for AR, and a published composer of music for the recorder, also much beloved, died on September 2, 1984.

Fortunato Arico, a cellist and viola da gamba player, was one of the first "early musicians" to succumb to the scourge that was AIDS, on October 7, 1984. Freddy was not a recorder player, but as a consummate performer on baroque string instruments he was very well known in the recorder world. He was also very much loved by his colleagues and friends. In an obituary in *AR* XXVI, 1, February, 1985, Judith Davidoff wrote:

> What stood out in Freddy's makeup was his total professionalism, without the cynicism that often accompanies it. Even more striking was his complete lack of malice, and his genuine interest in and support of his colleagues.

A.C. ("Cook") Glassgold died in February of 1985. He was vice president of the ARS from 1959–1963 and President from 1963–1965. Cook was talented in a number of areas, including both art and music. He was also a labor organizer and an extremely able administrator. From 1953 he was administrative director, then director of the medical center of the New York Hotel Trades Council. In a reminiscence in AR XXVI, 3, August, 1985, Cook's friend Ralph Taylor writes: "Cook was essentially a man of contrast. From his dignified appearance and demeanor, almost patrician, one could easily assume that he was an entrenched member of the establishment. On the contrary, he devoted a major portion of his life to the underdog, the disinherited, the martyr. Truly he was a man of many parts or, as the poet has it, a man for all seasons." As I have written elsewhere in these pages, Cook was very much under-appreciated and misjudged in his role as president of the ARS. Well, so were other presidents!

Father **Bernard J. Hopkins**, C.Ss.R., a Catholic priest (of the order of the Redemptorists), a self-taught musician, teacher and composer, music reviewer for *AR*, for a time the *Newsletter* editor and a faithful member of the Board of Directors of the American Recorder Society from 1976 to 1984, died in July of 1986. His death inspired a host of admiring and loving letters in *AR*.

The death of **Andrew Acs**, on February 3, 1987, although not unexpected, shook us up a great deal, at least partly because he was only 34 years old, another victim of the monster AIDS. A talented musician, teacher, and administrator, he wore many hats in his association with the American Recorder Society, as director of the New York Recorder Guild and later administrative director of the American Recorder Society and a member of the Board of Directors. He was both an ARS workshop teacher and an ARS workshop director. He played both the recorder and the viola da gamba. His death prompted his parents to found the Andrew Acs Scholarship Fund, later called the Andrew Acs Memorial Fund, with the proceeds of the sale of his instruments combined with their own very generous monetary contributions. The contributions of his many friends and colleagues swelled the fund. Originally planned for scholarships to ARS workshops, the giving has expanded to include aid to professional musicians as well. The first recipient of monetary support from this fund was Andrew's student, Roxanne Layton.

From a few of the tributes to him in *AR*:

> He was so talented and so full of promise, and he had so recently found out what it was in life that he was really good at [music education]. One's sense of loss is almost overwhelming.
> There is no understanding why Andrew's life should be cut short. It is a tragedy not only for his family and his friends but also for the world of music. All of us who loved him will miss him terribly.
> Thinking of Andrew evokes innumerable memories of exciting,

energy-charged activities, workshops, concerts, meetings, talk, and fun and games. Andrew brought the joy of music to a great many people, and that remains although he is gone.

Walter Bergmann died in January, 1988 at the age of 85. In Theo Wyatt's words in *AR* XXIX, 2: "Dr. Walter Bergmann held a unique place in the affections of recorder players." He was indeed an extraordinarily warm and friendly man, and I thought of him as a personal friend. Walter Bergmann was trained as a lawyer, but after defending a Jewish firm and being imprisoned by the Gestapo, he fled from Germany to England in 1939. Unable to practice law there, he gained employment at Schott & Co. and came to know Carl Dolmetsch and Edgar Hunt. When the Society of Recorder players resumed operations after a hiatus during World War II, it was Bergmann's students who formed the nucleus of the recharged Society. Walter became the musical director of its London branch.

Walter Bergmann was a teacher, an editor, and composer. Much of his music is still in the Schott catalog. In Wyatt's words again:

> There can be few amateur players in London who have not felt the influence, direct, or indirect, of his teaching, and few of the millions of children throughout the country whose introduction to instrumental music has been through the recorder who have not enjoyed their first taste of Handel or Purcell in his delightful arrangements.

Hans Ulrich Staeps died on July 25, 1988. Professor Staeps was an Austrian musician, a composer and teacher of recorder, piano, harpsichord, and theory at the Vienna Conservatory. He first came to the United States to teach at Bernard Krainis's International Recorder School held at Skidmore College in Saratoga Springs in 1965. Probably the work by Staeps that is best known to members of the American Recorder Society is his delightful *Saratoga Suite* for SAT recorders, which became No. 56 in the ARS Editions, published by Galaxy Music.

Professor Staeps was commissioned by the ARS Colorado Recorder Workshop to compose a piece for multiple recorders, piano, and percussion for their 1984 season, and the piece, entitled *Minstrels*, was later published by Sweet Pipes. The director of the workshop, Connie Primus, and her husband, Bob, met with Professor Staeps at his home in Vienna in the fall of 1983 to receive the manuscript, and remained friends with Staeps and his wife during the remainder of his life. In 1988 Staeps sent the Primuses an advance manuscript of a later work, *East-West*, which he considered his "secret farewell to America." The work was given its premiere performance at the Colorado Recorder Festival three days before the composer's death.

Another heartbreaking death due to AIDS was that of **David Hart**, who passed away in May of 1988. David was an extremely talented musician and friend to many, many people in the world of early music. He was a flutist and recorder player and a dabbler in early stringed instruments, such as the medieval harp, which he played in an unorthodox manner that horrified true harpists, but with great effect nevertheless. He was also a gifted teacher. Tributes to David appeared in *AR* XXIX, 3, August, 1988:

> I was dumbstruck by his playing. It made you want to drop everything and listen.
>
> There's a phrase in Matteo's [early 15th century] 'Le greygnour bien" where all three parts go off into completely different meters for about seven seconds, and are supposed to come together in a cadence at one single moment. Playing it with David was like letting go hands in a country dance, going through a separate figure alone in space, and finding the hand again exactly when and where you needed it. I feel he's spun off now into some figure or measure of his own and that when it all comes together at last, his hand, and his smile, will be exactly where it needs to be.

Marleen Forsberg Montgomery was another extraordinary person in a community of extraordinary people. She died on September 18, 1988. An accomplished pianist, harpsichordist, and recorder player, Marleen was a woman of exceptional magnetism who attracted students in droves, not only to study with her, but to perform with her. For 15 years her group called Quadrivium gave performances of medieval, Renaissance, and early American music, mostly in the Boston area where Marleen lived. It also served as a "training ground" for young musicians who went on to form other groups. From *AR*, XXX, 2, May, 1989:

> Marleen gave us the spirit and enjoyment of music. She knew how to encourage, uplift, and inspire so that we overcame our technical limitations and made marvelous music. Marleen cast a benign spell on everyone she knew.

Ted Mix's widow, Alice, died in 1989. With her daughter Madeline Alice retained the spirit of Magnamusic Distributors after Ted died, right up to the very end of her own life. Besides running the business and making many trips abroad as well as to places like the Boston Early Music Festival, Alice did a great deal of entertaining, extending hospitable friendship to her neighbors, friends, and business acquaintances, who were in fact really all her friends. Her cheerful demeanor, even in the face of some serious, painful illnesses, will never be forgotten. She was one in a million.

Administrative Angst in the '80s

I come now to a period in the history of the American Recorder Society that is very difficult to write about, as well as to re-live. It was an important time nevertheless, and must be recorded. The 1988 elections to the Board of Directors of the ARS changed the character of the Board. At that time everyone's term was for four years, and everyone went off the Board in 1988 except for Ben Dunham, who was first appointed in 1985, then re-appointed for another four-year term at the 1988 meeting, and Mary Maarbjerg, who had been appointed in 1986. Re-elected members of the Board were Louise Austin, Martha Bixler, Valerie Horst, Connie Primus (Valerie and Connie after a four-year absence each), and Jennifer Lehmann. Newly elected were David Barton, Marilyn Boenau, Scott Paterson, Neil Seely, and Phillip Stiles. Ken Andresen was an alternate.

It was astonishing to discover how much electricity was generated by this mix. The Board of Directors of the ARS divided rather quickly into two factions: those who looked for change, sometimes rather radical change in our administration and outlook, and those who sometimes rather desperately tried to retain the *status quo*.

The first Board meeting with new members was held September 30 to October 2, 1988 in my apartment in New York, as usual. Out-of-town members were hosted by New York members, friends, and neighbors, as usual. As outgoing vice president, I presided. (There was no point in having Shelley Gruskin, the outgoing president who was leaving the Board, come from faraway Duluth.) The "big meeting" also incorporated meetings of the individual committees of the Board.

Connie Primus, Louise Austin, Neil Seely at ARS Board Meeting in New York, 1988.

Much against my better judgment, I was flattered into running again for president of the ARS. I won the "election" (it was really a "selection," executed by members of the Board only) handily (it was easy—I had been around for a very long time). This time around, instead of saving, with the help of my friends, the ARS from the River Styx, I soon faced crises that I was unable to handle. Selected for vice president was newcomer Marilyn Boenau, a professional bassoonist and recorder player then living in California, although she was originally an Easterner. The secretary was Scott Paterson from Scarborough, Ontario. The treasurer was Mary Maarbjerg, which was logical, since she worked in finance.

Before anything terrible happened we managed, at that first Board meeting, to accomplish a number of tasks:

1. We appointed the indefatigable Connie Primus as chair of the chapter relations committee and we appointed other committee chairs.

2. We began preparations for ARS 50 celebrations in April, 1989.

3. We assigned a few chapters to each Board member for "chapter calls." These were telephone calls to be made from a Board member every few months to the representatives of each chapter to try to keep them interested in and connected to the national organization. As we were deciding on the individual chapters to be "assigned" to each Board member it became obvious that some were "plums" for the Board member who was doing the calling. He or she could use the friendly call to wangle teaching a workshop somewhere in that state, which was something many of us coveted at the time. Needless to say, some of us were not so quick at grabbing these plums. This "grabbiness" was typical of the kind of thing that went on during the tenure of this Board.

4. We reinstated life membership in the ARS at $1000.

5. We granted honorary life membership to Shelley Gruskin.

6. We decided on the next recipient (Bernard Krainis) of the Distinguished Achievement Award.

7. We decided to "abolish" the *Chapter Circular*.

8. We decided that the Katz Fund be designated the Erich Katz Memorial Fund.

9. We decided that ARS membership would be required of the director of every ARS-endorsed workshop (but not the participants), and that the director should be a member of the expanded workshop committee.

10. We gave raises to both the *AR* editor and the executive director of the ARS.

11. We redefined the publications committee as a **word publications committee** only, and created an **operations committee**, "instituted to help decide which matters of Society policy in the day-to-day running of the Society's business should be referred to the board and give Mr. Thompson assistance generally," ("Report of the Board Meeting," AR XXX, No. 2, February, 1989)

The American Recorder Society Board of Directors now had 13 committees chaired by its members:

ARS 50: Valerie Horst

Chapter Relations: Connie Primus

Development: Phillip Stiles

Education: Ken Andresen

Executive: Martha Bixler

Finance: Mary Maarbjerg

Katz Memorial Fund: Phillip Stiles

Membership: David Barton

Music Publications: Jennifer Lehmann

Operations: Martha Bixler

Scholarship: Mary Maarbjerg

Word Publications: Marilyn Boenau

Workshop: Mary Maarbjerg

Although I had misgivings about the two new committees, Operations and Word Publications, I did not totally understand the danger of the red flags they raised. Sigrid was not present at the publications committee meeting, because she usually did not come to any part of the Board meeting when she was not directly involved. The new configuration of the publications committee was transparently intended to give the Board more oversight of Sigrid and magazine matters. This was obviously necessary; it was becoming more and more difficult to get Sigrid to carry out her mandate of having the magazine reflect the direction of the Society. The long, boring, scholarly articles, the aspirations toward literary significance, her waning interest in chapter and national news, her seeming stubbornness manifested in refusals to print some things that were requested of her, and the continual requests for raises, whether the ARS could afford them or not, were driving all of us crazy. But the creation of this committee was the beginning of what Sigrid began to perceive as a persecution that interfered with her ability to edit the magazine, and eventually she felt she must resign.

But before her there was Waddy. Waddy arrived at the publications committee meeting Saturday morning only to be told that he was neither needed nor welcome. (And of course I was the one who was forced to tell him this.) Waddy was not, strictly speaking, a member of the publications committee, but he had a lot of ideas he wanted to present, and had assumed he would be welcome at the meeting.

Waddy was furious, and the rest of the Board meeting did not make him feel any better. Worst of all was the creation of the operations committee, offering him help with the running of the office, which he felt he certainly did not need, and which was, again transparently, an attempt to give the Board increased oversight of the executive director of the ARS.

Waddy resigned almost immediately after the Board meeting. I was absolutely stunned. I had agreed to assume the presidency partly because I had expected to be able to depend heavily on Waddy, as we had been doing since the beginning of the '80s. Waddy was to my mind indispensable. He was the one who had computerized the office and he knew everything there was to do. He was involved in running the ARS 50 Celebration. He kept all of us on track. I begged him to remain, but he was absolutely adamant. It was not the events of the Board meeting alone that prompted him to resign. There had been increasing friction between him and several members of the old Board, and there were immediate frictions with the new. Waddy had an orderly mind; he had become frustrated with Board members who did not keep their promises, were late with reports, or did not respond to his pleas for information, making his job much more difficult than it needed to be. I found out later that he had, in fact, been thinking of leaving us for several months. At first he agreed to stay on until December 1, but then a new job demanded his services earlier. In a great hurry we were able to get Gloria Berchielli, an active member of the Country Dance and Song Society and treasurer of the Westchester Chapter of the ARS, to take over in the office as a temporary administrator until we could find a permanent replacement for Waddy. "Gloria in Excelsis!" we wrote in the Winter 1989 *Newsletter* as we added her name to our list of saviors when the ARS was in crisis. We paid her $12 an hour. Gloria was there to answer the telephone, process memberships, respond to requests for information, and do routine clerical work, but there was a lot she had to put on hold, in particular ARS 50 affairs. One job that had to be done immediately was to put out the usual hopeful annual President's Appeal. This entailed sending a computerized letter, in several different forms for those who had given and those who hadn't given yet, etc. For people new to computers, like Gloria and me, it was somewhat baffling. Waddy helped as much as he could, on evenings and weekends, but it was hard.

As was everything else. We went on an immediate concentrated search for a new executive director. Al Gore's Internet wasn't in commercial use as yet, so advertising for a new director wasn't as easy as it later became. In the end we stayed close to home, persuading Andy Green, a flutist, musicologist, and erstwhile recorder student of mine, to take over as administrative director (we were wary of the word "executive"). Andy was finishing his Ph.D. at the City University of New York and working at various small teaching jobs at the time. He seemed perfect—young, extremely bright, personable, musically knowledgeable, a friend, and living on the upper west side of Manhattan, as so many of us did. Married, with two small boys, he was very much in need of the money as well.

This was a disastrous move. Andy was under the mistaken impression that the ARS job was only part-time and that he could continue to work on his dissertation. In addition he was a bit careless and not very computer-savvy. When he took the job Waddy was kind enough to take him on a tour around the office, explaining in detail what needed to be done and pointing out, particularly, the things Gloria had had to put aside. My heart sank when I saw how casual Andy was and how he tossed one set of papers on top of another as Waddy was showing him the ropes. One urgent job that needed to be performed immediately was to put out the Winter *Newsletter*. By holding Andy's nose to the grindstone I managed to help him to get it formatted and ready for production, but then disaster struck. The printer jammed, and in attempting to get it going again Andy managed to destroy it utterly. He was able to get it to a repair station, but when it was finally fixed he was so befuddled that he gave the person picking it up the wrong address, sending him rushing to the far east side of Manhattan instead of the far west, before he was able to stagger (printers were larger and heavier then!) back to the ARS office, then on lower Broadway, with the repaired printer. Spring was in full flower before the Winter *Newsletter* was printed.

Things went from bad to worse. Andy himself realized that we and he had made a colossal mistake. We were all grateful when Andy's wife was offered a job at the Eastman School of Music in Rochester, New York, and Andy moved up there along with her. He did make an attractive public appearance at the ARS 50 play-in at Symphony Space, and he was helpful at the Boston Early Music Festival that June of 1989, but by that time we had found Andy's successor.

Once again we interviewed with intensity, at one point seriously considering Sheila Levin, Philip Levin's wife, who was helping Philip run his instrument-building and repairing business in Newfoundland, New Jersey. But in the end we chose for our next executive director Alan Moore, who possessed both a BM degree from Eastman and a DMA from Stanford, as well as an MBA from Florida Atlantic University. He came well recommended by his previous employers, and made a good impression at his interview, especially when he had seemingly good ideas for grant proposals, in spite of the fact that he arrived winded and apologetic after taking the wrong subway train to get to my apartment in New York. We were also able, as a result of a good response to the President's Appeal, to hire for the first time a part-time office assistant, Lora Goodridge, who was to be membership secretary. With two paid professionals in the office we hoped to catch up with all the neglected back work and to see the ARS office running smoothly again.

I breathed a tremendous sigh of relief. Alan had a rather long commute to the ARS office in New York from his home in New Jersey, and at first he seemed not to mind. He worked diligently through the summer, putting the financial affairs of the ARS in order. At the fall 1989 Board meeting (September 21–October 1) we appointed Alan Executive Director. We also welcomed newly-appointed Peggy Monroe as a Board member. Also "accomplished" during this meeting were the resignation of Ron Cook as legal advisor and the appointment of Mark Jay. Mary Maarbjerg gave up her job as chair of the workshop committee (now called the Workshop Advisory Committee) and Neil Seely took over that rather difficult position. National dues were raised to $25.00.

Alan Moore, 1989.

The day before the full Board meeting, following the lead of SFEMS, the San Francisco Early Music Society, we spent a day with Dr. Robert Webb Crawford, a consultant to arts organizations. We paid him the magnificent sum of $100 or something thereabouts, and put him up at the B&B of a student and friend who was willing to give him the room gratis.

The night before Dr. Crawford's arrival I was "walking" my stepdaughter's dog when she suddenly began to run, pulling me after her. I tripped on a rough spot on the sidewalk and fell, literally flat on my face. A trip to the emergency room revealed a broken nose, and the physical evidence of my disastrous fall was fully apparent the next day: purple/black pouches under my eyes, a blue nose, and a badly swollen blue, black and purple face. I spent the weekend trying to assure the new Board members and Dr. Crawford that I really didn't "look like that." My accident was a bad omen of what was to come.

I hadn't particularly approved of having an expensive consultant come to spend a day with us, but hiring a consultant to help us "define our goals," was beginning to be a trendy thing at the time, and so I went along with the idea. Dr. Crawford had impressive credentials (he'd had a long association with the National Endowment for the Arts) and was both personable and amiable. One of the things our consultant perceived immediately was a lack of cooperative spirit among some members of the Board, who were passing notes to each other like school children, so transparently disdainful of what was going on at the meeting that he remarked upon it.

There was little that Dr. Crawford had to tell us that was useful, but he did make the suggestion that four years as an officer of the Board was a long time, and that perhaps we should limit the terms of the president, vice president, secretary, and treasurer, to two years, with a "re-election" or election of new officers after that time. This mild suggestion turned into a political football made of dynamite a short time after the consultant's visit.

Soon after the fall 1989 Board meeting Sigrid Nagle felt she must resign as editor of *AR*. In a somewhat melodramatic fashion she sent me her resignation in a note delivered by messenger. She had been angry with me for not preventing Waddy's departure and she was also angry with me for not protecting her from the increasing demands of the ARS publications committee: for a more folksy style and attention to the common man in the articles she accepted, and for a jazzier appearance of the magazine, in keeping with the modern magazine styles of the '80s. The tack she always took was that I should be more "presidential."

Of course I did not want Sigrid to resign either, but when she decided she must she still had, although she was terribly upset and disappointed, some trust in me to do the right thing when I was able. This trust was destroyed utterly when the Board instructed me that I must proofread Sigrid's final edition of AR before it went to press, just in case she tried to slip in something mischievous about the ARS, or the Board, or whatever it was that was feared. When I conveyed this request on the phone to Sigrid—it was really a command—her anger was immediate. She hung up on me abruptly, and really never spoke to me again except in public places where it was absolutely necessary.

We needed a temporary replacement for Sigrid immediately, and were lucky to get an offer from Ben Dunham to produce the next issue. *AR* Vol. XXXI, 1, March, 1990, was late, but it was a masterpiece—just what (some of) the Board wanted—and I was seduced as well. Gone was Sigrid's sedate cover, in the last issue a photograph from the National Portrait Gallery in London of a sculptured medieval angel playing a bagpipe. Instead we had a modern still-life: Ezra Laderman's spectacles and a recorder atop an open issue of *American Recorder*, with copies of various English early music magazines behind it. Overlaid was a photograph of Laderman's head framed in red, with the words "Laderman Premiere, Page 3, [the Michala Petri performance of our Fiftieth Anniversary piece] in white lettering. The name of the magazine, which had been The American Recorder for 30 years, was changed to *American Recorder* (without anyone's noticing!). A white banner was stretched across the upper left hand corner with "Summer Festivals, Page 16" in red lettering. In the lower right hand corner: "What are other Publications saying about the Recorder? Page 11." This was a rather clever provocative come-on for what was a fairly pedestrian (but interesting) article by David Lasocki on "The Recorder in Print: 1987–88: A digest of commentary on the recorder world-wide." This scholarly article was, by the way, the kind of thing Sigrid had been

Ben Dunham, 1995.

publishing for some time, but she had been drowning us with footnotes, and she hadn't thought of making the articles sound like something a little bit naughty. Inside, Ben's magazine was very different from Sigrid's as well. New departments, like "Tidings," bringing announcements such as the Michala Petri concert, and "Forum," presenting the ideas of various experts on aspects of recorder technique, were welcome. There were more photographs and, interestingly, drawings. I was especially pleased to find the Board minutes at the beginning of the magazine, instead of hidden away at the end. Fonts, particularly those used for headings, were larger, making everything in the magazine appear to be more exciting and important. Information concerning the summer workshops was attractively presented: an outline of a map of the United States appeared in a centerfold, with a picture of the fiftieth anniversary celebration at the Amherst workshop (cheering, clapping celebrants) super-imposed. Around the map were the usual descriptions of the various workshops being offered, again with bold headings in large fonts for June, July and August. Each workshop had a number, and this number was also on the map, showing at a glance the geographical (as well as the chronological) distribution of the workshops. Spread across both pages was the headline, again in a super-large font: "Eight Ways to Enjoy Your Recorder This Summer." The announcement of the summer workshops in the magazine has never been so eye-catching, before or since.

After Sigrid's resignation Ben Dunham was made the head of a search committee to find a new editor for the magazine. Those Board members who lived in the New York area were the obvious members of the committee. We went through the motions of looking for a new editor, but I suppose it was always a foregone conclusion that Ben would be the logical choice. As one Board member declared: "He knows what we want better than we do ourselves!"

There were more than 80 applicants for the position. We even had a would-be editor come down from Toronto for an interview. One young lady, a New Yorker, was rejected out of hand because she admitted to knowing nothing about computers. My choice was a brilliant young graduate student in musicology from City University. This applicant was super-qualified, possessing all the necessary skills: literary, musical, and technological. But he was tripped up by a trick question asked of all the examinees: "What would you like to improve upon or change in the magazine, if anything?" The poor applicant, thinking that we were perfectly satisfied with our (excellent) magazine, always replied that he/she would not change anything at all. During Robert's interview I sat mute, thinking I must not interfere (I should have) and watched him fall directly into the trap. My friend was not hired, of course. I was sick about it. He had wanted and needed the job very much and had felt certain he would get it. Needless to say he was extremely angry, with both the ARS and me, and like Sigrid, he never forgave me.

Ben Dunham was made permanent editor of the magazine and of the ARS *Newsletter* as well at the February, 1990 Board meeting. It should be noted that at the time Ben was not only head of the search committee but a member of the Board of Directors of the ARS as well. To his credit, it must be said that he did an excellent job on both publications. In addition, his work as "super-editor" of the Musicians Library Editions, on which I labored for so many years, was most welcome and helpful. He was always ready with help and advice, especially technological, and he made the whole endeavor much easier for me.

Things began to go badly for Alan Moore fairly quickly. Members of the Board had been so unhappy with Andy Green's performance that they started dogging our new executive director with phone calls, suggestions, and various demands, including requests for financial reports much more frequently than he would have liked. When it came time to arrange for a reception after Michala Petri's performance of the Laderman 50th anniversary piece I was instructed by some members of the Board to make sure Alan did a proper job of it, and when I tried to have the reception at my apartment, where it could have been done inexpensively and informally, Alan and I were undermined by another Board member's arrangements to hold the reception at the Stanhope Hotel across Fifth Avenue from the Metropolitan Museum, where the concert took place. The reception room was tiny and the expensive hors d'oeuvres uninspired, but a hotel address was grander than my West End Avenue apartment.

The above is a very small example of the kind of slight Alan felt he must endure. The operations committee was a watchdog that spent a lot of time peering over Alan's shoulder. He resented this mightily, and his response was to begin to slack off. He persuaded the ARS to move its office to New Jersey, near where he lived, so he would not have to spend so much time commuting (and where the rent was indeed cheaper), and this made sense, but it soon became apparent that Alan was taking more and more time off. The two factions of the Board became even more divided; the status quo people favored leaving Alan alone to do his job, and the "we must change" crowd thought he needed constant supervision. As president, I was expected by the latter group to ride herd on Alan and keep him in line. The ability to ride herd on someone was an ability I simply did not possess. Alan managed, in spite of his deteriorating relations with the Board, to hang on to his office until 1993.

I was having my own troubles with the ARS Board. Soon after the fall Board meeting of 1988 had passed and I was made President, I was persuaded to form an executive committee of the four chief officers of the ARS, the president, vice president, secretary, and treasurer. We met once monthly by means of a conference call. This was a very good idea, as we became more of a representative democracy instead of a dictatorship. But something started happening during our calls. I kept hearing the suggestion that I find out from our counsel, who was young and perhaps a bit inexperienced, whether it was "legal" for ARS officers to resign after two years. Of course it was "legal" for anyone to resign at any time. The idea that this should be done after two years in office had been put into our heads by Dr. Crawford himself. Since none of the other three officers gave any indication of a desire to resign, it became clear that they wanted me to go.

There were many other small indications that I was not the president at least some of the Board wanted, but this was the most overt, again a bit like the Chinese water-torture. Feeling somewhat persecuted myself, I talked to our counsel, in confidence I thought, about my fear that some of the Board members were anxious to get rid of me. To my astonishment he went immediately to those members and told them of my fears. I was told in no uncertain terms that there was absolutely "no conspiracy," and that I could fight for my job if I wanted to. Since I had already spent a most unhappy year and a half in the position it was an easy decision: I decided to make everyone happy and resign.

In all fairness, I have to say that the members of the ARS Board of Directors who were eager to see that I did not finish out my term as president were undoubtedly absolutely convinced that they were doing the right thing. I was a re-active rather than an active president, often in despair, rushing from crisis to crisis and trying to keep a finger in the dike, rather than entertaining and encouraging visions for the future as I was expected to do. It was probably a good thing that I had the sense to resign. When I announced this decision at the next Board meeting, in February, 1990, there was an immediate clearing of the air. Everyone was suddenly cooperative, and we began to work together as a Board again. The usual Board matters were taken care of. Ben Dunham was welcomed as editor of AR and the *Newsletter*. Louise Austin took over as chair of the chapter committee, although by this time there wasn't really much more to do for chapters, and we have pretty much left them alone since.

At the end of the February Board meeting Scott Paterson was good enough to inform me that the "forward-looking" faction had anointed him; he was to be the next president. My reaction was immediate: I was not going to let this happen. From that moment on I started on a resolute campaign to get the candidate of my choice, Connie Primus, into the presidency. First I had to persuade her—this was no small endeavor. Connie knew how difficult the position was; she was not at all anxious to take it. Finally I convinced her that the ARS would fall apart completely if she did not take over. Then I had to convince the other members of the Board of Directors. I embarked on a strenuous campaign, conducted by the slow medium of the U.S. mail in those days, and actually succeeded in getting a majority of the members of the Board to vote for her after I had officially resigned at the end of the fall 1990 Board meeting. The "other faction" accepted the results of the election graciously, and the '90s had begun. Connie Primus was the new president. Other appointments included Valerie Horst as vice president, Gene Murrow as treasurer, Judy Whaley as education chairwoman, and Judith Linsenberg as chairwoman of professional affairs. One of the innovations Judith Linsenberg brought about was the institution of the ARS CD club, which handles CDs made by professional members of the ARS, advertising them in a full-page ad in each issue of AR. Members may buy these CDs at a discounted price of $17, non-members for $20.

At the fall 1990 meeting Mary Maarbjerg was re-appointed and Gene Murrow, who was to assume an important role in the affairs of the ARS, was appointed to the Board. Connie ran the ARS for the next four years.

CHAPTER SEVEN

Afterword: the '90s and Beyond. More changes, and politics galore.

The ARS did not come to an end after its 50th birthday, nor did my involvement. I remained on the Board of Directors of the ARS for two years after my resignation, but the heavy duties fell upon Connie, who easily met my expectations for wise direction of the Society in times of crisis just as profound as mine. But lots of good things happened.

Although the ARS had ceased to endorse summer workshops and finally almost got out of the workshop business altogether, we retained a program of benefits for workshop members, later called "workshop affiliation." The $10 fee for a workshop listing in the magazine was soon rescinded. Any workshop that wanted to be listed could submit the information to AR. All this was to finally exclude any possibility of "accreditation" by the ARS. We would

ARS Presidents Martha Bixler and Connie Primus, 1992.

report on workshops, but that was all. The ARS continued giving scholarships through its various scholarship funds to these workshops and it still does.

Under the able chairmanship of Marilyn Boenau the **professional affairs committee** of the ARS finally began doing more for its professional players in the '90s. Recording grants were given to Nina Stern, Judy Linsenberg, and Alison Melville. While not covering all of their expenses, this aid from the ARS gave all of these players a leg up on their careers. In 1992 the ARS started subsidizing personal advertisements for professional members in *Musical America*. At the Boston Early Music Festival of 1993 the ARS started showcasing young professionals in short concerts called "Recorder Relays," which have continued at BEMF and the Berkeley Festivals ever since.

Ben Dunham continued to add new features to the magazine, among them a column by Pete Rose entitled "On the Cutting Edge," in which he wrote, most interestingly, about what was new in the recorder world. In 1992 Ben printed Pete's extremely informative overview of developments in the avant-garde that had transpired during the previous 40 years. Other new features in AR in the '90s included articles on electronic keyboards and wind instruments as well as electronic communication and music programs. The September 1991 issue focused on young professional recorder players in Europe and America. The editor also devoted part of the "Tidings" section to "Professional Potpourri."

In 1990 two new American music festivals appeared on the early music scene. The San Antonio Performing Arts Association announced a **San Antonio Early Music Festival** on May 7–13, 1990, with 35 concerts, a trade fair, master classes and a symposium.

A new **Berkeley Festival and Exhibition** took place on the Berkeley University campus, June 10–17, 1990. Planned to feature opera, dance, and early music, and a major exhibition of instrument makers, it was similar to the Boston Festival but smaller. Emphasis at this festival was more on performance than exhibition. At the first festival the featured performance, with the Philharmonia Baroque Orchestra, was Handel's *La Resurrezione*. Also featured were Tom Binkley's production of the original medieval *Carmina Burana* (lots of writhing on the floor) and Marion Verbruggen performing with Musica Antiqua Köln. The Berkeley Festival was held in all the even-numbered years since, alternating with the Boston Festival, until 2004 when it ran out of funding. A smaller, but very successful conference, on "the future of Early Music in America," sponsored by Early Music America, and a mini-concert series, "Berkeley Early Music on the Fringe," took its place.

In the summer of 1991 the ARS presented the Distinguished Achievement Award to former president Shelley Gruskin at the Boston Early Music Festival. Connie Primus, our new president, was the presenter. Shelley's years as president of the American Recorder Society from 1980–1988 were, as Connie stated in her presenting speech:

> . . . years of stability and growth for our organization. During this time the annual President's Appeal was established. Benefits have included a membership survey, workshop scholarships, chapter grants, the commission of a work by Ezra Laderman, and two recording grants.

Although Shelley might perhaps be considered a figurehead president, he was certainly inspirational, and he enjoyed the benefits of a dedicated group at headquarters, both paid and unpaid, and headed by Wonderful Waddy, who carried on the work of the expansion of the Society. Another development in Shelley's years was the formation of the various committees that steered ARS policy. They made the job of president many times easier than it had been in my day. I look back on the '80s with considerable nostalgia. They were in many ways the best years of the ARS.

In October of 1991 President Connie Primus made the first transfer of ARS historical materials to the University of Colorado (CU) in

Boulder for its American Music Research Center (AMC), which was under the directorship of Dr. William Kearns. This was the beginning of the ARS Archive. Previously, because of the foresight of CU's Dr. Gordon Sanford, working with Winifred Jaeger of Seattle, the Erich Katz Archive had been transferred to the AMC. In 2005 both the ARS Archive and the Erich Katz Archive were moved to the Recorder Music Center at Regis University in Denver, under the auspices of Dr. Mark Davenport, son of LaNoue Davenport. The Recorder Music Center has become the official repository for the American Recorder Society papers and related archival materials.

The 1992 President's Appeal brought in $14,000 in contributions to the ARS. These funds were used, in part, for chapter grants ($1,000), the President's scholarship to a summer workshop, chapter information packets, and representation at the EMA conference and a panel discussion and reception at the second Berkeley Festival in June, 1992.

The first "Play-the-Recorder Day" was announced with a certain amount of fanfare for March 28, 1992. Chapters and individuals were encouraged to organize special events to recruit members. About 200 people joined the ARS on that day. The Houston Historical Instrument Society led all chapters by recruiting 16 new ARS members. The chapter was awarded a Yamaha bass recorder, donated by Courtly Music, Unlimited, a music-and-instrument business. A second Yamaha bass recorder, donated by the Yamaha Corporation of America, went to the new Cuesta College chapter in San Luis Obispo, California. They added 11 new members to the ARS. A children's group from Winthrop, Maine also added 11 new members.

Besides gaining new members for the ARS, National Play-the-Recorder Day activities succeeded in spreading the ARS "message" far and wide. The Associated Press sent an article about ARS activities to over 1,000 newspapers around the country. Many local media outlets ran stories about local chapters and gave radio and television coverage to local groups. Station KLBJ in Austin, Texas, interviewed ARS

Executive Director Alan Moore in a live hook-up, and in southeastern Massachusetts, Continental Cablevision carried a four-hour phone-in marathon hosted by *AR* editor Ben Dunham. Guests included Friedrich and Ingeborg von Huene. The National Play-the-Recorder Day was Alan Moore's idea, one of his good ones. "Play the Recorder Month"—the month of March—with many chapters organizing successful ventures, continues to this day. Free recorders, raffles, and competitions for the most imaginative events held by chapters have been the incentives for new members. Sometimes publicity packets are sent to chapters with posters, ARS T-shirts to sell, and coloring books for a coloring contest for children. And many chapters have held special events.

In the '90s Board meetings began to be held "out of town," in places like Chicago, Baltimore, and Denver, enabling Board members to interact with members of the ARS outside of the New York area, and, finally, erasing some of the stigma that was attached to the doings of the "New York gang." Meetings were often hosted by chapters, and the annual meeting introduced many to the Board who might never have gotten to know them otherwise. This was a very big change. In 1991 the September Board meeting was held in Chicago. At this meeting annual dues for an individual were raised to $30 and we declared ourselves in good financial shape. (Dues for individuals were raised to $40 in 2000.) The final meeting of "my" Board, in February, 1992, was in the New York area again. The fall, 1992 meeting was held in Princeton, NJ, with new Board members Nancy van Brundt, Jack Anderson, Judith Linsenberg, Judith Whaley, and Nikolaus von Huene.

At this fall meeting, although I was again host to several out of town members of the Board, including President Connie Primus, I was suddenly informed that I was not invited to the Princeton meeting. Indeed, by this time my term was up, but I had been in the habit, heretofore, as had Valerie Horst and others, of attending Board meetings in New York simply as a non-voting interested bystander. This rejection was a rude shock, but somehow in keeping with things that

Peter Seibert and Connie Primus, 1980.

Scott Paterson and Judy Linsenberg at ARS Board Meeting in Seattle, WA, 1993.

had gone before. Undoubtedly the new ruling, that only current Board members could attend the meetings, was not intended to keep me away, but in my paranoid way I assumed that it was.

Subsequent Board meetings were held in Seattle (September 1993), Baltimore (February, 1994), and Toronto (November 1994). The first telephonic Board meeting was held in February, 1995, and since then a number of the Board meetings have been telephonic. The September–October 1995 meeting was in Denver at the new headquarters. The February meeting was telephonic again.

For the four years 1992–1996, the last two of Connie Primus's presidency and the first two of Gene Murrow's, I was somewhat "out of the loop," although the ARS continued to make demands upon me. I was very much involved with the Members' Library and the education committee, of which I was still a member. During the1990s the committee continued to tweak the education program of the ARS. In 1991 the Study Guides for Level I. II, and III were revised once again, producing a "Study Guide Handbook," available to all members. This was an ambitious project, containing scales, arpeggios, examples of melodic and rhythmic patterns, examples of Renaissance divisions, music lists, and a bibliography of reference books. At the Seattle Board meeting in September 1993, the education committee decided, and the board approved, that $50 each should be paid to the two evaluators of each Level III exam and consequently the fee for taking the exam would be raised to $100. A fee of $10 was instituted for those taking Level I and Level II exams.

In July, 1993 an interesting new organization, The American Recorder Teachers Association, was started at the first North American Recorder Teachers' Conference and Performers' Seminar run by Marie-Louise Smith at Indiana University. This was intended to be "a support network for recorder teachers that could also act as an advocate and source of information for recorder pedagogy." [From *The Recorder Education Journal* No. 1, 1995.] During the 1994 Conference a formal structure was created, The American Recorder Teachers Association, or ARTA, with co-chairs, committees, and a *Newsletter* editor. The organization had its ups and downs but under the determined leadership of, first Bruce Larkin, later Sue Groskreutz, who became president in 1997, and later LaVerne Sargent (2008), it thrived until 2010 when the state of Illinois shut it down as a 501 (c) 3 organization, as they had no "major accomplishments" to show.

ARTA published an informative, timely, and scholarly journal, *The Recorder Education Journal*, under the editorship of David Lasocki and Eva Legêne. ARTA supported a chat-line and put out a *Newsletter* in which many of the members' problems with teaching, choosing instruments etc., were discussed. Over the years the ARS and ARTA discussed the possibilities of joining forces, but their differing goals and the fears of one organization being taken over by the other have prevented any kind of affiliation. Since ARTA dues were small ($20) there was no hardship for individuals wishing to belong to both organizations. Finally the time, patience and energies of those devoted individuals who were keeping it afloat burned out. It was a great organization and its demise is a loss to everyone interested in teaching the recorder.

In 1993 the ARS education committee again involved itself with teacher certification. After a great deal of e-mail discussion among the members of the committee, we created certification requirements for teachers of both Levels II and III. The Level II applicant was to have "passed the Level II examination and have the expertise to teach all the material in the ARS Personal Study Program Levels I and II and in the Junior Recorder Society Leader's Resource Notebook. At least two years of recorder teaching experience would be expected." The Level III applicant was expected, of course, to have passed the Level III exam and have the expertise to teach all of the materials in the ARS Personal Study Program Levels I, II, and III. Three years' experience in teaching all levels of students in both private lessons and classes was required.

A $100 application fee was required of all who wished to take the exam at either level. The candidate also had to submit a résumé, letters of recommendation from students and colleagues, and a video- or audio-cassette of him/herself teaching a private lesson or a group. The candidate then was to take an open book exam with questions on music theory, recorder technique, and recorder repertoire and pedagogy, including teaching methods. In 1992 Betty Parker, a teacher of elementary school children in Santa Fe, was made a "Level II Teacher" upon submission to the education committee of a nearly perfect exam and an absolutely charming audio tape showing clearly how much she was giving to her children, instilling into them not only knowledge but a love of music and the recorder. In spite of other attempts, no other candidate has passed the examination for either

Level II or a Level III Teacher's Certificate, although by 1993 22 players had passed the Level III exam.

In 2000 the Education Committee tried to set up an alternative way to get teacher certification without satisfying all of the requirements. From the May, 2000 *Newsletter*:

> Criteria that will be considered by the Education Committee in granting exemptions from the full certification process include:
> 1. Institutions attended and degrees earned.
> 2. [Names of] recorder teachers of the applicant,
> 3. Positions held by the applicant,
> 4. Workshops where the applicant teaches or has taught.
> 5. Accomplishments of the applicant's students,
> 6. Recordings by the applicant.

The applicant was also required to be a member of the ARS, and had to submit a $20 fee.

The first and only applicant for teacher's certification in this "alternate" way was a person so controversial that she provoked an animated e-mail discussion among education committee members both for and against even considering her application. However, she had submitted a video-tape with her application, even though it was not required, and this was so very bad that it immediately disqualified her from any possible consideration. Nobody else has applied for either the "regular" or "alternate" method of attaining the ARS teacher's certificate since.

Political turmoil redux; Connie's ordeal

On January 1, 1993, a significant change occurred in the infrastructure of the ARS. The office was moved from New York City, where it had been since the very beginning, to Jackson, New Jersey. The idea was to save money on expensive New York rents, which we did, and to make it convenient for Executive Director Alan Moore to commute to work. Many of the Board members, always suspicious of Alan's motives, feared that this might tempt him to slack off, and unfortunately, their fears were realized. Alan cut down drastically on his hours in the office, claiming that he was working at home. It became more and more difficult to get an answer when telephoning the ARS office. Telephoning was still our chief method of communication, and it was particularly annoying for out-of-town board members not to get a live answer.

I am not in the know as to exactly how this happened, but things went from bad to worse between Alan and the members of the Board of Directors of the ARS. At the Seattle Board meeting in September Alan was "let go," and Sheila MacRae, a member of the Princeton Chapter who had been much involved with chapter affairs, was made temporary executive director while a search for a new executive director was quickly organized. This time the search was much easier than in the past, however, as electronic communication was already so well established in this country. After a four-month search headed by Nik von Huene, the ARS hired Gail Littleton, an arts administrator at Texas Tech University. Gail was eminently qualified: she holds two music degrees from Texas Tech, was/is an active performer on both recorder and flute, had served on the Mayor's Task Force on the Arts, and had hosted a bi-weekly public affairs and classical music radio show on KOHM-FM. She also possessed a familiarity with publicity (she had been publicity director for the Texas Tech School of Music) and grant writing. In addition she was/is totally computer-savvy. One surprising fact was that Gail had never heard of the American Recorder Society but, once acquainted with it, she became determined that more recorder players should know of its existence and that we should gain many more members—a nice determination in an executive director! Gail was introduced to the Board of Directors of ARS at the February, 1993 Board meeting in Baltimore, so that the whole Board could interview her. One of Gail's choices for a new location was Denver, where her mother lived. This made sense for the ARS, as

ARS Board Meeting, 1995. Left to right, front row: Gail Nickless, Judy Linsenberg, Connie Primus, Nancy VanBrundt, Peggy Monroe. Back row: Nikolaus von Huene, Gene Murrow, Valerie Horst, Jack Anderson, Judy Whaley, Scott Paterson, Ben Dunham, editor, AR.

President Connie Primus lived there, and there were four active chapters in Colorado. Miraculously, Gail, while not footloose, was fancy-free, and she was not only willing but happy to make the move.

Gail was a real find, another of the ARS saviors, and living proof that sometimes we could do something right. But Connie's difficulties were not yet over. She had to deal first with the fact that Sheila MacRae, who had managed to antagonize a number of people, including members and ex-members of the Board, had assumed that she would be the next executive director, and more or less refused to take no for an answer. It fell to Connie Primus and Ben Dunham to leave the Board meeting a day early in order to rush to Jackson, NJ to pack up the ARS office before Sheila could get there to prevent them. Connie and Ben sent the office materials to Denver, where Connie ran the ARS for six weeks from her home while Gail finished her job in Texas and then with Gail while our new executive director was being broken in. New office space was eventually found in Littleton, Colorado. This made a nice gloss on Gail's name, but she turned out not to be really fancy-free, after all; in May, 1995 Gail Littleton became Gail Nickless (Mrs. Wayne Nickless). Her assistant was Karen Voigt, a student of Connie's, who became membership secretary.

Significant events in 1994

In June the Berkeley Festival featured Jordi Savall and Marion Verbruggen. In August the Utrecht Festival had a recorder symposium. The first annual "Recorder Academy" at Indiana University gave 18 talented young players instruction from some of the top professionals in the world, headed by Eva Legêne. On June 11, 1994 the ARS presented its Distinguished Achievement Award to Nobuo Toyama, a Japanese engineer and pioneer in the manufacture of plastic recorders, and CEO of the Toyama Musical Instrument Company in Japan.

Toyama was the manufacturer of Aulos recorders, which entered the U.S. market in the late 1960s and revolutionized the recorder industry and recorder playing both here and abroad. Aulos recorders were the first decent plastic recorders ever made, cheaper, more durable, better in tune and more reliable than inexpensive wooden ones. Toyama was soon imitated by Yamaha, another Japanese instrument maker who produced inexpensive plastics that were better in tune, easier to take care of, more pleasant sounding, and easier to play than the Auloses. Toyama immediately improved its various models, and other makers like the Zen-On Music Company began making their own. Soon amateur players found themselves playing on "chests of recorders" that were entirely plastic. There is no question that Mr. Toyama was instrumental in a recorder revolution and deserved the DAA given by

ARS President Connie Primus presents the ARS Distinguished Achievement Award to Nobuo Toyama, surrounded by his family in Berkeley, CA, 1994

the ARS. I am told that this occasion was one of the most gala presentations of the ARS Distinguished Achievement Award, with Mr. Toyama and all his family from Japan in attendance. He died at the age of 75 on January 17, 1995.

Other happenings: Ben Dunham decided that beginning in September, 1994, AR and the *Newsletter* would henceforth appear five times a year at two-month intervals, except during the months of June, July, and August. This would give him a real vacation in the summer, which was reasonable. Of course there was more money in it for him as well.

10 scholarships were awarded by the ARS to individuals attending summer workshops. All were funded by the Andrew Acs Memorial Fund.

In September of 1994 Connie Primus, having served a valiant four years, stepped down from the presidency and Gene Murrow, who had been appointed to the Board in 1990, and had acted as treasurer from 1992 to 1994, was selected president for two years, then re-selected for another four. Gene had been a tremendous asset to the Board from the beginning of his tenure. It was Jenny Lehmann, who had known him at Pinewoods Camp, who first suggested that he be appointed. I offered a quick second, wondering why I hadn't thought of him myself. I had known Gene since he was a 19-year-old oboe student, and had hired him on the recommendation of his teacher Lois Wann, to teach recorder to beginners at Pinewoods Chamber Music Week. Lois was traveling to Europe with her husband that summer. Eric Leber and I, who were running Chamber Music Week (as it was then called) together at Pinewoods, needed a replacement fast. Gene set about teaching himself to play, and he was a great success. He soon integrated himself completely into the Country Dance Society, which ran Pinewoods Camp. He learned to dance, and he learned how to play the concertina as well as the recorder. Like Eric, he soon became proficient as both a musician and a dancer. When he assumed the presidency of ARS he had served three years as director of Early Music Week at Pinewoods Camp. Added to his musical skills were his high intelligence, his business and executive skills (he was a partner in Constructive Systems of Ossining, New York), his outgoing personality, and his astonishing powers of persuasion. While still new to the Board he was able to arbitrate disputes between Alan Moore and Ben Dunham that had threatened to become ugly. He was a natural for president of the American Recorder Society.

Gene Murrow, 1995.

    Other officers chosen by the ARS Board of Directors for their adminis-trative staff were: Valerie Horst, continuing vice president, executive director of Amherst Early Music; Scott Paterson, continuing secretary, chair of the wind department at the Royal Conservatory of Music in Toronto; new treasurer Nancy van Brundt, a former president of the ARS Chicago chapter; continuing assistant secretary Peggy Monroe, a founding member of the Early Music Guild in Seattle and an active professional recorder and percussion player; and continuing assistant treasurer Nikolaus von Huene, sales manager of the Von Huene Workshop, Inc. The Board meeting that September was held in Scott's home town, Toronto, and hosted by the Toronto chapter of the ARS, the Toronto Early Music Players' Organization (TEMPO). The September meeting was the first Board meeting for Gail Littleton.

The February, 1995 Board meeting was held as a conference telephone call, the first but by no means the last time this method has been used for a Board meeting. It lasted three hours.

Significant events at the Boston Early Music Festival in June 1995

The ARS finally gave the Distinguished Achievement Award to LaNoue Davenport on June 16 at a reception after a concert at the Boston Early Music Festival by Han Tol. Thus two of the greats were honored—the old and the young. LaNoue, who had felt passed over in earlier years, gave a particularly gracious speech of acceptance. Also at BEMF that year ARS President Gene Murrow and I gave classes for beginners, who, if they joined the American Recorder Society on the spot, received free recorders and method booklets. That year also Han Tol conducted both a Recorder Orchestra session and a master class, and the ARS held its becoming-traditional "Great Recorder Relay" featuring young emerging professional recorder players. One more event of note sponsored by the ARS was a day-long jazz recorder festival.

In June of 1996 I was presented with the Distinguished Achievement

Award at the Berkeley Festival. It was a really nice presentation, at an outdoor reception after Dan Laurin's concert. Gene Murrow made the presentation, and Connie Primus made a lovely speech. I very much appreciated this gesture on the part of the ARS, which came as a complete surprise. It had been rumored right after I declared my intention to resign as president, then retracted, then apparently forgotten. Of course it was gratifying to have my efforts on behalf of the ARS as well as my contributions to the recorder world from the "early days" of the '50s recognized!

In the spring of 1996, having taken temporary leave of my senses, I was persuaded to run once again for the ARS Board of Directors. I was still involved with committee work, and it did not seem as though I would be adding too much to my burdens to go to one or two Board meetings a year. I wondered why so few of the incumbent Board members were running again and after a few months I thought I had figured out why. This was the beginning of the age of e-mail letters; everyone was discovering how handy electronic mail was for communication, quicker and more reliable than snail mail, and in many ways easier than phone calls. We Board members were smothered in e-mails that took the place of face-to-face meetings. Sometimes this was a blessing; often it was a curse. Endless discussion via e-mail sometimes took the place of action. And this form of communication generated a lot of paper. I once took a great sheaf of e-mail communications with me to a workshop in California, left it at the home of my host, and never really retrieved the thread of discussion after that.

However, at the first meeting of the new Board of Directors of the ARS in September 1996 in Dallas, Texas, things seemed rosy indeed to the "class of 2000," as our president called us. Gene Murrow, one of only two "old" members on the Board, ran a brilliant meeting, insisting that we spend a morning getting to know one another before choosing our officers and the chairmen of the various committees. We persuaded Gene, who had already been president for two years, to continue in that office for another four, and we chose Judy Whaley, the other "continuing" member of the Board, as our vice president. The choice of Judy was particularly felicitous, as she later, during Gene's illness, found herself running the Recorder Society. Judy was also education chairwoman during this time and an exceedingly conscientious and hardworking one. Shelley Wold, who started out taking minutes, was a natural for secretary. Shelley had been a librarian and instructor of library science and her tidy mind and organizational abilities soon become obvious. Shelley was also chairwoman of the **scholarship committee**.

We did not have an obvious treasurer, but Israel Stein, a piano technician who had recently moved from Boston to California and had been active with the ARS on both coasts, agreed to act as assistant treasurer. Israel also took on the chairmanship of **chapters and consorts**. Virginia Ebinger, a former president of the American Orff-Schulwerk Association, seemed the perfect person to revive the **Junior Recorder Society**. Cléa Galhano, the vivacious and talented Brazilian recorder player who was/is also a dedicated teacher, was perfect for **special events/professional outreach**. Frances Feldon was made chairwoman of the **publications committee**. I sat on my hands when Gene made the call for volunteers to chair the various committees, but I continued as an active member of the education and the **Junior Recorder Society** committees. I was also on the **scholarship committee**, which meant helping to decide who should get scholarships for the summer and weekend workshops. I remained on this committee until 2012.

Gail Nickless prepared a very useful notebook for each new member of the Board with sections for various aspects of Board business: meetings, finances, reports of the president and executive director, and of the committee chairs. Among the sections was one entitled "Policy Book," a section containing various important decisions of the Board like: "The birth date of the ARS is established as April 1, 1939," and beside it the date this decision was made (9/30/88). The policy book has proved very useful over time, and has been continued up to the present.

In November, 1996 the education committee under the chairmanship of Judith Whaley issued a "Personal Study Program" to be given to all new members of the ARS and any other members who asked for it. This had three parts: a "Personal Study Program in Thirteen Stages to Help You Improve Your Playing," a checklist geared to the requirements for ARS Achievement Exams for self-directed study and also as a guide toward self-rating for classes and workshops, which was free to members; the ongoing "ARS Music Lists and Reference Materials for Levels I, II, and III," which not only listed music for the prepared repertoire for exams but also for guidance on purchasing music for personal use; and a "Guidebook to the ARS Personal Study Program," an expanded version of the Study Guide. There was a charge of $8 and $11, respectively, for the latter two. It seemed a pity to have to ask members to pay for these publications, but the ARS could no longer afford to give this kind of thing away free.

In 1997 the sputtering **Junior Recorder Society** was brought to life by our new and able Board member, Virginia Ebinger, who had been head of the American Orff-Schulwerk Association. Gin Ebinger formed a committee consisting of Elaine Clancy; Mary Halverson Waldo, a Suzuki recorder teacher; Cléa Galhano, a new member of the ARS Board of Directors, a brilliant recorder player from Brazil, and a dedicated teacher of recorder; Connie Primus; and me. We worked like maniacs in the waning years of the decade, putting together (partly by

Virginia Ebinger, 1991.

revising earlier work) three volumes of three issues of Junior Recorder Society *Newsletters*, as a three-year enrichment supplement, for use in public and private school classes, church and temple activities, and recorder clubs in an ongoing course of study. Each volume is devoted to a different area of recorder playing. Each *Newsletter* in each volume contains a Leaders' Guide, with suggestions for activities, information about the music and the composers, a list of other resources, and further bibliography, as well as a section directed to the students themselves with the actual music, illustrations, background information, and suggestions for performance. There are also ARS "buttons," part of the program from the beginning, and stickers for the children, to be used by the leaders in any way they like.

Volume 1 is concerned with folk music, the usual starting point of recorder playing by both children and adults. The first *Newsletter* in this volume deals with European music, the second with music native to the Americas, and the third with music of Africa, Asia, and Australia. The second volume deals with the recorder in history: "Music of the Middle Ages," "Music of the Renaissance," and "Music of the Baroque." Volume 3, "Music in the Modern Age," was in some ways the most difficult and in other ways the most fun to put together. The first *Newsletter* in this volume ("Modern Recorder Music") introduces children very gently to modern music (Bela Bartók, Erich Katz), the second is titled "Blues, Rags, and Jazz." The third issue, "Avant-garde music," presented a real challenge to the committee because we first had to study this subject for ourselves. We did, however, manage to come up with some truly avant-garde music that children could actually play, and a glossary of avant-garde terms.

The plan, which could be used loosely, was for the children to receive Newsletters at intervals during the school year, and to implement the activities suggested therein. It was hoped that by having some useful, well-organized material for presentation we would be able to get members for the Junior Recorder Society and see clubs or classes scattered throughout the country.

But instead of being bound into good-looking booklets the material was simply printed on loose-leaf paper and put into a notebook called a Leader's Resource Notebook. The rest of the notebook, indeed the bulk of it, consists of articles of interest to recorder teachers and leaders, some reprints of articles originally published in *American Recorder* and other educational publications, some written especially for the Junior Recorder Society. Topics include a short history of the recorder, four different approaches to recorder teaching, suggestions for "getting started," recorder technique, "tips for teachers," suggestions for the classroom and for recorders in religious settings, consort playing, and "beyond the notes,"—suggestions for ornamentation, composition, and playing dance music etc. There is also an extremely helpful chapter on resources: music, recorders, and reference materials.

All in all, an enormous effort was put into producing the notebook, which is available to ARS member teachers or leaders for $20, $40 for non-members. Membership in the Junior Recorder Society is $5. The material for children is attractive and very well thought out. The material for adults is extensive and helpful. But poor packaging and the lack of the right kind of promotion meant that we never brought in enough new members to the Junior Recorder Society to make it all worth the effort. There have never been more than a dozen Junior Recorder Society clubs in the country. Later members of the American Society Board of Directors tried to find better ways to produce and publicize this material and to attract new members, but finally decided too much revision would be necessary to put out an attractive package.

In addition to my labors for the Junior Recorder Society I found myself the self-appointed chairman, for a while, of a senior citizens committee. I tried to get a discount for membership for seniors, and when that turned out not to be feasible financially for the ARS, I dedicated myself for many months to trying to organize an Elderhostel program for beginning senior recorder players. There was already a summer Elderhostel recorder program for seniors called "Canto Antiguo," run by Shirley Robbins at the Thacher School in Ojai, California. At first I mistakenly thought Elderhostel programs were initiated by the Elderhostel administration in Boston but found out, finally, after many attempts to communicate with the Elderhostel brass, that Elderhostels were initiated by those wanting to run the programs themselves, and were overseen by regional directors.

I tried very hard to get Elderhostels for senior recorder players going at one of the several colleges in Rochester, NY, and at Franklin Pierce College in Rindge, New Hampshire, but was discouraged in Rochester by the promise of many meetings with the regional Elderhostel coordinator in Syracuse, and also an enormous amount of paperwork involved in setting up the program, and at Franklin Pierce by broken promises from the Elderhostel program director. However, others accomplished what I failed to do. Jennifer Barron ran a successful summer recorder workshop for Seniors at Holy Cross College in Worcester, Mass., and the "Canto Antiguo" workshop, now held at Chapman University in Orange, CA, (although it is no longer associated with Elderhostel) is still going strong. The sixth annual Elderhostel Recorder/Early Music Workshop was held November 6–12 and 13–19 2005 at the Hidden Valley Arts Institute in Carmel Valley, California.

During my four years on the Board of Directors of the ARS in the '90s I, like the other members of the Board, was swept up in a grand new capital campaign headed by our president, Gene Murrow. Like just about everyone else on the planet, we were somewhat awed and inspired by the fact that the world was entering a new millennium, and we thought we could create our own splash to go along with it. Gene was creative and inspiring, and soon we were all caught up in the idea that maybe this time we could actually raise some money and put the many activities of the ARS on a solid financial footing. In December, 1996 Gene persuaded Mel Mendelson, a professional fund-raiser, to be a member of our Board. At the February, 1997 meeting (another telephonic meeting, this time four and a half hours long!) Mel presented a plan for yet another capital campaign, but this one was to be more carefully thought out than any we had tried heretofore. At the September meeting, held in Judy Whaley's home town of Kalamazoo, we talked about almost nothing but the campaign, which we dubbed A.R.S Nova 2000. Gene created a Long-Range Planning Committee (I was on it, of course) that was to come up with a serious plan for what we would do with the money raised, and we launched a Capital Campaign to coincide with the 60th anniversary of the ARS in 1999. Besides thinking rosy thoughts about our financial future, we also elected newly appointed Howard Gay, a certified public accountant, to be our treasurer, relieving Israel Stein of his duties as interim treasurer. And we approved a handsome new logo designed for the ARS by Sheila Fernekes, a member of the Princeton, N.J. chapter (later a member of the ARS Board of Directors) to be used on all ARS communications, as well as on ARS T-shirts, mugs, and tote bags.

Then began lots of meetings, conferences, and the new trendy "focus groups" to plan the A.R.S. Nova campaign. Gene hired a facilitator named Cathy Robbins, Executive Director of the Chamber of Commerce Foundation in Colorado, who planned to conduct focus groups all over the country ("What do you want the American Recorder Society to do for you? What can you do for the American Recorder Society?"), then conduct a final focus group in Berkeley, California, where the September 1998 Board meeting was to be located. She was also to "lead the ARS Board in a retreat featuring in-depth discussions and prioritization of the feedback gathered in the regional focus meetings." With the self-assessment phase of the project completed, Robbins and an ARS long-range planning task force, comprised of current and former ARS Board members and other leaders, was to write an action plan. That document, once approved by both the task force and accepted by the ARS Board, was to become the basis for a well-organized resource development effort to "fund those projects considered most important by recorder players." [From the ARS *Newsletter*, September, 1998].

In the summer of 1998 I suddenly couldn't stomach any of this. I didn't see any point in any of the focus groups and I could not bear the idea of a retreat, of all things, where I was sure nothing substantive could possibly happen in the attempt to raise money for the ARS. In a fit of pique I resigned from the Board, mainly so I would not have to go to that Berkeley meeting. Mel Mendelson, who had by that time become disenchanted with the way his efforts were superseded by those of Cathy Robbins, also resigned at about the same time. Another Board member was appointed in my place, but I was in fact persuaded to get back on again, as sort of an eleventh member! But at least I missed the Berkeley retreat.

One important thing that happened during that Berkeley Board meeting in 1998 was a move to initiate a change in the bylaws of the ARS to allow for biennial elections of Board members and staggered four-year terms, providing the Board with more continuity. Staggered terms had always been impossible under the not-for-profit laws of New York State, but with the move to Denver it now became possible to have biennial elections, with only half of the Board at a time reaching the end of their terms. This change finally came about in 2000, when a few of us were persuaded to stay on the Board for two more years, and new elections were held in 2002. Finally we had a "staggered" Board, and were not faced with a possible situation in which all 10 members were ending their terms simultaneously.

Another good thing that happened that fall was that chapter rebates—that is, giving chapters a discount for new members who joined the ARS—were finally discontinued. I had never approved of the idea of "rewarding" chapters for bringing new members into the ARS when their members were supposed to be members of the ARS anyway. The rebates were introduced in the agenda and passed at one of the Board meetings when I was not on the Board, and I was glad to see them go.

Cathy Robbins was unsuccessful with the task she had assumed. After all the time she spent and all the money we paid her she came up with a short report with suggestions as to what we could do to satisfy our members. I believe it was about five pages long, and could have been prepared by any one of us in much less time.

There was nothing for it. The ARS Board itself had to buckle down and draw up a Long Range Plan. A much smaller committee consisting of Israel Stein, Gail Nickless and Gene Murrow worked extremely hard, and guessed at figures for a really super-duper plan that would raise tons of money and make all of our projects possible. I must say that here Gene was an inspiration because he really did make us all believe. At the ARS Board meeting of September 1999 President Gene appointed Ruth Albert of Cos Cob, Connecticut, to chair the A.R.S. Nova campaign. Ruth had been a realtor, and was an accomplished amateur musician and, most importantly, a volunteer but very talented money-raiser. She had just finished raising $1.5 million for a new library in Cos Cob.

Some Milestones of the '90s and 2000s

Jennifer Wedgwood Lehmann died of lung cancer on September 6, 1992. A granddaughter of the famous manufacturer of fine china, Josiah Wedgewood, Jennifer grew up in England and knew the Dolmetsch family. She attended preparatory school in the U.S.A., at the Putney School in Vermont, and Bryn Mawr and Radcliffe Colleges on the East Coast. Her B.A. degree in 1948 from Radcliffe was in mathematics. One of the first participants in the early music program administered at Sarah Lawrence by "Music for a While" (LaNoue Davenport, Sheila Schonbrun, Steven Silverstein, and Judith Davidoff) she received a Master of Fine Arts degree in early music performance from that institution in 1974.

She had lived in Princeton from 1954 until her death. A woman of many parts, Jennifer was employed by the Princeton University Computer Center from 1968 until 1979. She was an active volunteer reader for the blind and one of the founders of Princeton's Bryn Mawr Book Shop. Jennifer was best known to members of the ARS for her musical activities: she played the viola da gamba, bassoon, Renaissance reed instruments, and recorder professionally and semi-professionally. She taught recorder and was a devoted member of the American Recorder Society Board of Directors. One of her finest accomplishments was founding the ARS Members' Library Editions. Jennifer was also a loyal and very loving friend.

Howard Mayer Brown, a University of Chicago musicologist who was president of the ARS for a brief period in 1966, died on February 20, 1993 at the age of 62. Dr. Brown never really had much connection with the ARS except for his brief attempt at a presidency, but he was a musicologist who had a profound impact on the early music movement. One of his most important publications was *Performance Practice: Music Before 1600* (W.W. Norton, 1989), which he edited with Stanley Sadie.

One of the most important and influential figures in the 20th century revival of the recorder, **Carl Frédéric Dolmetsch**, died in July, 1997. He was 88 years old. Although he was born in France, Carl grew up in Haslemere, Surrey, England, and is strongly associated with the 20th century recorder movement in England. A son of the pioneering musical scholar, instrument maker, and early music revivalist Arnold Dolmetsch (1858–1940), Carl played a variety of instruments, including the viol, but is known best for his brilliant career as a recorder builder and performer in England and abroad. He gave his first full-length recital, with Joseph Saxby playing harpsichord, at the Wigmore Hall, London, in February, 1939. This was the first of his celebrated annual Dolmetsch Wigmore Hall recitals, at which he often played recorder pieces that he had himself commissioned by contemporary composers. Dolmetsch and Saxby (died June 23, 1997) played together in 40 of these recitals, and participated in 20 coast-to-coast American tours, as well as tours of Australia, New Zealand, Japan, North and South America, Alaska, Canada, and Europe.

Carl Dolmetsch and Edgar Hunt started the English Society of Recorder Players, with Max and Stephanie Champion, in 1937.

On October 6, 1957 the ARS (then mostly a New York organization) presented Dolmetsch and Saxby in a concert in New York City and also invited Dolmetsch to conduct a meeting of the ARS at the New York College of Music. Dolmetsch had by then been a noted performer for years and his instruments were household names. Professional recorder players in the U.S. were very partial to his instruments, particularly the altos. In those days one could buy a fine alto recorder by ordering one by mail from the Dolmetsch workshop in Haslemere, later receiving a bill for approximately $30.

Gerald Burakoff died at age 65 of a heart attack on January 6, 1998. Gerry was an instrumental music teacher in the public schools of Hicksville, Long Island who had the brilliant idea of getting his musically trained band members to learn to play the recorder as well as their flutes, clarinets, etc. These young people performed very impressively at MENC (Music Educators National Conference) meetings and wherever Gerry could find a venue. Gerry himself became very much interested in recorder pedagogy. He was a valuable member of the education committee of the ARS, and taught at his own and other ARS recorder workshops. In order to fill the demand for recorder methods for beginners, he started his own publishing firm, Consort Music, which became Sweet Pipes.

Fred Morgan, the remarkable Australian recorder maker whose instruments were sought by professional players the world over, was killed in an automobile accident near his home on April 16, 1999. Like Friedrich von Huene, Morgan made careful measurements and detailed drawings of surviving Baroque instruments in European museums. The success of his recorders at the first Bruges International Early Music

Competition in 1972 launched his career. In 1982 he visited the Rosenborg Castle in Denmark to measure and reproduce, for Eva Legêne, the two famous narwhal tusk recorders that are thought by some to be original "van Eyck" instruments. His very untimely death, at 59, was a great loss to the recorder world.

J.M. (John Mansfield) Thomson, founder and editor of the groundbreaking *Early Music* magazine from 1973 until 1983, died September 11, 1999 in his native New Zealand at the age of 73. As the founder of a journal devoted to the wider world of early music, Thomson was Sigrid Nagle's hero. She wanted desperately to turn The American Recorder into a journal like his, with scholarly articles as well as those conceived "for the masses." This brought about her downfall as editor of AR. Thomson, on the other hand, was extremely successful in his professional life as an editor, writer, and founding president of the National Early Music Association in the U.K. Like Fred Morgan, J.M. Thomson, although much acclaimed in England and Europe, felt the call of his homeland, and returned "down under" for the last 15 years of his life.

Gloria Berchielli, who "saved" the ARS in 1989, died in one of the first overt acts of terrorism directed against the United States—the crash of Egypt Air Flight 990 in October 1999. She was about to begin an Elderhostel trip in Egypt. This was a terrible end for the woman who did so much for the recorder world, not only the ARS but her own chapter, the Westchester Recorder Guild, and for the Country Dance Society as well. To the ARS she is still "Gloria in Excelsis," as we called her in one of our *Newsletters* when she came to our rescue after Waddy resigned.

LaNoue Davenport, my teacher and for years my mentor, died November 4, 1999, at the age of 77. He'd had a stroke and was very ill with emphysema when he died. One of his remarkable accomplishments after his stroke (in 1989) was to teach himself to use music publishing software on the computer with only one hand, and his father-son music publishing company, LaNDMark Press, continues with his son Mark to this day.

LaNoue began his musical career playing the trumpet with jazz bands in Texas before World War II, and in the Navy during it. After the war he came to New York to join his brother Pembroke in the world of pit bands and Broadway shows. The big change in his life came when he enrolled in the New York College of Music, where he became a protégé of Erich Katz. Although he was interested in all aspects of music, LaNoue found he had a prodigious talent for the recorder and an affinity for early music. In the words of LaNoue's son Mark:

> Those breaking new ground, such as LaNoue and Bernie Krainis, were simply left to their own intuition, musical aptitude, and musical ability to put what they had read in historical musical treatises into practice.

Both men had to invent for themselves the beautiful sounds they created on the recorder, and it is certainly possible that the jazz background of both contributed to their ability to do this. Hearing LaNoue play the recorder for the first time changed my life. I knew I had to study with him and do my best to imitate that gorgeous sound. I followed that Pied Piper to the end of his days.

Because of his association with Erich, LaNoue was drawn to the inner workings of the American Recorder Society. He was its *Newsletter* editor, and after the Society became incorporated he was its first president. After he joined the New York Pro Musica LaNoue had less time for the nitty-gritty doings of the ARS, but he always retained his loyalty to it and to amateur music making.

Bernard Krainis died on August 18, 2000. He was 75 years old. With LaNoue Davenport, Bernie was one of the "young Turks" of the '50s who met Erich Katz, got involved with the American Recorder Society, helped to found the New York Pro Musica, and became one of the giants of the recorder players of America in the mid-century. Like

LaNoue, he took his turn at being editor of the *Newsletter*, serving on the Board of the ARS, becoming president of the Society, and receiving the ARS Distinguished Achievement Award. As president of the ARS at the time (1989), I presented Bernie with the award and, as noted, he took the opportunity to voice, for the final time, all the reasons why he thought the ARS was falling down on its job of leading the recorder movement. By that time he was convinced that we were only interested in supporting the mediocre masses, and that we had no thought for improving the skills of the amateurs, as he did. The fascinating thing is that he was able to tell us how terrible we were with complete courtesy and impeccable manners.

Bernie himself was one of the first really professional recorder players in the United States. He performed widely, taught at various institutions and privately, and influenced hundreds of recorder players. There are many people today who still revere both his teaching and playing.

One thing that interests me is that despite the towering achievements of LaNoue Davenport and Bernard Krainis, they have left behind no "school" of American recorder players. There are plenty of us still living who can remember their wonderful playing and teaching, but with the exception of LaNoue's son Mark I can't think of any professional players who can trace their playing style back to either LaNoue or Bernie. Aspiring young people go to Europe to study, or they study with someone who has been to Europe to study. And the Europeans have come here in droves, bringing their "slant" to recorder playing in this country, which includes a virtuosic technique that is at times breathtaking. Bernie and LaNoue were not virtuosos, although they were often called that. Their legacy is different. They were jointly responsible for making the recorder-playing public aware of the possibilities for expressiveness on our instrument. A beautiful sound—what a concept! Believe me, this was brand-new in the '50s, and very, very exciting for those of us who were privileged to listen to and learn from them.

Manhattan Recorder Consort album cover, 1959. Left to right: LaNoue Davenport, Bernard Arnold (a student of LaNoue), Shelley Gruskin, Martha Bixler.

Bernard Krainis album cover, 1960s.

Medieval Jazz Quartet album cover, 1961. Left to right: LaNoue Davenport, Martha Bixler, Robert Dorough, Shelley Gruskin.

CHAPTER EIGHT

The Millennium —a very brief look

Unbelievably, when a new Board election came up in 2000, Frances Feldon, Cléa Galhano and I were persuaded to stay on for another two years in addition to the four years we had each already served; the reason given was to keep some continuity on the Board during its change from holding elections every four years to holding elections every two for staggered four-year terms. We joined continuing members Ruth Albert, Howard Gay, and John Nelson on the new Board. I was motivated by three factors: 1) Cléa and Frances had already agreed; 2) I really wanted to help get the Junior Recorder Society program geared up; and 3) frivolous as it now seems, Cléa had promised to get us all on *Prairie Home Companion* when the Board met in Minneapolis. I don't know what the motivations of the others were, but none of the three of us was terribly effective after the election. Frances disappeared almost completely; I was not able to do anything effective for JRS, although I tried; Cléa did keep her chairmanship of the **professional outreach committee**, which oversaw all recorder events at the early music festivals—the recorder relay, the recorder master class, the presentation of the Distinguished Achievement Award, the jazz improvisation classes, and panel discussions among professionals, but she never did get us on *Prairie Home Companion*.

At our September Board meeting there were few of us around who had even a clue as to the workings of the ARS, but luckily Gail Nickless was still with us as executive director, and she guided us through the meetings. Ever the power broker, I persuaded John Nelson to take over as president of the Society. Richard Carbone was vice president; Sheila Fernekes, secretary; Howard Gay, treasurer. Alan Karass was made chairman of **Chapters & Consorts**; Sheila Fernekes, **Education**; Janos Ungváry, **JRS** (served very briefly, having no clear direction as to what the job entailed); Frances Feldon, **Publications**; Carolyn Peskin, **Scholarship**. We still had Gene Murrow, we thought, as honorary chair, and Ruth Albert, as chair of A.R.S. Nova. Ruth had started in on her duties with high hopes. In her December 2000 report to the Board she was sanguine, having received material aid from Ben Dunham in organizing the campaign. As of December 2000, the ARS had received a total of $5,590 for the Fund, but she was still searching for donors who would be capable of gifts of $1000 each. The campaign was never a big success, and after we had raised a modest $30,000 in gifts and pledges Ruth resigned from both her post as chairwoman of A.R.S. Nova and the ARS Board in the summer of 2001, greatly disappointed over her lack of support from the Board and particularly from Gene, who had promised to help substantially in the campaign after he had resigned his presidency of the ARS and sold his business. This he was unable to do.

Membership in the ARS had been going down in the late '90s. We had 3,059 members in 1997. By 2002 we were down to 2,499 members. In that year, in a blow to the ARS, our magazine editor, Ben Dunham, left the Society to become editor of *Early Music America*. Gail Nickless expressed interest in becoming our new editor, and the Board of Directors thought that was a fine idea. But it meant that we were once again looking for an executive director.

Kathy Sherrick, a member of the Board of Directors of ARS, offered to step away from her membership on the Board and take over the administration of the Society. The office in Denver was dismantled and all materials taken to Kathy's residence in St. Louis, Missouri. Certainly, in view of the rapidly dropping membership, a restructuring of the ARS was necessary. The new administrative director of the American Recorder Society was able to tell me, in the summer of 2005, that the financial picture of the ARS had been stabilized and the ARS was on the road to financial recovery.

It is to be hoped that in its leaner form the ARS can maintain financial integrity while it continues with its essential programs. The scholarship program continues; so do chapter grants, and the activities of Play-the-Recorder-Month. A big step in the effort to give support to professional players was the establishment of a **professional development fund** by the Board of Directors at its February, 2005 meeting. This fund was proposed as a way to help support residents at the Sitka Center for Art and Ecology in Otis, Oregon. *American Recorder* (still of a high quality) and the *Newsletter* are still published four times a year. At its September 2005 meeting the Board of Directors decided to give up the idea of presenting the Junior Recorder Society materials in a better package. Too much revision would be necessary.

Mark Davenport, LaNoue's son and a professor of music at Regis

Mark Davenport, 2005, in front of the recorder display at the Grand Opening of the Recorder Music Center at Regis University, Denver, CO.

University, also founder and director of the Recorder Music Center at the University, was the next chairman of the education committee of the ARS, beginning in 2004. He worked to eliminate the exam-taking part of the education program as it had become too cumbersome and time-consuming for committee members and because there are now colleges and universities that offer accredited degrees and certificates in recorder more valid than the ARS Teaching Certificate. He also worked diligently toward his ongoing goal: using the resources of the American Recorder Society to help train music teachers who are teaching the recorder to children. Many of the materials developed over the previous decades by the Education Program committee members are now available on the ARS website as a service to the Society's members.

A major achievement for the ARS was the publication of the new *Consort Handbook* in January of 2006. This is a splendid volume. Some of the information in this book comes from articles previously published in *American Recorder*, (the English) *Recorder & Music Magazine* and other sources, and some is newly written. The publication of this handbook, which is especially designed for members or would-be members of consorts, had long been a cherished dream of the ARS. The material is arranged in five sections with sub-chapters: 1) suggestions for group interaction; 2) consort rehearsal technique; 3) gaining variety in consort playing; 4) public performance (this includes publicity and getting "gigs"); and 5) ensemble repertoire. Included are musical examples of what the various authors are talking about and a terrific bibliography.

On the bright note of this achievement I'll bring this history of the American Recorder Society to an end with the beginning of the new year in 2006. What will the future of the ARS be like? It will never be the organization every recorder player in the country *must* join, a situation we dreamed of in the heady years of the '80s; it will never be at the forefront in the education of recorder players, although it can certainly help. But it will always be *there* for the recorder players of America. I firmly believe it is because of the activities of the American

Recorder Society and its many devoted volunteer workers that so much more is known about the recorder now than 50 or 60 years ago, that so much music has been and is being published, that so many people play the recorder so much better, and that so many players, both professionals and amateurs, make use of its resources. We stand

ARS President Alan Karass presents the ARS Presidential Special Honor Award to Connie Primus in 2006 at the Berkeley Festival.

Connie Primus after receiving Presidential Special Honor Award with Valerie Horst, Ben Dunham, Berkeley, CA, 2006.

Gail Nickless, editor of AR magazine with Connie Primus, Berkeley, CA, 2006.

on the shoulders of those who came before us, and we must admire them for their achievements.

A Final Milestone

Suzanne Bloch, that fascinating, brilliant, talented, quirky, warmhearted, somewhat crazy lady and the founder of the American Recorder Society, died on January 29, 2002 at the age of 94. Suzanne was the daughter of the composer Ernest Bloch, and she was a great promoter of her father's work. Probably she was best known in American musical circles as a lutenist. She had studied that instrument with the antiquarian Arnold Dolmetsch in England, and after meeting Arnold's son Carl she become interested in the recorder as well. Suzanne taught at the Juilliard School from 1942 to 1985, and her ex-students remember her as demanding yet charming.

Born in Geneva in 1907, Suzanne came to New York with her family in 1916, when her father started teaching and conducting in America. She always spoke with a strong accent, talking very rapidly and in a very soft voice, which made interviewing her and trying to tape—and transcribe—the interview an absolutely maddening experience, particularly since everything she had to say was fascinating. Because of our mutual interest in the recorder Suzanne and I became personal friends in the 1970s. We also had a connection through our husbands. Hers was a mathematician, as mine was.

By the time I got to know her Suzanne had really lost interest in both the recorder and the American Recorder Society, but she was always graciously willing to talk about her musical past and the founding of the ARS. It took two long interviews to get her words on paper, but what was preserved is precious. Part of interview number two appears in AR XXIX, 4, November 1988, but the transcription of the full interview is preserved in the ARS archives at the Recorder Center in Denver. I cherish her memory, and American recorder players must be forever indebted to her for having the audacity to found what she called "the American Recorder Society." This is her lasting legacy.

APPENDIX I:

History of the American Recorder Society Chapters

Marcia Blue and Richard Sacksteder
September 9, 2006

The following pages record and summarize data on the local ARS chapters from the time of the founding of the first (in Boston) in 1955 through 1995. The information was compiled from *The American Recorder, Newsletters* of the ARS and local chapters, Board minutes, membership directories, national office records, and sometimes from the tribal memory of ARS veterans.

The developments of the chapters have been so varied that, to avoid tedious explanations, certain categories have been interpreted flexibly. Even such a basic issue as assigning a location to each chapter is more difficult than might be supposed. Usually a chapter could be located in a city, but in some cases a county was more appropriate. Sometimes, as with the Triangle Recorder Society of North Carolina, it was necessary to make a somewhat arbitrary choice among equally compelling possibilities. There are even cases like the Upper Valley Music Society, which has members in both Vermont and New Hampshire, for which the assignment of a state is debatable. Where there have been several chapters in a city, they have been distinguished by designations such as Buffalo I and Buffalo II.

There are also philosophical difficulties in determining when the identity of a chapter was maintained through a series of demises, revivals, name changes, and mergers. The decisions made here on all of these issues have been influenced more by common sense than any formal principle, but in keeping with the purpose of measuring regional activity, our policy has been to treat a renewal of activity in a location as a revival of a chapter even if no direct connection with a predecessor could be documented. This issue has been handled in presenting the data by identifying a putative chapter with a location, and listing dates of name changes, mergers, and period of activity within the location.

In cases where the exact date of an event could not be determined, it was arbitrarily assumed to have taken place on the first day of the month. The letters f, p, r, or s after the name of a chapter officer stand respectively for the founder, president, representative, or secretary. In cases where the office could not be determined, it is listed as representative.

The chapter records presented in Appendix II are alphabetized by state postal abbreviations and then by location within a state. Guam and Puerto Rico have been treated as states for this purpose. Locations outside the USA are listed at the end. Chapter affiliates and Junior chapters have not been included. The listings give the location in boldface on a line followed by the total number of the chapter's active years. The name(s) used by the chapter are listed in the column below the location. The beginning and ending dates for the use of a name are given in the row containing the name and following these in the row are the names of some officers of the chapter while that name was in use. When a chapter became inactive, but was later revived, separate lines correspond to the active periods.

The graph below shows the growth of the chapters. It is noteworthy that the number of chapters continued to grow even when the paid membership of the ARS was declining.

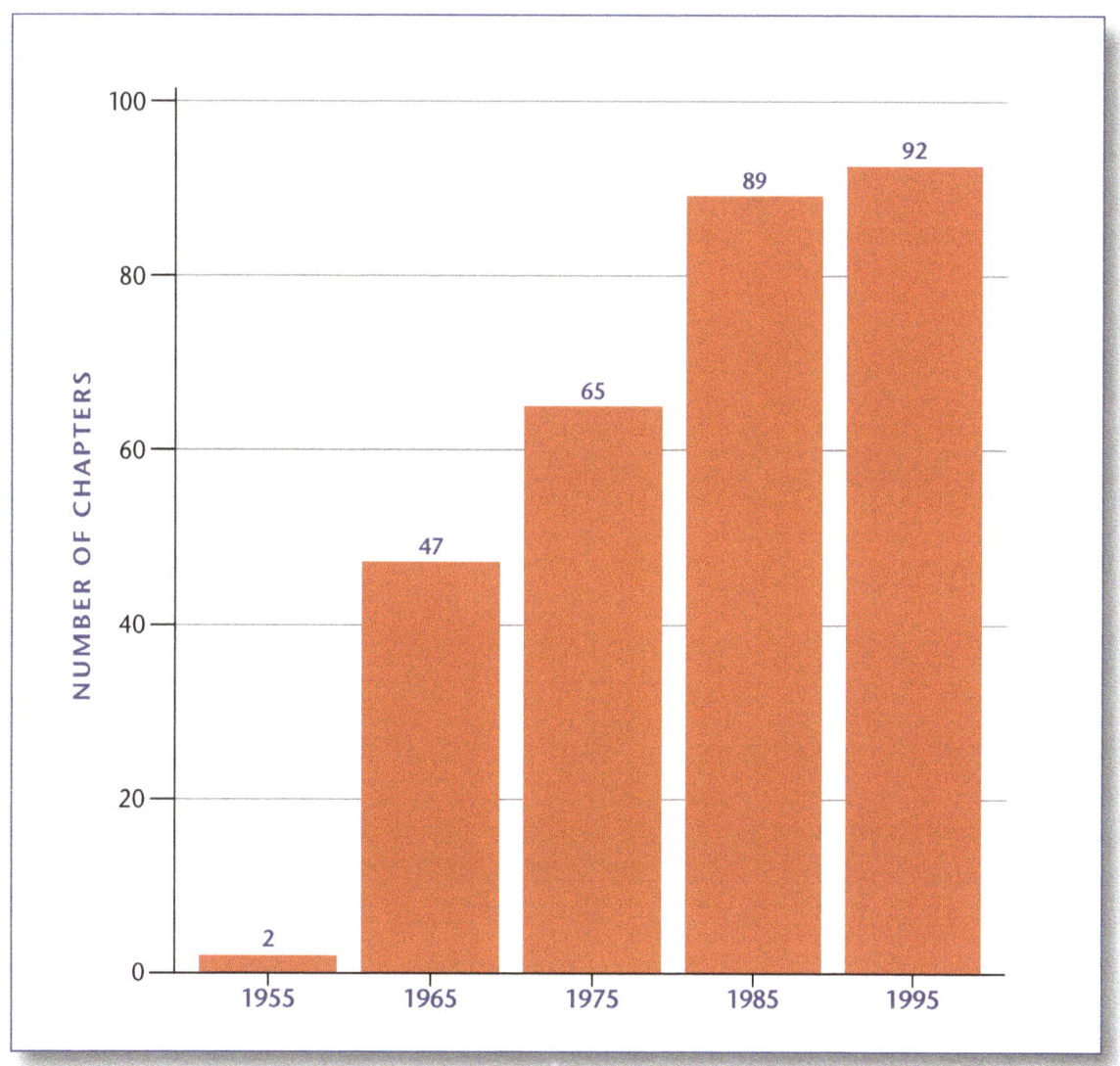

APPENDIX II

ARS Chapters (1939–1995)

USA

(Alphabetical by state postal code)

Birmingham, AL (14.41 active years)
Birmingham Chap   08/01/81–12/31/95   Phyllis Kirk, r

Montgomery, AL (17.42 active years)
Central Alabama Rec Soc   08/01/78–12/31/95   R. F. Kirkpatrick, r

Bella Vista, AR (1.16 active years)
Bella Vista Chap   11/01/94–12/31/95   Charles Whitford, r

Little Rock I, AR (0.75 active years)
Little Rock Chap   11/01/77–08/01/78   Maria Sylvester, r

Little Rock II, AR (14.41 active years)
Aeolus Rec Konsort of Central AR   08/01/81–12/31/95   Marybelle Nissly, r

Phoenix, AZ (26.34 active years)
Phoenix Chap   02/25/59–06/01/60
                                          06/01/61–08/01/78   Sanford Kaye, r
                                          02/01/88–12/31/95   JoAnn Trapp, r

Tucson, AZ (23.88 active years)
Tucson Chap   06/15/67–02/01/74   Mrs. Peter Madison, r
                                          10/01/78–12/31/95   Stewart Carter, r

Chico, CA (12.25 active years)
Northern California Rec Soc   05/01/66–11/01/77   Ewing England, r
Chico Area Chap   11/01/77–08/01/78   Ewing England, r

Fresno, CA (2.67 active years)
Fresno Recorder Consort   06/01/73–02/01/76   Alice Roth, p

La Mirada, CA (4.32 active years)
Rio Hondo Consort   01/06/76–05/01/80   Margaret Florence, p

Los Angeles, CA (34.86 active years)
Los Angeles Chap   02/18/61–02/01/74   Frank Plachte, r
Southern California Rec Soc   02/01/74–12/31/95   Charles Sauer, r

Marin County, CA (31.00 active years)
Marin Rec Soc   06/01/61–06/01/92   Leo Christiansen, r

Monrovia, CA (16.39 active years)
Monrovia Rec Consort   09/11/70–02/01/87   John Meehan, r

Morro Bay, CA (0.91 active years)
Coast Christian ISP Chap   01/01/95–12/01/95   Victoria Lowrie, r

Orange County, CA (21.16 active years)
Orange County Rec Soc   11/01/74–12/31/95   Donald Bowles, p

Redlands, CA (3.42 active years)
San Gorgonio Chap   09/01/83–02/01/86   Mary Jane
                                                                   Auerbacher, r
Redlands Recorders   02/01/86–02/01/87   Mary Jane
                                                                   Auerbacher, r

Riverside, CA (33.13 active years)
Riverside Chap   11/13/62–08/01/81   Elizabeth Zuehlke, r
Inland Chap   08/01/81–02/01/84   Elizabeth Zuehlke, r
Riverside EM Soc   02/01/84–12/31/95   Elizabeth Zuehlke, r

Sacramento, CA (13.31 active years)
Sacramento Rec Soc   01/24/67–06/17/68   Norman C. Peterson, r
                                          02/01/84–12/31/95   Richard Janes, r

San Diego, CA (23.67 active years)
San Diego Rec Soc   04/01/60–09/01/64   Frank Myers, p
San Diego County Rec Soc   01/01/75–02/01/76   Hugh Wade, r
                                          11/01/77–12/31/95   Hugh Wade, r

San Francisco/Berkeley, CA
(34.86 active years)
San Francisco Bay Area Chap   02/18/61–02/01/86   Kenneth Wollitz, f
East Bay Chap   02/01/86–12/31/95   Elizabeth Morrison, r

San Jose, CA (2.33 active years)
South Bay Rec Soc   09/01/93–12/31/95   Georgiana Rudge, r

San Luis Obispo, CA (3.58 active years)
Cuesta College Chap   06/01/92–09/01/94   John Warren, r
Central Coast Chap   09/01/94–12/31/95   John Warren, r

Santa Barbara, CA (27.82 active years)
Santa Barbara Collegium Musicum   4/07/61–02/01/89   Mrs. Cecil Thomson, r

Santa Cruz, CA (14.00 active years)
North Monterey Bay Rec   01/01/82–02/01/85   Carolyn Woolston, r
Monterey Bay Rec Soc   02/01/85–12/31/95   Carolyn Woolston, r

Santa Rosa, CA (11.00 active years)
Sonoma County Rec Soc   02/01/84–02/01/95   Elizabeth Hershey, r

Victorville, CA (11.22 active years)
Mojave Sandpipers   11/13/62–02/01/74   James E. Goodin, r

Boulder, CO (16.67 active years)
Boulder Chap   05/01/79–12/31/95   Steve Winograd, r

Colorado Springs, CO (10.91 active years)
Colorado Springs Rec Soc   2/01/85–12/31/95   Michael Richard, r

Denver, CO (31.27 active years)
Denver Chap   09/24/64–12/31/95   Lucile Gillespie, f

Ft. Collins, CO (4.83 active years)
Ft. Collins Chap   5/01/80–08/01/81   Jackey Canton, r
Ft. Collins Rec Soc   06/01/92–12/31/95   Betty Edmundson, r

Danbury, CT (6.90 active years)
Rec Soc of CT   02/05/89–12/31/95   Eleanor Fischer, r

Hartford, CT (22.32 active years)
Hartford Chap   10/09/62–02/01/85   Edward J. Miller, r

Wallingford, CT (6.90 active years)
Praetorius Players   12/06/70–11/01/77   David Langstaff, r

Washington I, DC (37.20 active years)
Washington Rec Soc   10/18/58–12/31/95   Todas M. Odarenko, r

Washington II, DC (14.17 active years)
National Capitol Suburban Rec Soc   06/01/64–08/01/78   Katherine Keene, r

Washington III, DC (21.16 active years)
Monday Recorder Group   11/01/74–12/31/95   Anne Oliver, r

New Castle, DE (5.83 active years)
Brandywine Chap   03/01/90–12/31/95   Lis Bard, r

Wilmington, DE (7.02 active years)
Wilmington Chap   01/24/67–02/01/74   Philip M. Levin, r

Cape Kennedy, FL (3.02 active years)
East Central FL Chap   08/26/66–09/01/69   Elisabeth Lauer, r

Daytona Beach, FL (3.50 active years)
Daytona Beach Chap   08/01/81–02/01/85   Richard S. Zelly, r

Ft. Meyers Beach, FL (1.50 active years)
Ft. Meyers Beach Chap   11/30/67–06/01/69   Lillian Guthrie, r

Gainesville, FL (23.41 active years)
Gainesville Chap   08/01/72–12/31/95   John Kitts, r

Jacksonville, FL (16.91 active years)
Jacksonville Chap   02/01/79–12/31/95   C. Harvey Peacock, r

Lee County, FL (7.91 active years)
Lee County Rec Soc   02/01/88–12/31/95   Ruth Purdo, r

Miami, FL (33.65 active years)
Miami Chap   05/08/62–12/31/95   Arnold Grayson, f

Orlando, FL (11.30 active years)
Mid-FL Rec Soc   09/11/70–02/07/75   John W. Rata, r
FL Tech University Chap   02/07/75–08/01/78   Patricia Steinberg, r
Central FL Chap   05/01/79–08/01/81   Patricia Steinberg, r
                                            11/01/94–12/31/95   Ann Cook, r

Sarasota, FL (11.91 active years)
Sarasota Chap   02/01/84–12/31/95   Barbara Venon, r

St. Petersburg, FL (14.50 active years)
St. Petersburg Chap   08/01/72–11/01/77   Mrs. Paul Dunsing, r
Suncoast Chap   11/01/77–02/01/87

Tampa, FL (17.00 active years)
Tampa Chap   02/01/72–02/01/79   Mrs. A. C. Mathieson, r
Tampa Bay Chap   02/01/79–02/01/89   Arthur Allison, r

Atlanta, GA (21.85 active years)
Atlanta Rec Soc   04/11/62–06/17/68   George Kelischek, r
                                            05/01/80–12/31/95   Jan Kapoor, r

Augusta, GA (4.92 active years)
Augusta Chap   03/01/84–02/01/89   Tish Berlin, r

Savannah, GA (3.20 active years)
Savannah Rec Consort   06/19/66–09/01/69   Mrs. Robert Herndon, r

Agana, GU (2.92 active years)
Guam Rec Soc   12/01/74–11/01/77   Henry M. Meinecke, p

Honolulu, HI (19.54 active years)
Hawaii Chap   06/17/67–02/01/74   Larry Stevens, r
                                            02/01/83–12/31/95   Janet M. Callender, r

Des Moines, IA (5.75 active years)
Des Moines Chap   11/01/66–08/01/72   Roger W. Tate, r
Iowa City, IA (11.91 active years)

Iowa City Chap 02/01/84–06/01/90 Judy Cottingham, r
Eastern Iowa Rec Soc 06/01/90–12/31/95 Ruth Williams, r

Charleston, IL (8.38 active years)
Eastern IL Chap 09/16/75–02/01/84 Robert W. Weidner, r

Chicago I, IL (37.25 active years)
Chicago Chap 09/29/58–12/31/95 Ray Anthony, r

Chicago II, IL (15.67 active years)
West Suburban EM Soc 05/01/80–12/31/95 Gretel Dunsing, f

Evanston, IL (31.76 active years)
North Shore Chap 02/25/60–12/01/91 Virginia McCollum, r

Quincy, IL (1.00 active years)
Quincy EM Consort 05/01/79–05/01/80 Larry Lowery, r

Ft. Wayne, IN (3.08 active years)
Ft. Wayne Chap 12/01/92–12/31/95 Wayne Peterson, r

Indianapolis, IN (15.67 active years)
Indianapolis Chap 05/01/80–12/31/95 Kathy Smith, r

Lafayette, IN (8.17 active years)
Lafayette Chap 12/01/65–02/01/74 Carol Purkhiser, r

Muncie, IN (26.54 active years)
Northeastern IN Chap 06/17/68–01/01/95 Thomas Cirtin, p

South Bend, IN (23.31 active years)
South Bend Rec Soc 10/10/61–02/01/85 Robert J. Lauer, r

Topeka, KS (1.33 active years)
Topeka Rec Soc 09/01/94–12/31/95 Cheryl Myers, r

Wichita, KS (32.99 active years)
Wichita Chap 03/03/60–03/01/93 George E. Vollmer, r

Louisville, KY (2.83 active years)
River Cities Chap   02/01/89–12/01/91   Johanna Bos, r

Baton Rouge, LA (16.91 active years)
Baton Rouge Rec Soc   02/01/79–12/31/95   John Waite, r

New Orleans, LA (30.03 active years)
New Orleans-Woodvine Chap   12/19/65–06/17/68   Milton Silverman, r
New Orleans Chap   06/17/68–02/01/80   Barbara Henry, r
EM Soc of New Orleans   02/01/80–12/31/95   Simone Fischer, r

Shreveport, LA (5.50 active years)
Shreveport Chap   08/01/81–02/01/87   Edith Elliot, r

Boston, MA (40.75 active years)
Boston Rec Soc   04/02/55–12/31/95   Elna Sherman, f

Fall River, MA (1.33 active years)
Fall River Fipplefluters   09/01/94–12/31/95   Judith Conrad, r

Oak Bluffs, MA (2.72 active years)
Oak Bluffs Rec Soc   02/10/75–11/01/77   Charles Grey, r

Springfield, MA (14.67 active years)
Pioneer Valley EM & Rec Soc   05/01/81–12/31/95   Robert Castellano, r

Worcester, MA (24.74 active years)
Worcester Chap   05/08/62–02/01/87   Walter E. Knapp, r

Baltimore, MD (19.89 active years)
Baltimore Chap   06/27/61–06/17/68   Anne C. Tremearne, f
Soc for EM of Northern MD   02/01/83–12/31/95   Robert Lauer, p

Columbia, MD (21.09 active years)
Columbia Chap   11/27/74–12/31/95   Carlton King, r

Aroostook County, ME (2.97 active years)
Aroostook Rec Soc   11/11/74–11/01/77   Tammy Ladner, r

Camden, ME (3.54 active years)
Penobscot Bay Chap   06/19/66–01/01/70   Mrs. Raymond Gowdy, r

Falmouth, ME (4.00 active years)
Pine Tree Chap   02/01/85–02/01/89   Frances Bove, r

Ann Arbor, MI (15.72 active years)
Ann Arbor Rec Soc   11/13/62–08/01/78   Marion Wirick, r

Detroit, MI (26.09 active years)
Metropolitan Detroit Rec Soc   03/01/66–11/01/77   Alma L. Fry, r
                                          08/01/81–12/31/95   Mary Johnson, r

Holland, MI (10.63 active years)
Holland Chap   03/17/67–11/01/77   L. M. Hoepfinger, r

Kalamazoo, MI (20.91 active years)
Kalamazoo Rec Players   02/01/75–12/31/95   Edwin E. Meader, r

Lansing, MI (7.00 active years)
Round-about-Lansing Rec Plyrs   01/01/89–12/31/95   Dorothy Lansing, r

Muskegon, MI (8.91 active years)
Muskegon Baroque Rec Ensemble   02/01/87–05/01/91   Frances Pearsons, r
Muskegon Rec Players   05/01/91–12/31/95   Frances Andrews, r

Duluth, MN (2.51 active years)
Zenith City Whistle Soc   01/26/76–08/01/78   William van Druten, r

Minneapolis/St. Paul, MN
(34.00 active years)
Twin Cities Chap   01/01/62–12/31/95   Mrs. Benjamin Grey, r

Columbia, MO (3.75 active years)
Columbia Chap   11/01/77–08/01/81   Janet Welsh, r

Kansas City, MO (3.63 active years)
Kansas City Rec Soc   02/12/60–06/01/61   Ethel McAfoose, r
                                          02/01/84–06/01/86   Janice Lee, r

Springfield, MO (17.42 active years)
Heart of the Ozarks Chap				08/01/78–12/31/95		Judy Mignard, r

St Louis, MO (4.31 active years)
St Louis Chap					05/08/62–08/28/66		Pat Gausch, r

Asheville, NC (6.02 active years)
Overmountain Rec Soc				01/26/78–02/01/84		Ellen Moore, r

Chapel Hill, NC (28.79 active years)
Triangle Rec Soc				03/17/67–12/31/95		Katherine Ormston, r

Greensboro, NC (1.00 active years)
Triad EM Soc					01/01/95–12/31/95		Donna Yaniglos, r

Salisbury, NC (9.35 active years)
Piedmont Chap					09/25/64–02/01/74		Dale Higbee, r

Lebanon, NH (4.08 active years)
Upper Valley EM Soc				12/01/91–12/31/95		Barbara Prescott, r
some members from VT

Peterborough, NH (15.25 active years)
Monadnock Chap					09/29/80–12/31/95		Dorothy Fitch, r
some members from VT

Atlantic City, NJ (11.91 active years)
South Jersey Chap				02/01/84–12/31/95		Dahlia Fayter, r

Bergen County, NJ (28.08 active years)
Bergen County Chap				11/30/67–12/31/95		Irene Engsberg, r
formed by some No Jersey members –

Highland Park, NJ (7.67 active years)
Highland Park Rec Soc				05/01/88–12/31/95		Donna Messer, r

Lakewood, NJ (3.08 active years)
Squankum Players				12/01/92–12/31/95		Hilda Borcherding, r

Montclair, NJ (22.30 active years)
North Jersey Chap   11/13/62–03/01/85   Phoebe Larkey, r
1967, Bergen Co Chap created from

Navesink, NJ (16.91 active years)
Navesink Rec Soc   02/01/79–12/31/95   Eleanor Larson, r

Princeton, NJ (19.84 active years)
Princeton Chap   02/26/65–02/01/74   Jennifer Lehmann, r
Princeton Rec Soc   02/01/85–12/31/95   Joan Wilson, r

Somerset, NJ (21.91 active years)
Somerset Hills Rec Soc   02/01/74–12/31/95   Virginia Kennedy, r

Las Cruces, NM (4.08 active years)
Rio Grande Chap   12/01/91–12/31/95   Joyce B. Henry, r
some members from TX

Los Alamos, NM (30.33 active years)
Los Alamos Chap   09/01/65–12/31/95   R. E. LaBauve, r

Santa Fe, NM (13.67 active years)
Santa Fe Rec Soc   05/01/82–12/31/95   Hazel Mosley, r

Albany I, NY (13.08 active years)
Capital District Chap   11/01/77–05/01/79   Eloise Scherzer, r
merged into Hudson Mohawk Chap   5/01/80–12/01/91   William Rawley, r

Albany II, NY (4.08 active years)
Hudson Mohawk Chap   12/01/91–12/31/95   Jeanne Ammon, r
Capital & NE Chaps merged into

Buffalo I, NY (26.75 active years)
Buffalo Rec Consort   04/01/59–10/09/62   Mrs. Richard Ament, r
Western NY Chap   10/09/62–02/01/74   Alice L. Sprague, r
Buffalo Rec Soc   02/01/84–03/01/90   Charles Hall, r
Buffalo S. Tn Chap merged into   03/01/90–12/31/95   Charles Hall, r

Buffalo II, NY (20.96 active years)
Buffalo South Towns Chap   03/14/69–03/01/90   Robert Kidder, r
merged into Buffalo Rec Soc

Cooperstown, NY (8.20 active years)
Cooperstown Chap   04/04/60–06/17/68   Katherine Ketcham, r

Corning, NY (8.17 active years)
Painted Post Chap   06/01/73–08/01/74   Richard S. Perry, p
Southern Tier Rec Soc   08/01/74–08/01/81   Richard S. Perry, p

Garden City, NY (5.45 active years)
Garden City Rec Players   02/18/61–08/01/66   Mrs. Philip Hardie, r

Ithaca, NY (1.00 active years)
Ithaca/Finger Lakes Chap   01/01/95–12/31/95   Marsha Evans, r

Long Island, NY (18.16 active years)
Long Island Rec Soc   11/01/77–03/01/79   Dorothy Partridge, r
Rec Soc of Long Island   03/01/79–12/31/95   Dorothy Partridge, r

New York City, NY (35.33 active years)
New York Rec Guild   09/01/60–12/31/95   Bernard Krainis, f

Potsdam, NY (3.26 active years)
North Country Rec Soc   04/27/69–08/01/72   Lorraine Sterns, r

Poughkeepsie, NY (3.48 active years)
Poughkeepsie Chap   12/08/61–06/01/65   Katherine Creelman, r

Rochester, NY (30.03 active years)
Rochester Chap   12/19/65–12/31/95   Helen Benz, r

Rockland County, NY (4.33 active years)
Rockland County Rec Soc   09/01/91–12/31/95   Lorraine Schiller, f

Saratoga Springs/Schenectady, NY
(25.37 active years)
Northeastern New York Chap   07/18/66–12/01/91   Margaret S. Demarsh, f
merged into Hudson Mohawk Chap –

Westchester County, NY
(9.91 active years)
Westchester Rec Guild   02/01/86–12/31/95   Claire Horn, r

Cincinnati, OH (3.00 active years)
Cincinnati Rec Soc   09/01/83–09/01/86   Lawrence Brown, r

Cleveland, OH (28.33 active years)
Greater Cleveland Area Chap   09/01/67–12/31/95   Cornelia Hayman, r

Columbus, OH (22.42 active years)
Columbus Chap   08/01/72–01/01/95   Suzanne Ferguson, r

Dayton, OH (9.33 active years)
Miami Valley Chap   02/01/83–06/01/92   Robert Cogburn, r

Toledo, OH (21.71 active years)
Toledo Rec Soc   06/17/68–11/01/77   James Rudolph, r
                                               09/01/83–12/31/95   Marilyn Perlmutter, r

Youngstown, OH (7.56 active years)
Youngstown Rec Consort   06/10/63–01/01/71   Beth Schultz, r

Midwest City, OK (2.76 active years)
Midwest City Chap   05/01/82–02/01/85   John Hillabolt, r

Oklahoma City, OK (13.25 active years)
Oklahoma City Chap   10/01/82–12/31/95   Sherry Phillips, r

Tulsa, OK (21.34 active years)
Tulsa Chap   05/08/62–09/01/64   Thomas H. Galey, r
Tulsa Rec Consort   12/22/76–12/31/95   Richard F. Neal, r

Eugene, OR (4.24 active years)
Eugene Chap   09/21/65–12/19/69   Evelyn Thomson, r

Newport, OR (1.33 active years)
Oregon Coast Chap   09/01/94–12/31/95   Corlu Collier, r

Bethlehem, PA (11.32 active years)
Lehigh Valley Rec Soc   04/07/61–08/01/72   Robert Young, r

Carlisle, PA (4.77 active years)
Carlisle Chap   04/27/69–02/01/74   Daniel Bechtel, r

Lancaster, PA (5.83 active years)
Lancaster Chap   02/01/86–12/01/91   Patricia Miller, r

Philadelphia, PA (40.59 active years)
Philadelphia Rec Soc   05/31/55–12/31/95   Herbert Koslow, f

Pittsburgh, PA (30.54 active years)
Pittsburgh Chap   06/18/65–12/31/95   Dorothy C. Bund, r

State College, PA (17.72 active years)
State College Chap   06/10/75–03/01/93   Arabelle Carlson, r

San Juan, PR (12.61 active years)
Lewis C. Richardson Rec Soc   12/19/69–05/01/79   Mrs. Lewis Richardson, r
EM Soc of Puerto Rico   09/01/83–12/01/86   Adaimberto Jurado-Bas, r

Bristol, RI (8.90 active years)
East Bay Chap   09/07/72–08/01/81   James Bartram, r

Providence, RI (31.72 active years)
Providence Chap   10/10/61–06/03/63   Jacqueline Bachaud, r
                                12/04/65–05/01/82   Ilse Schaler, r
Rhode Island Rec Soc   05/01/82–12/31/95   Richard Carbone, r

Columbia, SC (3.00 active years)
Columbia Chap   02/01/85–02/01/88   Craig Kridel, r

Chattanooga, TN (3.24 active years)
Chattanooga Rec Soc   03/06/58–06/01/61   David Dzik, p

Knoxville, TN (14.41 active years)
Eastern TN Chap   08/01/81–12/31/95   Andrew Peed, r

Memphis, TN (4.67 active years)
Memphis Chap   10/01/56–06/01/61   Virginia van Hook, s

Nashville, TN (14.41 active years)
Nashville Parks Chap   08/01/81–12/31/95   Wayne G. Hill, r

Alpine, TX (4.25 active years)
Texas Mountain Chap   06/01/91–09/01/95   Eve Trook White, r

Austin, TX (36.82 active years)
Austin Chap   03/08/59–12/31/95   M/M Don W. Morgan, f

Dallas, TX (18.50 active years)
Dallas Rec Soc   07/01/76–01/01/84   George Kriehn, r
                                         01/01/85–12/31/95   David Barton, r

El Paso, TX (7.25 active years)
El Paso Chap   11/01/77–02/01/85   Robert Hyland, r

Ft. Worth, TX (2.46 active years)
Ft. Worth Chap   02/16/79–08/01/81   Michael Burke, r

Houston, TX (18.23 active years)
West University Chap   06/10/75–02/01/85   Lauren Boehme, r
Houston Hist Instrument Soc   02/01/85–02/01/89   Gregg Hill, r
                                         03/01/90–12/01/90   Michael R. Cooper, r
                                         03/01/92–12/31/95   Barbara Duey, f

San Antonio, TX (7.32 active years)
San Antonio Chap   05/08/62–09/01/69   Roy Miller, p

Provo, UT (4.41 active years)
Utah Central Chap   12/01/70–05/01/75   Clarence Bushman, r

Salt Lake City, UT (18.83 active years)
Salt Lake City Chapter   12/01/70–11/01/77   Lynn Carson, r
                                         02/01/84–12/31/95   Paul Dorsey, r

Falls Church, VA (7.91 active years)
Northern VA Rec Soc   02/01/88–12/31/95   Linda Waller, r

Fredericksburg, VA (4.04 active years)
Fredericksburg Chap   06/01/64–06/17/68   Robert H. Shaw, r

Richmond, VA (5.67 active years)
Richmond Chap   12/01/66–08/01/72   Donald Tennant, r

Virginia Beach, VA (4.06 active years)
Virginia Beach Chap   01/01/63–01/24/67   Charles W. Hardin, r

Williamsburg, VA (13.12 active years)
Peninsula Rec Soc   06/17/68–08/01/81   David R. Brooks, r

Burlington, VT (9.50 active years)
Lake Champlain Rec Soc   09/01/83–03/01/93   David Russell, r

Marlboro, VT (5.88 active years)
Marlboro Chap   12/01/65–01/18/69   Edmund Brelsford, r
                                        08/01/72–05/01/75   Edmund Brelsford, r

Bellingham, WA (5.83 active years)
Bellingham Rec Soc   03/01/90–12/31/95   Carol Hoerauf, r

Kirkland, WA (15.67 active years)
Moss Bay Chap   05/01/80–12/31/95   Mary Whittington, r

Richland, WA (4.08 active years)
Columbia Basin Rec Soc   12/01/91–12/31/95   Drew Rutz, r

Seattle, WA (31.58 active years)
Seattle Rec Soc   06/01/64–12/31/95   Beverly Bush, r

Madison I, WI (28.62 active years)
Madison Chap   09/25/64–01/24/67   S. Barrett Williams, r
                                        06/17/68–08/01/72   James Margenau, r
Madison Rec Consort   02/01/73–08/01/74   Beverly Inman, r
                                        05/01/75–06/01/90   Beverly Inman, r
Winds of Southern Wisconsin   06/01/90–12/31/95   Virginia E. Dobson, r

Madison II, WI (7.50 active years)
Encore of Madison Ltd. Chap   02/01/75–08/01/81   Ruth Feige, r
                                        02/01/84–02/01/85   Margaret Peterson, r

Milwaukee, WI (29.92 active years)
Tosa Musica Antiqua Chap   11/01/59–02/01/74   Martin Kuban, f
Milwaukee Chap   05/01/80–12/31/95   Gertrude Stillman, r

St. Croix County, WI (2.56 active years)
St. Croix Valley Chap   01/08/70–08/01/72   William Abbott, r

Follansbee, WV (0.67 active years)
Rec Soc of West Virginia   05/01/95–12/31/95   Vincent Richards, r

Brazil

Sao Paulo (5.63 active years)
Sao Jose dos Campos Chap   06/17/68–02/01/74   Angelino de Jesus
                                                              Rosa, r

Canada
(Alphabetical by province postal code)

Calgary, AB (10.92 active years)
Calgary Rec Soc   02/01/84–12/01/90   Patricia Barton, r
Calgary Chap of ARS   12/01/90–01/01/95   Pam Witten, r

Edmonton, AB (3.75 active years)
Edmonton Rec Soc   02/01/74–11/01/77   Louise Dawson, r

Winnipeg, MB, (11.89 active years)   03/13/62–02/01/74   Stefan Carter, r

Ottawa, ON (1.73 active years)
Ottawa Chap   09/25/64–06/19/66   Seymour Sokoloff, r

Toronto, ON (11 active years)
Toronto Chap   02/01/74–05/01/75   N. E. Russell, r
                                  09/24/84–02/01/87   Shirley Peters, r
T.E.M.P.O.   02/01/87–12/31/95   Lois Dove, r

Montreal, QC (31.58 active years)
Montreal ARS Musica   06/01/64–02/01/88   Donald Cash, r
ARS Musica Montreal   02/01/88–12/31/95   Mary McCutcheon, r

Mexico

Mexico City (16.57 active years)
Mexico City Chap   04/07/61–11/01/77   Frederick V. Field, r

www.ingramcontent.com/pod-product-compliance
Lightning Source LLC
Chambersburg PA
CBHW041410300426
44114CB00028B/2969